Beverle
Blake

BY LAWRENCE LANGNER

BOOKS

G. B. S. and the Lunatic   1963

The Play's the Thing   1960

The Importance of Wearing Clothes   1959

The Magic Curtain   1951

PLAYS

Suzanna and the Elders (with ARMINA MARSHALL)   1939

On to Fortune (with ARMINA MARSHALL)   1936

Pursuit of Happiness (with ARMINA MARSHALL)   1934

Henry Behave   1927

These Modern Women   1926

Moses   1924

G. B. S. AND THE LUNATIC

G. B. S.
AND THE
LUNATIC

Reminiscences of the Long, Lively and
Affectionate Friendship between
George Bernard Shaw and
the Author

LAWRENCE
LANGNER

ATHENEUM

NEW YORK

1963

TO ARMINA

FOREWORD

MORE than a decade has passed since the death of Bernard Shaw stilled one of the most stimulating, witty, wise and argumentative voices in the modern world.

If there is a heaven reserved for Creative Evolutionists, the name which Shaw gave to the small but elite band of converts in his personal religion, I feel sure he is there gaily challenging its social customs, poking fun at the dignity of the angels and suggesting improvements in the behavior of the saints. Meanwhile, time has relentlessly set about the re-evaluation of his life work in relation to Posterity. Despite the years which have passed since his death at the age of ninety-four, his barbs of humor and wisdom are ever popular, and his plays are given in hundreds of professional and amateur theatres annually throughout the world. One of these, *Pygmalion,* has been made into the musical *My Fair Lady* and has carried his fame to millions of people who would never have heard of him otherwise, and the end is not yet.

For many years, along with my colleagues at the Theatre Guild, I worked on the productions of Shaw's plays in the United States. Of these, six can be considered world premières, these being *Heartbreak House, Back to Methuselah, Saint Joan, Too True to Be Good, The Simpleton of the Unexpected Isles* and *The Millionairess.* Other plays were revived by the Theatre Guild in New York, and by me and Armina Marshall and our colleagues in Westport, making a total of twenty-five major Shaw productions with which I was associated in the United States.

Being three thousand miles away, Shaw could express his pleasure or displeasure with our efforts only by letters and postcards, in which he was prolific; he also used cables, but sparingly, since he hated to waste money on them. This led to the exchange of a series of letters, addressed mainly to me, which form an entertaining and revealing record of Shaw's views on many of his plays and on a variety of other subjects ranging from sex to Socialism. I have presented the most interesting of these in the present volume, together with some addressed to my colleague Theresa Helburn, who worked with me on most of the New York productions mentioned in this book.

Letters from Shaw are no novelty. Two famous collections of his love letters to well-known actresses, Ellen Terry and Mrs. Patrick Campbell, have been published to the world, and more recently a third collection addressed to an American painter (and erstwhile actress) Molly Tompkins of Atlanta, Georgia, has come to light. For all I know, there may be more collections of love letters still to be discovered. The Shaw letters included in these pages are decidedly *not* love letters. Indeed, many of them are brimful of anger, of irritation, of controversy, and a few have their moments of affection. But the revelations in these letters are mostly confined to art and business, two subjects with which he dealt realistically and never in terms of amorous fantasy or poetry.

The "lunatic" in the title of this book refers to me. It is based on the fact that in my more optimistic days I asked Shaw to let me have a contract for the Theatre Guild to produce his dramatic epic *Back to Methuselah,* which consisted of five separate plays in eight scenes, with a total of forty-five characters as well as supernumeraries.

"Don't bother about a contract," Shaw replied, as I stood at the door of his London apartment before leaving for New York with his promise that we might produce the plays if we liked them. "It isn't likely that any other lunatic will want to produce *Back to Methuselah!"*

After some months of agitation with my confreres at the Theatre Guild, who realized that we were risking our future on a single throw, I persuaded the more practical members of our Board of Directors that we should proceed with this monumental undertaking, which in sheer size, length and conception dwarfed any other theatre work in the history of the world theatre. O'Neill's long major plays *Strange Interlude* and *Mourning Becomes Electra* were child's play by comparison.

On July 28, 1921, after many months of argument back and forth, I was at last able to write to Shaw jubilantly:

> *The lunatic has prevailed!* God and yourself willing, the curtain will ring up on *Back to Methuselah* in February or March of the coming year. . . .

Later on Shaw himself remarked that the production of this

play was "an exploit still unique, which so amazed me that I have hardly yet recovered my breath after it." Of the foolhardy band of young men and women who performed this gigantic task, only two are still living as I write these words: Lee Simonson, who designed the magnificent scenery and costumes, and I. The others, Theresa Helburn, Philip Moeller, Helen Westley and Maurice Wertheim, have all gone the way of all flesh. My wife, Armina Marshall, as associate producer, also participated in the later Shaw productions. This account of my relations with Shaw over so many years and so many plays is a record of their efforts as well as mine, the brilliant stage direction of Philip Moeller and the scenery of Lee Simonson being particularly outstanding. But special mention must be made of Theresa Helburn, who served as Executive Director of the Theatre Guild during most of the time we were producing Shaw's plays, who worked side by side with me and others, and who was particularly responsible for the brilliant casting of many of the plays.

This book is dedicated with love and affection to their memory, which is forever enshrined in the contributions they made to the maturity of the American theatre at a time when it was coming out of its swaddling clothes.

LAWRENCE LANGNER

Weston, Connecticut
1962

CONTENTS

Part One

Part Two

Part Three

ILLUSTRATIONS

George Bernard Shaw   FRONTISPIECE
(E. H. Galsworthy)

FOLLOWING PAGE 20

Two scenes from *Heartbreak House*
Dudley Digges, who directed the play and also portrayed Boss Mangan
(Ira Schwartz)
A scene from Part II of *Back to Methuselah*
A set designed by Lee Simonson for *Back to Methuselah*
Other sets by Simonson for *Back to Methuselah*
(Francis Brugiere)
Roland Young as General Burgoyne in *The Devil's Disciple,* shown here
with Basil Sydney and Lotus Robb
Other scenes from *The Devil's Disciple*
Winifred Lenihan as Joan of Arc in *St. Joan*
Philip Leigh with Miss Lenihan, in the original *St. Joan*
The cathedral scene and the trial scene from the 1923 *St. Joan*
(Vandamm)
Uta Hagen as Joan in the 1951 revival of the play
(Talbot Giles)
Helen Hayes as Cleopatra in the production of *Caesar and Cleopatra*
Scenes from *Caesar and Cleopatra*
(Francis Brugiere)
Alfred Lunt and Lynn Fontanne in *Arms and the Man*
Tom Powers on the tour of *Arms and the Man*
(Vandamm)
Henry Travers and Romney Brent in *Androcles and the Lion*
In the same production, Edward G. Robinson as Caesar
(Vandamm)
Scenes from *Garrick Gaieties of 1925*
Richard Rodgers and Lorenz Hart

FOLLOWING PAGE 116

Lynn Fontanne in *Pygmalion*
Reginald Mason and Henry Travers in scenes with Miss Fontanne from
Pygmalion

Part One

CHAPTER ONE

Introducing a Very Peculiar Character

T H E shock created by Shaw on the modern world was that of an alert intelligent mind—armed with the weapons of rapier-like wit and bludgeoning horseplay, intent on destroying the shibboleths of Victorian morality—whose thrusts delighted the younger generations which followed him. He was not the first to use the theatre for the explosion of obsolete social ideas. Ibsen had done the same thing just before him. But where Ibsen was solemn and dour, Shaw was humorous and gay. He attacked with laughter and comedy where Ibsen had attacked with solemnity and tragedy.

Shaw's major contribution to the modern theatre was to provide a galaxy of brilliant theatrical experiences which both entertained and stimulated his audiences. His ideas flowed in an ebullient stream out of the theatre into the lives of the intelligent public of his day, and what he did not wish to dwell on in his plays he enlarged on in his Prefaces. Before his advent, the theatre of ideas was like a church in which a little congregation of so-called intellectual theatregoers took itself so seriously that its influence was confined to a group which regarded itself as the elite custodians of modern thought. Shaw himself in his play *The Philanderer* satirized these heavy-going intellectuals as members of what he called the Ibsen Club, and he transported the theatre of ideas into the wider world of the popular theatre.

No writer for the theatre has affected his times as much as Shaw has, and for this very reason, some of his plays have become seemingly obsolete because the social customs against which they were directed have also become obsolete. Once when I discussed with Shaw a revival of his play *Man and Superman,* I mentioned the fact that the idea of women pursuing men on which it was based had now lost its novelty, and that the reception of the play would be affected as a result. "Nonsense!" said GBS. "When the play was first done, the audiences were so shocked that they were unable to laugh. Now that they are no longer shocked, they laugh heartily at the play itself. Indeed, it is actually now possible to appreciate my play as a comedy and not as a social document." However, there are several of Shaw's plays, such as *John Bull's Other Island,* which deal with historical or social situations that no longer exist. While the same is true of almost all of Shakespeare's plays, the latter are always of current interest because Shakespeare was not attempting to change the social customs of his day, whereas Shaw was nearly always intent on demolishing some current injustice or folly. When he succeeded, as he often did, the plays which accomplished this lost much of their topical interest. But this may easily change in the years to come, when such plays may be revived for their playing values or historical interest.

Having worked on the production of so many plays of O'Neill and Shaw, the two outstanding theatre geniuses of my time, I was interested in learning their opinions of each other and in comparing their attitudes toward each other's work. I once asked O'Neill to what extent Shaw had influenced his own writing. 'Gene said he had been more influenced by Shaw as a man and as a writer than as a playwright. When he went to school in Stamford, Connecticut, he was wildly excited about Shaw's *Quintessence of Ibsenism.* It was his favorite reading during his last year at school. He kept underlining in red ink the places where he agreed with Shaw until every page of the book was almost entirely covered with red lines. Whenever 'Gene indulged in an argument on the theatre, he told me, he would slay his opponents by quoting from Shaw.

Shaw greatly admired O'Neill's work as a dramatist, but

with his old-maidish temperance attitude, he could never quite avoid being shocked by 'Gene's early drinking. When I told him at Stresa that 'Gene had not touched a drop of liquor for years, and had sworn off it for life, Shaw replied, "He'll probably never write a good play again." I explained that 'Gene had already written many good plays since he had stopped drinking, including *Strange Interlude* and *Mourning Becomes Electra.* This seemed to make very little impression on GBS, however, for a few years later he asked me the same question again.

"How is O'Neill feeling?" asked Shaw when I called on him while I was in England in 1947. I said that he was well, but that he took a pessimistic view about the state of the world and was of the opinion that our present civilization was on its way downhill and headed for ultimate disaster. "Tell him not to worry about that," said Shaw cheerily. "If mankind turns out, as I suspect, to be a failure, it will destroy itself and be replaced by some other creature." Their outlooks appeared to be the same, but O'Neill, the writer of tragedy, was tragic about it, while Shaw, the writer of comedy, was cheerful, and this difference in attitudes existed despite Shaw's being the older man by thirty years.

My first contact with Bernard Shaw began when I was working as an apprentice in the office of Cruikshank and Fairweather, a Scottish firm of chartered patent agents in London. My employer and teacher, Wallace Cranston Fairweather, was an amateur Fabian and gave me a ticket to a lecture with the intriguing title, "The Position of the Artist under Socialism," to be given by Shaw at the Fabian Society. Shaw, aflame with his red beard and his subject, made a profound impression on me, although I was no older than fifteen at the time. The position of the musician, author or actor under Socialism, according to Shaw, would be that of a capitalist millionaire. "My income," said Shaw, "as a state dramatist would be enormous!" "And serve you right," cried someone in the audience.

Shaw was not entirely mistaken in his prophecy, for years later Stanislavsky, the famous founder of the Moscow Art Theatre, told me that Chaliapin, a national hero in Soviet Russia, was paid handsomely for each performance. One day he was set upon by robbers in a remote Russian village. "I'm Chaliapin!" he announced imperiously to the footpads. They apologized profusely, gave him a present of an heirloom they had stolen, and escorted him on his way to safety.

My first actual introduction to GBS came after I arrived in the United States from England in the year 1911. Thanks to my friend Alice Raphael, I met a small but interesting group of young people interested in politics and plays, of whom the leaders were Walter Lippmann, Philip Moeller, Waldo Frank, Alice Raphael, Clare Raphael Reis (who later founded the American Society of Composers), Theresa Helburn, Edward Goodman, Kenneth MacGowan, Russell Herts, Josephine A. Meyer and a number of others, some of whom were in the habit of reading plays aloud in the homes of Moeller and Goodman. One of the plays selected was Shaw's *Press Cuttings,* and because of my English accent rather than any inherent acting ability, I was asked to play in it opposite Theresa Helburn, who took the role of Egeria, thus beginning an active if not acting relationship which was to continue for many years. This was my one and only appearance in a Shaw play, and mercifully there was no audience beyond the other readers. Many of this same group joined me in forming the Washington Square Players, which became the first "off-Broadway" theatre of that period, at the little Bandbox Theatre on East 52nd Street.

One of the most ambitious projects of the Washington Square Players was to produce Shaw's *Mrs. Warren's Profession* at the Comedy Theatre on March 11, 1918, with which we stormed the doors of Broadway. The role of Mrs. Warren was played by Mary Shaw, a lady who imparted an air of Bostonian respectability to the part of Mrs. Warren, who operated a Shavian house of prostitution. While earlier performances of this play at the Garrick Theatre in the year 1905 had resulted in all the actors' being arrested and the play closed, by the year 1918 when we produced it with Mary Shaw and Diantha Pattison, Shavian prostitution had become so dull that we limped by with about forty performances and an average business which paid neither Shaw his royalties nor our landlord, Lee Shubert, his theatre rent. Thus our first venture with a Shaw play was not profitable in terms of money, scandal or prestige.

When I listened to Shaw lecture at the Fabian Society years earlier, I had not yet fallen under the spell of his personality and his writings. He struck me not so much as a great man lecturing to a crowd of his admirers, but rather as a genial, warmhearted intellectual casually addressing a group of his friends and equals, of which I formed no part. His general appearance impressed me as being tweedy and eccentric as to dress, since he wore "plus fours" of green Jaeger wool, while his head, which seemed slightly too large for his tall thin body, rose out of his shaggy growth of red beard. His complexion, hair and beard were so ruddy that one carried away a feeling of a woolly bundle of greens framing a Mephistophelian countenance with blue eyes always smiling, and I carried this picture of GBS for many years, long after I counted myself as one of his admirers.

However, the Shaw I came to know later on was quite other than this. The greater part of my association with him took place at a time when middle age had written its moderating influence on his expression. A kind of benevolent geniality had taken the place of the sardonic smile which, while it still danced often in his eyes, was not as ever-present as it had remained in my memory or imagination. Shaw when I first met him personally had gained the force and dignity of a great man, but without any pomposity or outward show. The difference may have been in me, but to me he had mellowed in appearance and showed his greatness, not in attitudes or expressions which called for admiration, but rather the reverse. He put his visitors at ease by the warmth of his welcome, and then entertained them with a constant stream of humorous anecdotes in which his visitors could join with him on the same free and easy level of companionship. This geniality, this desire to entertain, was perhaps one of the outstanding characteristics which one observed on first meeting GBS, and it continued throughout his life. At times, GBS deliberately played the role of a "star" entertainer, assuming an easy responsibility for keeping his guests stimulated and amused by his conversation. In this mood, which was displayed more often as he grew older and more accustomed to being admired, he was a fund of delightfully good-humored conversation and he illustrated any points he wished to make with a wealth of witty stories. Yet when occasion called for it, he could be quite stern, almost frighteningly so, but this was usually only when he became involved in business arguments, on which he was just as positive as in matters of his plays or politics.

Although he was almost sixty-four when I first met him, GBS seemed toweringly tall, held himself as straight as a rod, and walked as lightly as a man twenty years his junior. He carried his head high on his shoulders and had a habit of tossing it back in laughing. This youthful bearing continued until he reached his nineties. Indeed, it was so remarkable to see him bent over at the age of ninety-four, as shown in one of the photographs which appears in this book, that I was greatly saddened by the depredations of age on his body, if not on his spirit. When he smiled (and he usually smiled while he talked) his eyes seemed actually to twinkle.

Nothing I can write can tell the story of what Shaw looked like as well as some of the informal pictures I took of him at Stresa, in the year 1929 when he was seventy-three years old. When Shaw posed for a formal picture, he usually appeared serious and stiff; when I caught him in a snapshot, he was vivacious and unself-conscious, and a much better picture resulted. He was particularly proud of the posed picture which he gave to Mrs. Langner. He drew my attention to his forehead, which he said was "as high as a house." He was as flirtatious as any callow youth when he was "snapped" with my wife, Armina, while he acted the part of the affectionate husband with hilarity when he kissed Mrs. Shaw for my benefit (not hers). This was probably the only picture ever taken of them kissing. These earlier pictures should be contrasted with those taken of Shaw in his later years, those in his little workshop and the one taken of him in 1950, about four months before his death. All the pictures mentioned are included in this book.

Shaw's manners were always courtly, almost old-fashioned. With women he was gallant in an old-world way. He seemed always to want them to like him, and his letters to Theresa Helburn, whom he nicknamed Tessie, were full of affection. I am sure he enjoyed writing love letters to such actresses as Ellen Terry and Mrs. Pat Campbell as exercises in imaginative literature, and I am sure that he would have been greatly embarrassed had the recipients of these love letters desired to have these affairs become physical instead of literary.

St. John Ervine, in his book *Bernard Shaw, His Life Work and Friends,* says that Shaw's marriage with Mrs. Shaw was never consummated. How could he possibly know for sure? He quotes as his authority for this a letter Shaw wrote to Frank Harris in 1930 in which he said, "Not until I was past 40 did I earn enough to marry without seeming to marry for money, nor my wife at the same age without suspicion of being driven by sex starvation. As man and wife we found a new relation in which sex had no part. It ended the old gallantries, flirtations, and philanderings for both of us." I maintain that the above passage alone is not convincing proof. It could mean that "as man and wife we found a new relation in which sex had no part" after a certain length of time. The very fact that he mentions "a new relation" suggests that before this new relation, there was an old relation in which sex played a part and which ceased some time after their marriage, and this is confirmed by the sentence, "It ended the old gallantries, flirtations, and philanderings for both of us." Add the words, "with each other" to the end of this sentence, and it makes more sense than that a woman of Mrs. Shaw's temperament and breeding was in the habit of carrying on "old gallantries, flirtations, and philanderings."

In any event, this one letter of Shaw to Harris is a flimsy bit of evidence on which to characterize a marriage, which can be explained in the normal way, especially since, as St. John Ervine points out, his alleged affairs with other women ceased after he married Charlotte. Ervine, who knew both GBS and Mrs. Shaw extremely well, evidently had no personal information from either of them on this subject, or else he would surely have included the fact in his excellent book, which is a mine of valuable information.

In *The Apple Cart,* which I, as well as many others, believe to be partly autobiographical, there are many remarks which clearly explain the very old-fashioned attitude of GBS toward Charlotte. They are found in the words of Magnus in his Interlude with Orinthia, his alleged mistress, who wishes him to divorce his wife Jemima and marry her. To this suggestion he replies:

> Being your husband is only a job for which one man will do as well as another, and which the last man holds subject to six months notice in the divorce court. Being my wife is something quite different. The smallest derogation to Jemima's dignity would hit me like the lash of a whip across the face. About yours, somehow, I do not care a rap.

Whatever may be the facts about GBS's private personal sex life (and no doubt scores of psychologists, psychiatrists and other self-styled authorities will speculate about it), I am able to inform all and sundry that I never saw at any time the slightest trace of effeminacy in Shaw's bearing, and having spent a long time in the theatre in contact with all the varieties of sexes,

I believe that I would have been fully aware of any deviation from the radiant masculinity which was characteristic of him. And I know many women who knew him well and will bear me out. Moreover, in all my encounters with Mr. and Mrs. Shaw, there was never the slightest suggestion that they were other than a most conventionally happily married couple, with an affectionate attitude toward each other which was often illuminated by a sense of humor on her part toward his shortcomings. Once, after he had made an extravagant speech on the virtues of vegetarianism, she remarked quietly to me, "Of course, Mr. Shaw is a strict vegetarian, but I've noticed when he is traveling, he doesn't inquire too closely into the origins of the soup!"

On one occasion when Alfred Lunt and Lynn Fontanne were lunching with the Shaws, I was seated next to Mrs. Shaw and GBS was at the other end of the table. While he entertained Alfred, Lynn and the Theatre Guild director Philip Moeller with a stream of amusing anecdotes of the theatre, I asked Mrs. Shaw why GBS always refused to visit America. "I'm afraid he's liable to get overexcited, meeting so many people, and getting so much publicity," said Mrs. Shaw. "But we could arrange to protect him," I replied. A particularly loud burst of laughter came from the other end of the table. "I'm sure you'd do your best to keep him quiet," she replied, "but you see, there's Mr. Shaw himself!"

As to my own relationship with Shaw, I found that the best way to get on with him was to fight back when attacked and to attempt, as well as I could, to match my wits with his. I soon learned that I got nowhere by treating him with the respect and admiration which I felt for him. Once when he called me by telephone while I was in London, asking me to come to lunch, I replied, "I'm sorry. I've arranged to take my daughter Phyllis out this morning." "Well, bring her along," was the joking reply. "She can say when she grows up that she once met the great Bernard Shaw." "I'm sorry," I replied, "I've promised to take her to the zoo, and I think it'll mean much more to her!" On another occasion, when Shaw dropped in to see me at my London hotel, Phyllis was in the room and made a drawing of GBS which she showed him. "I'll autograph this," he said, and wrote under it, "This is me. GBS." The postcard is reproduced in the book.

An occasion I remember with pleasure was bringing GBS

and A. A. Milne together. Having produced A. A. Milne's *Mr. Pim Passes By* and with other plays by him under consideration at the Theatre Guild, I telephoned him for a luncheon appointment on one of my visits to London. On the morning we set for this I received a call from GBS asking me to lunch. "I'm sorry I can't come," I said, "I'm lunching with A. A. Milne." "Bring him along," said the genius at the other end of the line. "I'd like to meet him." "But suppose he doesn't want to come?" I asked. "Don't you worry about that," said GBS. "I'm sure he'd like to meet *me*." Milne, of course, was delighted and we met at Mr. Shaw's apartment.

Milne was a slight, boyish-looking young man, genuinely bashful and an excellent listener. This suited Shaw to a tee and we sat there listening to GBS discoursing on the subject of playwriting. "Now take *At Mrs. Beam's,*" said Shaw. "C. K. Munro, its author, has done a good job, but his observation is not good. He has a character remark that he dislikes going to church and sitting among a group of smelly people in dirty clothes. Now, as a matter of fact," said Shaw, "the people who go to church usually take a bath on Saturday night—their only bath in the week—and put on their 'Sunday best' clothes, so church is probably the only place where these people are ever clean. Good observation is essential to good playwriting."

Milne, who was later on to write *Winnie-the-Pooh,* which made him famous in every English-speaking nursery, was charming and self-effacing. When at last we were alone together he showed me a snapshot of his wife and child with a butterfly flying over them, of which he was inordinately proud. As an amateur photographer he was apparently far more interested in the detail of the butterfly than in his wife, his child, his plays or me.

In the season of 1923-24 we engaged Arnold Daly, one of the most famous actors on the American stage, to appear in special performances of a German play, *The Race with the Shadow* by Wilhelm von Scholz. Besides being a magnificent actor, he could justly claim the honor, along with Richard Mansfield, of having first introduced the plays of Bernard Shaw to America. Arnold, who had been extremely handsome in his youth, was a middle-aged man when I first met him. He was of medium stature, with dark hair and dark eyes which constantly danced under his busy brows as he would recount one amusing story after another about his relationship with Shaw, with whom he ultimately quarreled violently in London. He once described to me how Shaw directed his own plays. "All that it is necessary for you to do, Arnold, is to say my lines so slowly and clearly that the audience can understand every word." "What about my acting?" asked Arnold. "As long as they can hear my lines, you can act or not as you please." This, of course, was Arnold's version of the story.

"After I write my plays," Shaw once told me, "I take a chessboard and move the pieces from position to position. Each piece represents an actor, and I write the stage directions into my plays after I have worked them out in detail on this chessboard. If the actor follows the stage directions exactly as they are written in the play, he cannot possibly go wrong."

Shaw's stage directions are indeed masterly, but they do not leave the actor and director any latitude. A creative artist with the temperament of Arnold Daly was constantly in hot water with Shaw for departing from his instructions. After the break between them, Shaw vowed that Daly would never again appear in a Shaw play. They were both Irish and explosive about each other, Shaw being the more tolerant of the two, while Arnold took to drink, being at heart deeply unhappy over the rift.

Before we engaged Daly to appear in *The Race with the Shadow,* Arnold had been drinking heavily but he seemed then to be on his good behavior. He was magnificent in the part. But one Sunday evening he arrived at the theatre tragically inebriated. He could barely repeat his lines even though the stage manager, Philip Loeb, fed them to him one by one from the wings, until the pages of the prompt script fell out of his hands and scattered all over the stage. We were forced to ring down the curtain on the pretense that Arnold was ill. Despite this, we engaged him for other plays after he had had a long spell of good behavior, so greatly did we admire his acting talents.

Unfortunately, Daly won the ill-will of the well-known dramatic critic Alexander Woollcott, who fluctuated between being an angel to his friends and a hellion to those he disliked, with an emotional instability which made it impossible to know at any given moment whether he was going to kiss you on the cheek or stab you in the back. Daly appeared in two failures in succession, followed by a third. "Arnold Daly went down last night for the third and last time," wrote the irrepressible Woollcott, going far beyond the bounds of dramatic criticism and human decency. Arnold never recovered and died horribly in a sordid rooming house by accidentally setting fire to himself with a cigarette, apparently while in a state of intoxication. Thus, lonely and without friends, one of the greatest actors this country has ever known made his tragic final exit.

The day after his body was discovered, there were blazing headlines on the front pages of the newspapers: "Bernard Shaw says of Arnold Daly's death that spontaneous combustion, while rare, sometimes occurs!" I could hardly believe my eyes when I read these cruel words. Surely Shaw was misquoted, I said to myself, and the next time I saw him I raised the question. "GBS, I don't believe you actually made that statement about Arnold Daly dying from spontaneous combustion, and I've told people so." "No, you are wrong, Lawrence," he replied. "I did say it, and for this reason: Arnold was no more sentimental about death than I am. He adored publicity, and his death was getting very little of it. Had I made a few pious remarks, they would have gone unnoticed, but I knew that if I made a sensational statement it would make front-page headlines, so I invented the story about spontaneous combustion sometimes occurring, and it had exactly the desired effect. Arnold, had he been alive, would have been delighted to see his name in large headlines in every important newspaper in the English-speaking world." I looked at GBS in amazement, but I had no reason to doubt his sincerity. I had seen so many instances of his kindness that I believed him incapable of intentional unkindness to Arnold.

It is not my intention in this book to evaluate any of Shaw's writings in the various fields in which he was interested, outside of the plays which he sent us for production or on which I worked at the Theatre Guild and the Westport Country Playhouse (these are listed in the Addenda). Shaw has probably expressed himself more voluminously on the subjects of music and musical criticism, drama and dramatic criticism, religion, politics, economics, socialism, sex, Marxism, medicine and evolution than any other man, living or dead. The task still remains for an energetic admirer to codify his ideas on all these subjects, and it will take almost a lifetime to do it.

Shaw was supremely a thinker and a writer, but not a man of revolutionary action. Nothing more dramatic occurred in his life than attendance at meetings of the St. Pancras Town Council at the turn of the century, interminable lectures, Socialist meetings, soap-box oratory at Hyde Park and enormous activities in meetings of the Fabian Society and the Independent Labour Party of which he was one of the founders. He led no rebellions, took part in no violence, and chained himself to no lamp posts to help woman's suffrage, of which he was an ardent supporter. His weapon was his pen and he wielded it bitingly and effectively as an agitator and propagandist. On one occasion I told him of an idea I had for restoring Jerusalem as the center of religions for over a billion peoples. "A splendid idea, Lawrence," he said. "Why don't you write a play about it?" Had I told him of my plan to build a Shakespeare Festival Theatre for the United States, he would have probably suggested that I write an article for it. He did as much for the proposed British National Theatre in London. He even wrote a play about it, *The Dark Lady of the Sonnets,* with a plea for building the theatre, which at this time still remains to be built, although it is apparently on its way after all these years.

Shaw had a great interest in reforming the teaching and spelling of the English language, including the formulation of a new alphabet, and in his will he left a large sum with the British Public Trustee to carry out this work—work he did not do himself, but left for others to do after his death. Had he been a man of action instead of a man of literature, he would have started this work himself, so that by the time he died, an English language institution would have been founded under the impetus of his enthusiasm, and the British courts would not have had to void this part of his will as a practical matter because of the difficulty of carrying out Shaw's wishes as a legal "charity."

Shaw had many collisions with the Lord Chamberlain on the subject of censorship, and here again he attacked the situation vigorously with his pen alone. He led his revolutions on paper but did not lead any revolutionists in a march on the office of the Lord Chamberlain. (For that matter, nor did anyone else.) This perhaps illustrates the difference between Shaw and Aristophanes, the two greatest playwright-critics of the social systems under which they lived. As Shaw stated in the preface to *Heartbreak House,* he largely kept his mouth shut during the First World War and did not write plays against the conflict, because "you cannot make war on war and your neighbour at the same time." Yet he took time out to write an antiwar pamphlet, *Common Sense and the War,* which accomplished little more than to raise an outcry against him which took him out of public life and gave him the time to write his longest play, *Back to Methuselah.*

Aristophanes, also a rebel against war, did not hesitate to write antiwar plays during the Peloponnesian Wars. He incurred the animosity of the populace and the Athenian leaders by his satire *Babylonians,* which criticized the high-handed treatment by Athens of her allies. According to John Gassner in *A Treasury of the Theatre,* an effort was made to declare him a foreigner who had no right to comment on Athenian politics, and he would have been sent "back where he came from" had he not been born in Athens. Shaw, born in Ireland, was one of Britain's severest critics during his lifetime, but thanks to the hospitality of the British people, as well as Shaw's own ability to plead his causes entertainingly as well as convincingly, he was never forced to defend himself against more than censorship or accusations of blasphemy or immorality in his writings. It is unthinkable, for example, that Shaw would have played a character in one of his plays because all the available actors were afraid to play it. Yet this is what Aristophanes did, when no actor would venture to impersonate the politician Creon in one of his plays.

Despite Shaw's polemics against marriage, he was one of the most exemplary married men I have ever known, conventional in a mid-Victorian middle-class manner, and in my opinion as much bound as a Church of England Bishop by the so-called "respectability" of his day against which he inveighed so fearlessly in his plays. I feel sure that Mrs. Shaw, knowing of his protracted love letters to the actresses Ellen Terry and Mrs. Pat Campbell, regarded them as bits of Irish whimsy, coupled with the practical fact that he wanted these actresses to appear in plays written by him, probably the only consummation he ever achieved with these actresses, since he was successful in this respect with both of them. But we must not underestimate the fact that he was also stage-struck and no doubt idealized both women as artists, as stage-struck authors often do. It represented a high order of creativity coupled with worldly wisdom to be inspired by an actress and at the same time to secure her employment in the pursuit of your own artistic aims, to say nothing of your livelihood. Shaw, more than any other man I have known, succeeded in this. I am somewhat bewildered by the new group of love letters he wrote to Molly Tompkins, a young actress from

Atlanta, Georgia, who gave up the stage and became a painter, for here he cannot be accused of combining romance with artistic expression as a playwright.

What impelled Shaw to leave Ireland for England might be indicated by the poetic speech given to the character of Doyle in Act I of his now obsolete play *John Bull's Other Island* in which he castigates Ireland and Irishmen with the following:

> Oh, the dreaming! the dreaming! the torturing, heart-scalding, never satisfying dreaming, dreaming, dreaming, dreaming! [Savagely] No debauchery that ever coarsened and brutalized an Englishman can take the worth and usefulness out of him like that dreaming. An Irishman's imagination never lets him alone, never convinces him, never satisfies him; but it makes him that he cant face reality nor deal with it nor handle it nor conquer it: he can only sneer at them that do, and [bitterly, at Broadbent] be "agreeable to strangers," like a good-for-nothing woman on the streets. . . . And all the time you laugh! laugh! laugh! eternal derision, eternal envy, eternal folly, eternal fouling and staining and degrading, until, when you come at last to a country where men take a question seriously and give a serious answer to it, you deride them for having no sense of humor, and plume yourself on your own worthlessness as if it made you better than them.

Shaw, the bright, imaginative, dreaming young man from Ireland who came to England to sell his literary wares and to deride the stolid humorless qualities of the British which he unconsciously admired, was the last and greatest of a procession of precocious Irish wits who were "agreeable to strangers" and whose number included Dean Swift, Daniel Defoe, Richard Brinsley Sheridan, Oliver Goldsmith and Oscar Wilde; among them, the last-named three and Shaw wrote some of the most entertaining comedies of the English theatre, many of which are still popular today. Yet of these brilliant playwrights, Shaw alone wrote as a social moralist, with an acid pen and a pungent wit, with intent to destroy the hypocrisies of his day, a work which is still to be completed.

During our long relationship with GBS, neither Terry Helburn nor I entered into arguments with him on the subject of politics, and it was not until we rejected *Geneva* in 1938 that any strong differences of opinion on this score developed between him and the Theatre Guild. As these were always in the intellectual realm and never carried over into personal disagreements, we were able to maintain our friendship on both sides over the years without disturbance on this count. Most of our differences were on business subjects, and although he sometimes exploded violently, his outbursts did not last long.

At the time I am writing these lines, most matters of world politics are seen in terms of the "cold war." This was not so in the twenties and thirties. Two facts about Shaw and his social and political teachings which should be remembered are extremely important in terms of the present. Working to establish the British Labour Party at a time when very little responsibility was assumed by the British government for the well-being of the working classes, Shaw and his group of associates in the Fabian Society preached the possibility of a better life without class warfare and bloody revolution. Thanks to the reform measures advocated by this group, of which Shaw was one of the most vocal members, Britain (followed later by the United States) adopted the economic and social reforms which now make it possible for the Western World to challenge the Soviets in the cold war. Their ideas, all advocated by GBS, included unemployment insurance, higher wages and greater consumption of food and goods by the working classes; anti-child-labor laws; income taxes and heavy death duties breaking up the large landed estates; state aid to agriculture and farms; old-age pensions; free medical assistance; extension of free education; low-priced housing, slum clearance and numerous other reform measures to provide improvements in the status and employment of women. Almost all these ideas have been embraced now in both England and the United States. And all this has been accomplished without loss of human rights, including the freedom of expression of creative writers and the press and the right to criticize the government without being liquidated. Bad conditions still exist on both sides of the Iron Curtain, but without the reforms for which GBS fought during most of his early life, on balance we should have lost the cold war long before this.

Anyone reading Shaw's Prefaces, essays, and drama and music criticism must marvel at the range of his reading, and his extraordinary memory which enabled him to reach into his mind and pull out examples from the world's literature and the lives of great men of the past, and sometimes little-known men. He was an avid devourer of books and periodicals, and there were always foreign newspapers and magazines strewn over the table in his living room.

On the occasion when we stayed at the same hotel with the Shaws at Stresa, we noted at those meals (usually lunch) which he and Mrs. Shaw ate together that they always had their noses buried in books and seemed to be far more interested in what they were reading than in what they were eating or in conversation. It was perhaps the lack of a formal university education that caused Shaw to educate himself along informal lines. As a result, he was as erudite in music, painting, sculpture (but not poetry) as he was in sociology, history, philosophy and the medical and biological sciences of his day. In his late eighties he tried to master the physics of the atom bomb but understood the subject only dimly, although he understood clearly such mathematical concepts as the quantum theory. He could argue against Darwin's theory of evolution with a Darwinian and cover him with confusion; he could argue acting with an actor and show him how to speak and act; he could talk politics with politicians and outplay them at their own game; and he could argue business with his theatrical managers and tell them how to advertise and sell theatre tickets. And he did all this with a fund of good humor, a gaiety of expression and an irresistible sense of the value of laughter in making a controversial point which, had he expressed it seriously, might never have been accepted.

Readers who peruse my letters to GBS may wonder why I so often wrote flippantly or attempted to make my points humorously. I found that I could accomplish far more by this method than by solemn correspondence, for I too did not wish to be derided "for having no sense of humor." One of the few occasions when he responded angrily was when I teased him, in his nineties, about his constant reference to being treated as dead. His tart reply left no doubt that he was still very much alive.

Readers may be amused by my habit of trying to protect GBS from the onslaught of unfavorable dramatic critics, especially with reference to *Saint Joan, Back to Methuselah* and his later plays. In retrospect, I seem to have tried to play the part of a mother hen shielding her chick from critical unpleasantness. I soon discovered that in general unfavorable criticism affected Shaw—to use another barnyard simile—about as much as water falling off the proverbial duck's back, and in the case of *Saint Joan* some of the notices which I regarded as unfavorable and tried to soften were regarded by him as excellent. Having been a critic himself, he was generally kindly toward other critics, remembering how difficult it was to earn one's living by enforced attendance at the theatres where only a few plays each season were worthy of important critical attention. "Pity the poor, hard-working drama critics" might be regarded as Shaw's attitude toward them—a benevolence which I am afraid I did not attain until far too late in life to serve any happy purpose.

As to what it was like to work with Shaw, my readers will learn in the correspondence which passed between us how he managed to control us over a distance of three thousand miles. His reluctance to visit the United States and to assist personally in the production of his plays here resulted in far more correspondence passing between us than would have been the case had he given us verbal instructions. It is my hope that this record of the productions of some of Shaw's most important plays, from *Heartbreak House* on, during the latter part of his life will be of interest to admirers and students of one of the greatest geniuses and reformers in the history of the world as well as the theatre.

CHAPTER TWO

Heartbreak House

O U R interest in Shaw's unproduced play *Heartbreak House,* which had been published in the year 1919, with a Preface under the alluring title of "Heartbreak House and Horseback Hall," was stimulated by the postwar attitude of GBS. He was, as always, against war in general, and against war from the air in particular. The play's last scene with giant bombers droning over London was prophetic enough to make many of us feel uncomfortable, and even more of us scared to death, notwithstanding the fact that we had just won a war "to make the world safe for democracy," as the high-sounding slogan of Woodrow Wilson succinctly put it.

In *Heartbreak House,* while delivering a host of scoldings on a host of subjects, Shaw sounded a warning blast against the possible world destruction which would ensue if mankind continued to fail to find a remedy other than war for disputes among nations. Alas, it seems that we of this century must always live under the dread of airplanes or rockets screaming in the skies above us and threatening to bring down a rain of horrible mass destruction on us and our civilization. Three times in my own life I have witnessed periods when this play was top-

Two scenes from *Heartbreak House,* which opened November 10, 1920 as the first Shaw play presented by the Theatre Guild

Dudley Digges, who directed the play and also portrayed Boss Mangan

A scene from Part II of *Back to Methuselah*. Shown here are Claude King as Lubin and A. P. Kaye as Joyce-Burge, thinly veiled portraits of Asquith and Lloyd George

The tree in the Garden of Eden, a set designed by Lee Simonson for *Back to Methuselah*

Other sets by Simonson for *Back to Methuselah*

Roland Young as General Burgoyne in *The Devil's Disciple,* shown here with Basil Sydney as Dick Dudgeon and Lotus Robb

Other scenes from *The Devil's Disciple*, staged by Philip Moeller

Winifred Lenihan as Joan of Arc in *St. Joan* in the Theatre Guild production of 1923, a world premiere
Philip Leigh as the Dauphin, with Miss Lenihan, in the original *St. Joan*

The cathedral scene *(above)* and the trial scene from the 1923 *St. Joan*

Uta Hagen as Joan in the 1951 revival of the play

Helen Hayes as Cleopatra in the production of *Caesar and Cleopatra*
which opened the new Guild Theatre, April 13, 1925

Scenes from *Caesar and Cleopatra*. Lionel Atwill as Caesar, Helen Westley as Ftatuteeta

Alfred Lunt as Bluntschli and Lynn Fontanne as Raina in 1925 production of *Arms and the Man (above)*

Tom Powers in the Lunt role on the tour of *Arms and The Man*

Henry Travers as Androcles and Romney Brent as the Lion in *Androcles and the Lion,* presented in 1925
In the same production, Edward G. Robinson as Caesar

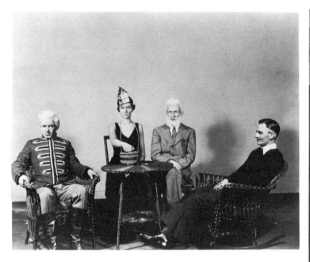

Scenes from *Garrick Gaieties of 1925,* which satirized some Guild productions of Shaw; Romney Brent *(right)* as Alfred Lunt in *Arms and the Man;* Rosalind Russell *(above)* in a scene with "Shaw"

Richard Rodgers and Lorenz Hart at the time of this, their first collaboration

ical, the last being now upon us. *Heartbreak House,* unlike some of Shaw's plays, did not accomplish the destruction of the target at which it was aimed, so it will unfortunately continue to be of contemporary interest for many years to come. The play contained many other important social implications which will be discussed in relation to some of the later plays in Chapter 9.

Heartbreak House was produced by the Theatre Guild in the United States before it appeared on the stage in London. The theatregoing public of the United States recognized Shaw's genius long before the English did. Indeed, his first financial successes as a playwright came from productions by the American actor-manager Richard Mansfield, and later by Arnold Daly, who eventually played a repertory of Shaw plays in New York City and on tour. At the time when we of the Theatre Guild began to interest ourselves in *Heartbreak House,* Shaw had received full recognition as a major dramatist with such highly successful plays as *You Never Can Tell, Arms and the Man, Pygmalion, The Devil's Disciple, The Doctor's Dilemma, Captain Brassbound's Conversion, Androcles and the Lion, Major Barbara, Getting Married, Misalliance* and *Fanny's First Play.*

However, in the years just before World War I, nothing of Shaw's had been played in the New York theatre since *Pygmalion* in the year 1914. Our production of *Heartbreak House* was historically interesting as the first to break GBS's theatrical silence for several years, and it was produced at a time when, because of his attitudes toward the war, he was by no means popular in either this country or England.

The writing of *Heartbreak House* was started by Shaw in 1913 and the play waited almost seven years before our production in 1920. It ran for 125 performances in New York and was rated a great success for the Theatre Guild and Shaw. The London production, which had the benefit of Shaw's personal assistance, was prepared with a great deal of acrimony between the author and the producer on the subject of casting, and despite its New York success and reputation, the play was pronounced a failure. Many English critics have since eaten their words and have rated it, as we did, one of Shaw's finest plays.

Our production of *Heartbreak House* came after the Theatre Guild had started its third season rather disastrously with a production of Pinski's *The Treasure,* which some of our brighter young directors had cast with an ill-assorted group of Irish actors led by Dudley Digges. The directors followed a Broadway tradition that if you are producing a play about Jewish people, you should use Irish actors to play the roles, thus showing that Jewish people are just like any other people, and especially like Irish people. This set us pondering on the Irish, and particularly on the famous Irish playwright then living quietly in partial retirement in England, so unpopular was he after writing and speaking for years against the efforts of the Allies in World War I. But if he did not approve of the British, neither did he approve of Kaiser Wilhelm and his embattled Teutons, with the result that he was as much disliked on one side of the trenches as on the other.

In order to secure the rights to the play, I cabled Shaw for permission for the Guild to present it. GBS, not having heard either of the Guild or of me, telegraphed curtly to my friend St. John Ervine, WHO ON EARTH IS LANGNER? Ervine told Shaw that Langner and the Guild could be safely trusted with the play, having already successfully produced Ervine's own play *John Ferguson*. Then GBS wrote to Theresa Helburn that he wondered if the Guild was "bold enough and clever enough to know that the alternative to pleasing an audience for two hours is to put the utmost strain upon their attention for three, and send them home exhausted but inspired."

Somebody had told us of Shaw's difficult contract terms, and we discussed the situation with John Drinkwater, whose play about Abraham Lincoln had had a long run in New York. Shaw wrote Drinkwater asking him his opinion about the Theatre Guild, and the latter cabled back:

> HAVE SEEN TWO THEATRE GUILD PERFORMANCES "JOHN FERGUSON" AND "FAITHFUL" VERY MUCH WORTHWHILE AND THEY ARE NOT RICH SOME LUNATIC HAS FRIGHTENED THEM ABOUT YOUR TERMS THEY ASK MY INTERCESSION WHICH I KNOW IS NOT NECESSARY.

Our first business contact with GBS was made through the intermediary of a friend, Ralph Block, who happened to be in London at the time. On May 19, 1920, we cabled Ralph as follows:

> ACCEPT TERMS HEARTBREAK UNDERSTAND ROYALTIES SEVEN ONE HALF ON FIRST SEVENTYFIVE HUNDRED TEN NEXT TWENTYFIVE HUNDRED TWELVE NEXT TWO THOUSAND FIFTEEN ABOVE CORPORATE NAME THEATRE GUILD INCORPORATED.

Ralph must have discussed this with GBS over the phone, for we received the following cable in reply:

HAVE HEARTBREAK DEFINITELY

On May 22 we sent Ralph the following cable:

IF POSSIBLE INCLUDE OPTION DEVILS DISCIPLE HEART-
BREAK CABLE ANSWER THE GUILD.

Ralph sent this original cable to GBS on which he wrote, "This explains itself. I sail May 31. At the Savoy until then." Shaw returned the cable to Block who sent it on to us. On it GBS wrote the following: "They want the earth now. But they must just do their trial trip with *Heartbreak House* first. GBS." Ralph also received the following letter from Shaw dated 23 May, 1920, before he left England:

The enclosed, without committing either of us, will give the T.G. a notion of the sort of agreement I shall propose if *Heartbreak House* is produced by it.

A good deal will depend on a successful carrying out of the scenic idea. The T.G. should get the same designed by an artist to be carried out by a scene painter. If the two are the same man, so much the better; but that does not always happen. The problem is to find an artist who likes the magnificent storm galleries and gold framed windows of the old Dutch deckers and Spanish galleons, and sees how a room could be made to look like the cabin of a XVI century admiral.

I should like very much to see a sketch of this, or a photograph of a sketch. I enclose a ground plan of the scene to save the artist the trouble of puzzling out the positions of the doors, etc., from the text.

Bon voyage!

Along with this letter came two enclosures, one a plan of the stage setting of the play, and the other the rough draft of a printed contract, on the top of which was written in Shaw's own neat handwriting the following:

This is the sort of thing you may expect if the Theatre Guild decides to do business with me. It is only a sample, not a draft.

At the bottom of the contract he wrote the following:

To the above clauses I shall probably add one obliging you not to break the run as long as the receipts exceed a certain figure, but allowing you to transfer to another theatre when this comes into conflict with your obligation to produce five (is it?) plays every year.

After Shaw had granted us permission to produce the play, I was told to communicate with his lawyer, Benjamin Stern, a charming and urbane gentleman who had represented Shaw's interests in this country for decades without showing any appreciable signs of accompanying wear and tear. Whether instructed to do so by Shaw or as a personal favor to me, Stern in a fatherly manner did his best to frighten me into a panic. "I must warn you," he said, "that Shaw will not permit you to alter as much as one single word in his play. He once closed Faversham's production of *Getting Married* because the actor dared to cut it without his permission. And lest you think," he proceeded, fixing me with his penetrating eyes, "that you can tamper with the play without Shaw knowing about it, let me also warn you that he has the most uncanny way of knowing exactly what you are doing. Once Arnold Daly wanted to present one of Shaw's plays at the Maxine Elliott Theatre on Fortieth Street. Shaw cabled his refusal because the street was being repaired!"

I learned later from Shaw that a lady, one of his early admirers, had been in the habit of attending the performances of all his plays in New York with the book in her lap and wrote Shaw instantly if anyone deviated from the printed word. She undoubtedly also kept him informed of the condition of the New York streets.

After considerable discussion with Mr. Stern in New York, an agreement was worked out which is a historic document so far as both Shaw and the Guild were concerned, for which reason it is reprinted in the Addenda. All the changes were made in Shaw's own handwriting, and the single witness was J. M. Barrie, who described himself as "Author," of Adelphi Terrace House, Strand, London, W.C. I like to picture the tall Irishman and the little Scotsman, the most eminent men of the English theatre, as they sat down at a desk on August 24, 1920, in Shaw's apartment and inscribed their names to this document. This was the only contract which existed between us for over twenty-five plays. The other signature was mine as Treasurer of Theatre Guild, Inc. and it was witnessed by Mr. Stern. The amount of the advance royalty payment to Shaw was $2,500, and this was the only advance he ever asked for or that we ever made to him during our long association.

The selection of an opening date for the play presented many difficulties, for Shaw refused to give permission to open the play until after the presidential election of 1920 had taken place. In vain we pleaded for an earlier opening. INEXORABLE, he cabled, economizing on his cable costs. Later he addressed the following letter to Theresa Helburn, after we had written to St. John Ervine asking him to intercede on our behalf:

> It is useless to trouble Mr. Ervine or to expostulate with me. I have been through it all before. The Theatre is so out of touch with politics that it never even knows a presidential election is on until it finds that the public is not paying the slightest attention to it and *won't* until the Monday following the first Tuesday in November relieves its mind as to who will be President next year. My lawyer (Mr. B. H. Stern of 149 B'way) has the strictest instructions to pay not the smallest heed to your entreaties to be ruined by throwing away your trump. You will find him inexorable. You must carry on as best you can until the third week in November. Then you can go ahead; and very thankful you will be to me for having saved you from a disastrous blunder. You will be wiser four years hence. This is your first election. I forgive you for not being aware of the danger.

Having already hired a cast and started to work on the production, we continued to expostulate, believing that GBS was hopelessly out of date about the effect of American elections on the theatre. It took us many years to learn how right he was. The latest occasion was the Kennedy-Nixon election of 1960, when the debates over television had a disastrous effect on theatregoing. Shaw wrote Terry further on a postcard:

> It would be far better to produce *H.H.* with the first cast you could pick out of the gutter on the 15th of Nov. than to produce it on the 15th of October with Sarah Bernhardt, the two Guitrys, Edwin Drew, Maude Adams, Charlie Chaplin and Mary Pickford.

A running play may do very well, because people already know about it, and it needs no press. But a new production has no chance. The presidential candidates play
the author and the cast off the stage: and the election
crowds out the theatre. If you doubt me, try—but with
somebody else's play. You will never try again.

I am sorry to upset the arrangements; but a new management has to buy its experience; and it mustn't do so
at the cost of an old—too old—author.

If any producer or author reads the above and is contemplating a September or October opening during an election year, I
solemnly abjure him to heed the Old Sage's advice. He was as
good a businessman as he was a playwright, and he knew much
more about the effect of American elections than we did.

We engaged a cast of competent players for the play, among
whom the best-known were Effie Shannon and Lucille Watson.
The leading role of Captain Shotover was played by Albert
Perry and Ellie by Elizabeth Risdon, neither of whom were
prominent at the time. Our production itself, directed by Dudley
Digges with scenery by Lee Simonson, was excellent, and while
I have seen several other productions since, including one
which employed a galaxy of stars, I still think ours was not
only the first but also the best. This is because this particular
play does not lend itself to star performances, and the best results are obtained by a group of actors who play and interplay
with one another. In one of the last performances I saw of the
play, each star actor hardly seemed aware of the presence of the
other people on the stage. The result turned the play into a series of monologues.

After the presidential election resulted in the victory of Warren G. Harding with his slogan "Back to Normalcy," our first
Shaw production, *Heartbreak House,* had its world première on
November 10, 1920. *Heartbreak House* was well received by
the press, which praised both the play and the acting, as well
as the Theatre Guild for producing it.

At the outset of rehearsals, we were faced with a difficulty,
for after engaging the beguiling blond-haired Effie Shannon for
the part of Hesione Hushabye, we noticed she was described by
Shaw as having "magnificent black hair." In the text of the
play, Ellie, another character, says to her, "Oh, you don't mean
to say, Hesione, that your beautiful black hair is false." Effie

was approached by us and requested either to dye her hair black or to wear a black wig, but her reaction to both proposals turned our approach into a retreat, if not a rout. The six Guild Directors put their heads together and hit upon the ingenious plan of having the line slurred in the reading. Nobody in the audience realized what was happening, and we thought we had succeeded in overcoming our little difficulty without breaking our agreement with Shaw, which did not permit us to alter a single line.

The play ran for almost five months at the Garrick Theatre and cemented our relationship with Shaw in the best possible manner, for there is no better bond between an author and a producer than a successful first production. (This statement must be modified since the advent of the Hollywood talent agencies, most of which now do almost everything possible to destroy such a bond, for fear that it may interfere with their "ownership" of the author.)

Shaw wrote us, some time later, "I am threatened with a London production of *Heartbreak House* now, as Nigel Playfair has returned from New York full of the impressions made on him by the Guild's production at the Garrick."

At the end of November, 1920, at a meeting of the Guild Board, I informed them that I was going to England for business reasons, and that while there I would try to obtain from Shaw a contract for the Theatre Guild to produce all of his plays in the States.

After the war, the accumulation of inventions which had been made or held over during the war, as well as the large number of new clients who entered into foreign trade for the first time, overwhelmed our international patent office with work, and it became necessary for me to take a trip to England and the Continent to establish a London office for my firm and also to make contacts with leading European authors, directors and actors who would be helpful to the Guild. So after our successful opening of Shaw's *Heartbreak House,* I set sail for England with the happy feeling that my office and the Theatre Guild were in good shape and that I could devote some time and effort to strengthening the European connections of both. I also resolved to call on Mr. Shaw, to ascertain whether the Guild could represent him in the States.

The idea of representing GBS in this country took a very firm hold in my mind, as I was not thinking in terms of a single play, but of a series of plays which could form, so to speak, a solid foundation for the Guild's subscription system, based on Shaw's so-called "congregations" throughout the United States, which could be counted on to support his plays at a time when it required a selected audience to do this. It should be remembered that at the time we produced *Heartbreak House,* GBS was anathema to the British people because of his attitude toward World War I. Instead of being purged or shot, as would undoubtedly have been the case with this particular artist at such a time under Communism, he had retired to his home in the country to work in peace and quiet. The series of plays which he wrote during this time was entitled *Back to Methuselah* and was actually five separate plays. This I was to learn later on, after we had our discussions about *Heartbreak House.* On December 8, 1920, before departing for Europe, I wrote GBS as follows:

> The writer, who is one of the founders and directors of the Theatre Guild, is taking this opportunity of dropping you a line on the subject of possible future relations with the Guild. I am leaving for England about the middle of January, and want to take up with you, on my arrival, the question of doing some of your other plays. *Heartbreak House* continues to go extremely well, and we expect to have a prolonged run.

In another letter I asked for the right to make *The Devil's Disciple* our next Shaw production. I received a postcard in reply:

> When you come to London ring me up (Gerrald 331— not in the book, so make a note of it) or drop me a line to say where you are staying.
> Mansfield squeezed the last farthing out of the *D.D.:* its success was the turning point of his career as far as his final conquest of New York was concerned; but that was more than 20 years ago.
> Still, the play remains essentially a star melodrama, and, as such, not so much the Guild's business as, say, Barrymore's.
> We can discuss it when we meet: this is only to prepare you for my point of view.

Arriving in London in the winter of 1921, I called on St. John Ervine, whose fine play *John Ferguson* was the Guild's first success. He gave me some advice as to how to achieve my objective to produce all of Shaw's plays in America. "He's really a very kind man," said St. John. "When I lost my leg in the war, he sent me a postcard saying that every tree is better off for a little pruning. This was his way of telling me not to dwell too much on my troubles."

This did not sound very reassuring, and I left Ervine with the impression that a difficult task lay ahead of me. The morning arrived when I was instructed to call at 10 Adelphi Terrace, and I walked up the stairs to the entrance to Shaw's apartment. A low fan-shaped grill of sharp iron spikes separated the staircase landing from the lower floor of the building, and I speculated on how easily a precipitous retreat might result in one's being impaled on this formidable barricade. The door opened, and I was shown into the study, a comfortable Georgian room, crowded with photographs and busts of Shaw including the famous one by Rodin and dominated by a cheerful fireplace on the white mantel of which were carved the words "They say—what say they—let them say!" I innocently supposed that this was Shaw's own personal formula for iconoclasm but learned from him years later that this legend was on the mantelpiece before Shaw moved into the apartment. Perhaps this was why it appealed to him. Paraphrasing the motto, I said to myself, "Shaw says—what says he—let him say!" and I waited with a little more courage as a result.

After a few minutes, Shaw came in, lean, white-bearded and erect, looking rather like Father Christmas on a hunger strike, minus only the red cloak and the bell. His face was pink and red, his eyes alive and keen and his manner very cheerful and sprightly. He greeted me warmly, put me at my ease and after discussing the production of the play, asked to see the photographs I had brought with me. His sharp blue eyes scanned the very handsome set Lee Simonson had provided—"Quite good," he said rather severely, in the manner of a schoolmaster appraising an examination paper, "only the room should look more like a ship's cabin. Simonson has made the tops of the doors rounded instead of flat. Doors on ships are never rounded." I murmured apologies, and said that it hadn't hurt the play—no one had noticed the tops of the doors anyway, they were so engrossed in his dialogue! His severity relaxed until he came across the picture of Effie Shannon. "Isn't she playing the part of Hesione?" he asked sharply. My heart momentarily stopped beating. The vision of being permitted to produce more Shaw plays began to fade. I nodded, and the sharp blue eyes regarded me angrily. "But she has blond hair—you must have cut one of the lines!" "Well, not exactly," I replied. "We just mumbled it—what would you have done?" The fate of my mission hung in the balance. Shaw smiled. "That's all right," he said, and the crisis was passed.

I broached the subject of producing more of his plays. He evaded me—plunging into an account of his latest work, *Back to Methuselah,* which he had been writing during the war and which he assured me was probably the longest and best play ever written. It was based on the theory that mankind could extend the span of human life from the Biblical threescore and ten to many thousands of years, by leading a spiritual and somewhat vegetarian existence on lines laid down by Shaw. The play itself was in five separate parts, and since it began with Adam and Eve and stretched over millions of years, it seemed that no member of our Theatre Guild audiences was likely to live long enough to be able to disprove any of Shaw's prophetic conclusions. My interest was excited, and I asked for a copy. "On your way back from the Continent, drop in to see me again, and I'll have the plays ready by that time." "And about a contract?" I asked. "We'll discuss that too."

After a while, Mrs. Shaw entered. She was a gentle gracious lady with plain, pleasant features, of medium height and comfortable build. She was about the same age as Shaw, whom she seemed to regard in much the way a mother would a brilliant young son who needed careful guarding. Perhaps her maternal attitude came from the fact that she married him after nursing him through a rather dangerous illness. Shaw seemed a little quieter in her presence, as though on his good behavior, but I sensed a relationship between them which I was to learn afterward was based upon the deepest respect for each other's qualities.

Upon the death of Mrs. Shaw many years later, the American newspapers printed a ridiculous story that she had left her personal fortune "to teach the Irish good manners" because of Shaw's lack of them. During the years I was to know them both, I was constantly amazed at Shaw's courtly old-fashioned manners. If Mrs. Shaw started to leave the room, Shaw would leap from his chair, dash like a sprinter to the door with his beard waving so as to arrive ahead of her, and he would hold it open with a deep bow until she had passed into the hall. When I first met her, Shaw introduced her in the grand manner, like an impresario displaying a prima donna, a role which did not fit Mrs. Shaw in the least. He ostentatiously seated her in a chair and showed her the photographs of the production, which she admired. However, when Shaw pointed out his objection to the doors with the rounded tops, she replied simply, "What difference does it make?" to which the great man made no reply. I was to learn from many years' friendship with Mrs. Shaw that "the Genius," as she lovingly called him, was guided by her excellent common sense, which often served as an antidote to his tendency to explode fireworks on all occasions. Moreover, she suggested the subjects of some of his best plays, including *The Doctor's Dilemma* and *Saint Joan*. Mrs. Shaw was most kind to me and invited me to lunch with them when I came back from the Continent.

Returning to London a month or so later, I called again on the Shaws. The iron spikes had lost their terror and seemed even a little friendly as I rang the bell. After being told politely by Shaw that I was not to smoke in the dining room (a wholly unnecessary precaution, since I did not smoke at all then), we had lunch, during which GBS gave me his views on the war and the peace which was in the making. "I have seen the end of the German Empire," he said, devouring a goodly helping of cabbage, "the end of the Russian Empire, and as for the British Empire——" he winked, and ate some more cabbage.

We talked about *Back to Methuselah* and the best way to present it. Shaw's idea was to have all five plays produced consecutively, so that the audience would have to take the entire dose in one helping. On leaving, he said he would send me the printed proof sheets, and I asked for a contract. "Don't bother about a contract," he said, as I stood at the door taking my leave. "It isn't likely that any other lunatic will want to produce *Back to Methuselah!*"

And he was right, as usual.

CHAPTER THREE

Back to Methuselah

S H A W' S genius for selecting subjects for his plays which would continue to be topical and controversial long after his death was well exemplified in his longest play (or group of plays), *Back to Methuselah,* which deals with the question of whether man will ever be able to live long enough to acquire sufficient wisdom to govern himself successfully. But this was only one of the many subjects of topical interest encompassed by this play. Prominent among these are the questions of why mankind was placed on this earth, and also the workings of Darwinian evolution, with which Shaw only partially agreed, while following the teachings of Lamarck and Bergson with some additional ideas of his own, which he called "the religion of Creative Evolution."

The quarrel between various groups of scientists in attempting to explain the history of man's evolution from the animal world is still continuing today with renewed vigor. Not a promising subject for entertainment in the theatre, yet Shaw managed to present his profoundest thoughts and ideas in the play both entertainingly and theatrically effectively.

Back to Methuselah represents the most monumental intellectual accomplishment in play form in the history of the thea-tre. This is not to say that it is the greatest play or even that it is among the world's greatest masterpieces, for it is excelled in sublimity by many dramas and in execution by many lesser works. But in the breadth of its conception and its quality of imagination it stands head and shoulders above any other work in the theatre, and in its field of intellectual speculation it stands alone.

Reaching from the beginning or creation of man to as far as thought can go in the future, Shaw attempts in this group of plays to show how man can ultimately live long enough to acquire Godlike wisdom. Whether philosophers, scientists and teachers agree or disagree with Shaw's conclusions, there is no doubt that nobody else has conceived the portrayal in theatrical form of scenes which take place thousands of years in the past, in the present, in A.D. 2170, A.D. 3,000 and A.D. 31,920. More-over, Shaw prognosticated the effect of creative evolution on the lives of humanity in those periods lying in the remote future. Shaw regarded this work as a gospel, and his subtitle for the play was "A Metabiological Pentateuch."

Unfortunately for the popularity of the play, there is an aridity about the lives of the He-ancients and She-ancients with which Shaw peopled the earth thirty-two thousand years hence. However, he does not set forth these museum-piece creatures as a desideratum, but rather as the result of the accumulation over long, long lives of the knowledge and experience which constitute human wisdom. But wise old men seldom do the daring things, the gallant things, the leaps ahead which take chances and lead humanity to the heights. We listen to the wisdom of the aged, but creation results only when succeeding generations refuse to follow in the footsteps of the past. I feel that GBS may have overreached himself by placing too much faith in the power of the mind and too little in the power of human intuition and emotion. His treatment of love and sex as childishly immature manifestations in the later plays of the cy-cle suggests a blind spot in Shaw's sense of values. "There are no passions as strong as the passions of the mind," Shaw once wrote. How true this is when one considers the passions of men such as Hitler, Savonarola, Torquemada or the other fanatics of the world. "I love humanity but I hate people," one of Dostoev-sky's characters says in *The Brothers Karamazov,* and a hundred other writers have noted this same defect in those who conceive

idealistic societies and then force men to participate in them.
Shaw had more than a touch of the fanatic in him, and nowhere
is it more manifest than in the ideal social systems he envisaged
in his later plays and Prefaces.

We welcomed *Back to Methuselah* in our younger days because it seemed to say, "We have only to live longer and we
will become wise enough to find the cures for all the ills of
humanity." Alas, the life expectancy of man is growing greater
every year, but is he also growing wiser? I found that while
Shaw was still alive and approaching the years of Methuselian
adolescence (about ninety) he was not wiser but more gullible.
He began to repeat himself, and in his plays he often had nothing new to say. Creation stopped with the sheer wearing out of
his faculties. And even if science could renew the faculties,
there would still be missing in the renovated aged the spark of
creation that happens when a young mind, innocent of too
many preconceptions, meets a new or old problem. Shaw himself was extremely conscious of this toward the end of his life.
He wrote the following in his Preface to *Seven Plays,* published
in the year 1898:

> But alas the world grew younger as I grew older; its vision
> cleared as mine dimmed. . . . In my weekly columns,
> which I once filled full from a magic well that never ran
> dry or lost its sparkle provided I pumped hard enough, I
> began to repeat myself; to fall into a style which, to my
> great peril, was recognized as at least partly serious. . . .
> The younger generation, reared in an enlightenment un-
> known to my schooldays, came knocking at the door too: I
> glanced back at my old columns and realized that I had
> timidly botched at thirty what newer men do now with
> gay confidence in their cradles.

One of the most important aspects of *Methuselah* when it
reached the public of its day was that it caused them to think
of such important subjects as the future of humanity, its inabil-
ity to govern itself, the folly of its senseless wars and the supreme mystery of life and death. To me it said in the end,
"How welcome is death when life is too long." To others it offered a nostrum: "How to live for a thousand years! All you
have to do is to desire it sufficiently!"

At the time when we decided to produce *Back to Methuselah,* we did not concern ourselves with any of the ultimate

truths of the play. It represented a job to be done in the theatre, and we were the lucky people chosen to do the job. We screwed up our courage and took the plunge.

The possibility of presenting *Back to Methuselah* was first mentioned at an interview between me and Mr. Shaw in London during the spring of 1921. Shaw had evolved the idea of the "ancients" from studying some experiments made in Austria by Dr. E. Steinach. At that time, he told me in brief the stories of the various plays; although "in brief" may not be the right phrase, since he took at least two hours. At the end of that time, I was satisfied that while the plays were not consecutive, the work as a whole was nevertheless extraordinary, and just the kind of thing for the Theatre Guild to do. I wrote back to New York describing the play in a general way, and I was authorized by the Guild to deal with Shaw regarding it. GBS's answer to my request for a copy of the script was as follows:

> The only set of proofs I am not actually working on is in the hands of Granville Barker. If he returns them in time, I will hand them to you before you go to Paris: if not, remind me when you come back.

The impression made upon Shaw by our production of *Heartbreak House,* which was very highly praised by his English friends Granville Barker and Nigel Playfair, established a strong feeling of confidence on his part that the Theatre Guild could give an adequate production to *Back to Methuselah.* He agreed to let us produce the play if we wanted it after reading it over, but he warned me that *Heartbreak House* was like a musical comedy compared to it.

The day before I sailed for New York the proof sheets arrived at my London hotel together with a letter from GBS dated March 9, 1921, reading:

> At last I have got a complete set of proofs of the forthcoming volume.
>
> You will understand that I am breaking faith with my publishers in letting them out of my own hands for export and that I must place you under the most blood-drinking sacred obligation not to show your colleagues in the T.G. of America. If any account of them or quotations of them reach the press in either country there would be the devil to pay for me. Further, as they are not finally corrected for

press will you send them back to me when the book is published or else write me an assurance that you have destroyed them with your own hands. If you once let an imperfect text loose, you can never overtake it and I always have to destroy my unused proofs with the greatest care. Bon voyage!

His postscript read:

The final corrections will not involve any change that you need take into account. Also you may regard the dialogue as drastically cut, so the producer has nothing more to hope in that direction.

When I looked over the three hundred closely printed pages and realized that this was the play which was drastically cut, I had a sinking feeling which increased when I began to read the script on board ship. Whether this was due to *Back to Methuselah* or the rather stormy weather we encountered, I am still not entirely sure, although I must admit that as the weather improved, so did my liking for the play. By the time I had reached the States, I had written to GBS expressing the belief that the Guild would want to do the play and that I for one would vote for it. I also calmly suggested he might want to make some changes in the second part, *The Gospel of the Brothers Barnabas,* as the various political events which he discussed in so much detail were generally unfamiliar to American audiences. I qualified this in a later letter:

Of course, to make the play real, it is just as well to deal with real facts and the way real people react towards them. I felt on reading this play that it was parochial, and would not be understood in America. I think now that it does not matter very much whether America understands it or not. It shows very clearly the kind of men the politicians are, and illustrates the necessity of having them live a couple of thousand of years or so. That ought to be sufficient.

My first task on arrival in New York was to ensure the secrecy which Shaw had imposed on me as a "blood-drinking sacred obligation." One of the difficulties of the youthful Theatre Guild arose from the fact that six tongues can wag six times more frequently than one, and the problem of keeping theatri-

cal news out of the New York newspapers was almost as difficult then as it is today, when some of our newspapers employ
reporters with all the talents of private detectives to spy on our
doings. On arriving in New York, I swore my colleagues to
secrecy and then let them read *Back to Methuselah*. They did,
and realizing the length and expense involved, as well as the
fact that we were nearing the end of the theatrical season, we
decided to postpone the play over the summer. Meanwhile,
Shaw wrote me that he wanted the play published in book form
before the performances, which seemed illogical in view of his
earlier admonition to make no mention of the plot. On April
6, 1921, I explained the situation to him as follows:

> I have made the various members of the Theatre Guild
> sign a letter to the effect that they will not disclose the
> contents of your play, and I am therefore a little more at
> ease about the subject matter getting into the press. About
> two months ago, a photograph of you appeared in Vanity
> Fair with a statement underneath to the effect that you
> had just completed a play, the beginning of which was laid
> in the Garden of Eden, while the end went thousands of
> years into the future. I have not divulged any more than
> this to the numerous press correspondents who literally
> besieged me when I arrived.
>
> On reconsidering the letter I wrote you on board the
> ship, I think it was somwhat nervy on my part to ask
> whether or not a new version of the second play could be
> written. . . .
>
> Now as to the publication of the play in book form, I
> think it will very seriously affect the success of the play on
> the stage. If we were to give the play early in September,
> would you be willing to arrange that the American edition
> did not come out until after the play had been put on?
> When I say September, I suppose I really mean any time
> before Christmas of the coming year, as it will undoubt-
> edly be a big job. Perhaps you could let me hear from you
> on this subject. By the way, a big firm of publishers here
> called me up and were very anxious to let me permit them
> to read the script which I refused point-blank, notwith-
> standing the fact that they have published nearly all your
> plays in the United States.
>
> If you would like to come over to the States at the time

when we give the play, the Guild would be prepared to pay for your passage and expenses in New York. You would not be required to give any lectures or be anything more than a plain gentleman, giving us the benefit of your assistance in managing a play. We would shield you from all publicity by every possible method. What suggests it-self immediately is that you enter the country clean-shaven, so that nobody will recognize you. What could be simpler?

P.S.: I think there is every chance that the Guild will do the play. The committee is now immersed in it.

Shaw replied to this in a letter dated 3 May 1921 from the Shakespeare Hotel, Stratford-on-Avon:

I have been travelling about for more than a month, delivering political orations; trying to recover from the too long spell of unbroken work that *Methuselah* brought on me; and writing nothing but the most urgently neces-sary letters on picture postcards. Hence my delay in re-plying to the letter you wrote on the Aquitania on the 18th. March.

The second play will not mean Asquith and Lloyd George to your public; and so far it will not produce the effect it will produce here on the few people who have any sense of political personalities. But in *Fanny's First Play,* the American public knew nothing about Walkley, Gilbert Cannan and A. E. Vaughan (for that matter very few people outside a little ring in London were any better informed). Nevertheless Trotter, Gunn, and Vaughan went down just as well in America as here. I therefore believe that if Joyce Burge and Lubin fail here, they will fail everywhere; and if they succeed here they will succeed just as well in America. However that may be, the thing must stay as it is now. The job did itself that way, and I cannot pull it to pieces and do it some other way.

As to the first play, it produced such an astonishing ef-fect when I read it to an audience consisting mostly of women that I never ventured on the experiment again. I gather that it missed fire with you. It may be so with your public; but I assure you it *can* explode with shattering con-sequences. To play it and the second play at the same performance is impossible. You will have to make up your mind to the three evenings and the two matinees. You must sell the tickets in batches of five, all five tickets on one sheet with perforated card divisions. If people buy them that way they will not throw them away. They may be bothered and disappointed by the first two plays as you expect; but their bewilderment will not take the form of throwing their tickets into the fire, especially if you charge enough for them. You can warn them that the prologue in the Garden of Eden will last only an hour (or perhaps 50 minutes; you can time it at rehearsal) and that no assumptions must be made as to the duration of each part of the play. Mark: each part of the play, not each play. The wording of your programmes and announcements must always rub in the fact that what the public is going to see is one play, with sections of various lengths.

Later on we can see about giving separate performances of the sections; but for the first ten performances (say) it must be impossible to take less than the whole dose.

The book will be published on the first of June or thereabouts. I note your calm suggestion that it should be held back until you are ready to produce. I told you you wanted the earth. If you want to produce simultaneously with the publication you must hurry up very smartly indeed.

I scrawl this in great haste in a hotel after a day's driving.

I replied to this on May 16:

Your letter from Stratford-on-Avon is just at hand, and I have very carefully noted what you say. You will gather from a letter I wrote you in the interim that I am inclined to believe that the second section will act better than it reads. I still maintain, however, that the first two sections are largely a preparation for the last three. Your ideas about the tickets seem very sensible, and if we decide to give the play I shall endeavour to persuade the others to follow them.

I note what you say regarding the publication. However, man proposes, the labor unions and God do the rest. There is a printers' strike at the present time, and we may not have to hurry quite as much as would otherwise be the case. I am sending you the programmes of two plays now running, as well as an announcement of our next season's subscription plans. If we decide to do *Methuselah,* it will naturally have to be done as a special proposition, and probably in a larger theatre.

I gather from reading *Methuselah* that if you want to live three hundred years, you will live three hundred years. If we keep on wanting the Earth consistently enough, we shall probably get it.

The question of the expense of this enormous undertaking was bothering us considerably more than my letters to Shaw indicate. *Back to Methuselah* is in reality five separate and complete plays, each calling for quite different sets, actors and costumes. We had the Garrick Theatre on lease, the seating capacity of which was so small that it was impossible to operate on a profitable basis there, no matter how well the play was attended. While we were debating the matter, I reported to GBS:

The general consensus is that it is a stupendous piece of work, and the Guild stands awed. The greatest difficulty seems to be the second play. The majority of the Guild are in favor of putting it on next season during a lull, so that we can all work on it, but we are all worried about the second play. I have never heard from you about this, and hope I may do so shortly.

My next letter to Shaw on July 7, 1921, explained what had been happening over the summer.

Things have been moving rapidly since I last wrote you in regard to *Back to Methuselah.* I have completed the financial plans (by this I do not mean I have secured the money, but I know how much we need which is almost the same thing). I have talked a lot to the newspaper reporters on the subject and they are all featuring it just as though the Guild had actually decided. What I have really done is to stir up public interest in the play to such an extent that my opposition on the Board of Managers has visibly weakened. Give me a little more time and I shall be writing to you for a contract.

My idea is to start selling seats six months ahead of the opening of the performance so that we can sell every seat in the Theatre for two weeks solid. The only practical way of putting on the plays having regard to the fact that you must make some concessions to those of the public who have to earn their bread by the sweat of their brow, is to start about 6 o'clock in the evening, play section 1; allow one and a half hours for dinner, then play section 2, getting your people home fairly early. This will take care of Monday. Sections 1 and 2 should also be played on Tuesday. Sections 3 and 4 should be played in the same way on Wednesday and Thursday. Section 5 to be played on Friday and Saturday.

The purpose of giving two sets of performances in this way is to allow a breathing spell of one night. Otherwise the physical task would be too much. A playgoer can see sections 1 and 2 on Monday, spend Tuesday grumbling at it; see sections 3 and 4 on Wednesday, spend Thursday "enthusing" over it; see section 5 on Friday and spend the week-end puzzling over it. We hope to be able to pull it off in February if we have any money left in the treasury. We expect to put the venture through on a cooperative basis; the theatre, the Guild, artists and actors all sharing in the profits. You could help me very much to stir up the necessary public enthusiasm by sending me copies of any articles which have been written, damning you as thoroughly unscientific, together with your answers. I can get these in all the newspapers. You have lost a great deal of prestige over here because you picked Carpentier to win the prize fight [over Jack Dempsey], and we are now all inclined to doubt the truth of any statement made by you on the subject of science, whether it be pugilistic or otherwise.

My appraisal of the kind of theatre work we were doing in the States did not move GBS to visit us, but he spent considerable time commenting on our ticket-selling plans. This is what he wrote me from Yorkshire on the 29th of July, 1921.

If *Barnabus* and *The Elderly Gentleman* can be played in two hours, then your 6 to 11 plan will work; and I see no objection to your Monday-Wednesday-Friday and Tuesday-Thursday-Saturday performances instead of consecutive nights. But you will sell 3 tickets per head per set instead of 5, but no doubt you will sell more sets and gain on the whole.

I have not worked out the question of the strain on the actors. If you have a separate performer for each of these parts, this need not be considered; but that would be extravagant and would spoil the unity of the show. Here are a few doublings which suggest themselves.

Adam, Conrad, the Accountant General, the Envoy (unsympathetic character actor).
Eve, Mrs. Lutestring, the Oracle, the She-Ancient (dignified leading lady).
Cain, Burge, Burge-Lubin, Napoleon, Ozymandias.

Lubin, Confucius, Elderly Gentleman, Pygmalion (must have a gentle and very distinct voice).
Savvy, Zoo, the Newly Born.
Franklin, the He-Ancient.

All these would have to be good actors. The Serpent should have a very peculiar and fascinating voice, and an articulation that would be excessive in any other part. She could double Ecrasia, but if she plays the Serpent only, neither her appearance nor her age will matter. The Negress (who must be real) might double her.

Do not bother about the reviewers: They will do the work themselves.

My remarks on the prize fight between Carpentier and Dempsey seemed to interest GBS at least as much as the play; he prided himself on his knowledge of prize fighting and he wrote indignantly in the same letter:

I must insist that I did not pick Carpentier to win the fight. I expressly warned the punters [bettors] that Carpentiers had been beaten by Dempseys very often, instancing Macy by King, as I might have instanced Corbett by Fitzsimmons and Johnson by Willard (if that was genuine). What I did say was that the betting was absurd, and that though I had never seen Dempsey and knew nothing about him at first hand, it was humanly impossible that he could be so superior to Carpentier as to justify odds of 4 to 1. I said that on Carpentier's achievements the betting was 50 to 1 on him; and after the fight I said it should have been 500 to 1 on him. Dempsey, according to the reports and the films, made no defence at all: Carpentier literally smashed his fists on him, but this time had not the luck to get on the elusive spot which he found in Beckett. Dempsey is one of those terrors whose simple plan it is to take whatever the other fellow can give him and hammer him to pieces afterwards. But that is a very chancy plan when the other fellow is such a tremendous hitter as Carpentier. Dempsey escaped falling to C's right by a millimetre; and that is not quite good enough to back 4 to 1. The next step would seem to be to put up a gorilla for the championship.

By the way, if Carpentier had been an Englishman he would quite possibly have gone ten rounds by keeping on the retreat when he found that hitting was no use. But Carpentier will fight; and this silly infighting which he picked up from the Americans enabled Dempsey to thump him on the back of his neck and serves him right, too. In the old days the champions were all middle weights, and the giants mere chopping blocks for them. However, all that is stale drivel now; that fight has disgusted everybody with the ring.

GBS returned to the same subject in an attack on Heywood Broun, for reprinting the above letter with my permission, but without his.

Broun had no right to use my letter to disparage Dempsey. He did not mean that perhaps: I think he really wanted to disparage me as a boxing expert; but my reason for writing to correct him was that Dempsey especially on the verge of a big fight, has just the same right not to be damaged in repute as any member of the learned professions; and Broun's use of my letter was distinctly damaging to him. You cannot trust journalists with private letters: they always make a mess of it.

Meanwhile my colleagues and I at the Theatre Guild finally decided to present the series of plays on a "Festival" basis, which I triumphantly reported to GBS.

The lunatic has prevailed. God and yourself willing, the curtain will ring up on *Back to Methuselah* in February or March of the coming year (unless some dire financial calamity happens to the Theatre Guild).

Meanwhile, I am writing to ask you to let us have a contract of some sort. It need not be a formal one, but I leave that to you. The question of terms has been bothering me. I confess that with the idea in mind of a "Festival," which will last perhaps only two weeks (it will be essential, in order to put the thing over, to crowd everybody into the Theatre in as short a time as possible, owing to the heavy expenses), I am somewhat perturbed at the idea of paying the usual Shaw royalties.

We are going to ask everybody who takes part in the venture to do it on a profit sharing basis; that is, the theaatre, the actors, the Guild and the scenic artists would each receive a minimum amount and if there is any profit, this profit will be divided. It is only by securing the cooperation of a large number of people willing to help, making it a sort of semi-public affair, that we can hope to handle the "Festival," and this is the way we propose to go about it.

Will you, therefore, let me know what you think about royalties, making the arrangement such that it would not hamper us in launching the "Festival," because I can assure you we are not doing it for the purpose of making money, although if we did make a financial success, we would not be disappointed. Perhaps one way of doing it would be to give us a low royalty for the first two weeks. We should only extend the run if it were a financial success, and you could give us two more weeks at a somewhat higher royalty. If we decide to run it after the two additional weeks, we could pay you the regular royalty. I do not think this is an unfair arrangement, in view of the fact that a number of the actors will be playing only two nights a week, which means an exceptionally large company.

We shall, of course, perform the play without any cuts (unless you, yourself, want some), and will endeavor to give the very best possible production.

How about coming over in the Spring and assisting us in the affair? We promise you full police protection and immunity from speech-making and social duties. We should like you to come, not only because we want your help, but also from the box office standpoint, because we are sure that your presence would stir up a tremendous interest in the proceedings which would be reflected in the play. . . .

This is an extremely mercenary letter upon so idealistic a conception as *Back to Methuselah,* but I feel that your job is only half done if the play is written and not performed. It would be too bad if a tradition grew up that the play was only meant for reading, and not for acting. Having written a sort of Bible, your missionary work is not completed until people become familiar with it, and it requires something in the nature of a Billy Sunday revival spirit or the bombast of a Barnum & Bailey circus to get the crowds to come in droves and be converted.

We think that we have one thing to surprise you, and that is the excellence of our acting, our production, and our scenic investiture. I am convinced that we are doing better work than is being done anywhere in Europe today, so far as the "production" of plays is concerned, and I believe you would enjoy a visit from that angle alone.

Shaw's reaction to my "mercenary" letter was to ignore it completely.

Back to Methuselah was put into rehearsal early in the year 1922. We decided that the first four plays should be given two at a time, which made a somewhat lengthy evening, and the openings were to be a week apart. As this called for more work than our stage director, Philip Moeller, could possibly handle, we decided to share the production with the Neighborhood Playhouse, connected with the Henry Street Settlement, and their directors, Alice Lewisohn and Agnes Morgan, staged the first play, *In the Beginning.*

The costumes of Adam and Eve presented a problem, since they were in the prefig-leaf period of the story, and the difficulty was to find a compromise between stark-naked realism and what the New York Police Department would permit to appear on the stage of a so-called "legitimate" theatre. Our scenic artist, Lee Simonson, decided to swathe Ernita Lascelles, who played Eve, in heavy pink tights with hair of cloth of gold. Her pink fleshings simulated nudity to such an extent that we feared the possibility of intervention by the police. She created a minor sensation on both sides of the footlights. Never in all my experience in the theatre, either before or after her performance, have I seen the stagehands stand on stage and watch every movement of a play from the rise to the fall of the curtain. But I am afraid that GBS had very little to do with their interest.

Adam, played by George Gaul, was also given pink tights and a pair of bathing trunks of the same bright gold material. On the day of the dress rehearsal, the Garrick Theatre was filled with prim lady social workers from the Neighborhood Playhouse, who brought with them an atmosphere of Social Welfare and Higher Morality not usually associated with the theatre. On the stage Margaret Wycherly was trying to hide herself behind a bush out of which her arm, garbed as a Serpent, protruded as she moved it in sinuous undulation—it being our intention that Margaret's head should be hidden by the bush, but the bush was not quite large enough. "I can still see your head," cried Theresa Helburn from the rear of the theatre. "Can you see it now?" asked Margaret, shrinking into an impossible position behind the bush. Suddenly George Gaul, resplendent in his cloth-of-gold loincloth, appeared from the wings as Adam. As he walked into the spotlight, nothing was visible on stage but his highly illuminated gold loincloth which sent a gasp through the assembled ladies. "If you think we can't see it, you're very much mistaken," shouted Theresa Helburn to Margaret Wycherly. George Gaul, thinking the remark was addressed to him, rushed off the stage in frightened embarrassment, while the Social Welfare and Higher Morality ladies rocked with unashamed laughter for ten minutes before order was restored.

On February 14, I reported progress to GBS:

I don't know whether anyone in the Guild has written to you regarding the progress of work on *Back to Methuselah,* but they expect to be ready to open in two weeks. It has been a tremendous undertaking, but owing to the fact that we have, for the last three years, been building up a personnel of producers, actors, etc., we expect to be able to make a thoroughly effective production.

We are following your suggestions carefully about the tickets. They are all on one sheet with perforations as you suggested. You will be pleased to hear that we have very few seats left for the first eight complete performances. We are not allowing anybody to buy single seats; they must take the whole dose, to use your own expression. I am inclined to believe that if the press notices are favorable, *Back to Methuselah* will be playing right into the summer. People over here like a sensation, and the fact that this play is about four times as long as any other play appeals to their interest in the same way that a bridge that is four times as long as any other bridge would appeal to them. Given a favorable press (which I think is almost assured), it will be a riot!

We shall send you copies of the criticisms, photographs, posters, printed matter, etc., in due course. We are advertising the production widely as "A Shaw Festival," and the idea is catching on.

We have engaged Walter Pritchard Eaton, one of the best dramatic critics in the country, and he is giving lectures on your plays at different colleges, writing special articles, etc., as part of our publicity campaign.

You would be amused at the various discussions we have been having as to what costume or lack of costume, would be proper (or improper) for Adam and Eve. We would be more than delighted to have your suggestions.

Since the various members of the Theatre Guild read *Back to Methuselah,* they made up their minds they would all live three hundred years, but now that we are in the throes of the work, it looks as though we shall shorten our years rather than increase them.

Meanwhile, you will be interested to know that Lee Simonson smokes a great deal less and whenever he lights a cigarette, does so with evident nervousness and a guilty hesitant look in his eyes.

Finally, on February 27, 1922, the first two plays of the cycle opened. They were enthusiastically received by the audience, but not by the press, to my bitter disappointment. It is always a mistake to count on the critics' approval in advance. It is a good rule to assume they will dislike everything, and you will sometimes be pleasantly surprised. I have no record of my letter to GBS after the opening, but on March 6 I wrote him as follows:

We have just finished the second lap of *Back to Methuselah.* Last night we had a dress rehearsal and press performance, and it went excellently. We were somewhat afraid of the length of this bill, but the audience stayed on enthusiastically until the end. I feel quite sure that the press notices for the second batch will be better than the first.

Unfortunately, as usually happens when you don't want it, there was some hitch in the lighting of *The Brothers Barnabas* which caused the curtain to delay, and while it was usually over by 11:15, on the night when the critics were there, it wasn't over until quarter to twelve. So while *The Brothers Barnabas* did not make a very good impression on the critics, it went excellently with the public the next day. I was right, however, in telling you when I first read the play that parts of *The Brothers Barnabas* were too parochial for American audiences. It was not a question of their not knowing the political personalities involved. People simply howled when Lloyd George and Asquith appeared. Both of these parts were played excellently. Such dullness as there was, was due to allusions to things about which the people here know nothing. Lines which would have caused the people to laugh in London, such as references to "Welsh disestablishment," "National Liberal Federations," etc., went for nothing here. However, we did not cut a single line so you yourself have had to take the consequences. Not that it matters very much what the critics have to say. You will appreciate that the majority of them are sitting on their brains. Consequently they are more conscious of the length than most of the other people. The average critic, faced with the problem of writing a review of a play, naturally grasps at the most unusual feature and if it happens to be the length, that serves. The first cycle of eight performances (three weeks solid) is completely sold out, and a second cycle of an additional three weeks is well on its way.

We took a formal canvass among our subscribers and found that very few of them would be able to attend afternoon performances. There is really no leisure class in America. Such leisure class as we might have had emigrated to England where it is introducing the democratic principle into the House of Lords. People here simply cannot come to afternoon performances, and as our subscribers and particularly the poorer members are made up of people who work in the daytime, we decided that if the play was to be given at all it had to be given in the evening. During the present bill we are serving coffee and refreshments in the lounge between the acts, and this has given the play a considerable amount of extra publicity and interest.

I have seen a good many productions of your plays from time to time, both here and in England. Putting aside such prejudices as I might be expected to have as a member of the Theatre Guild, I have never seen such splendid acting as has characterized the performance of each part at the Garrick Theatre. This is reflected in all the press notices and in the response of the audience. I have postponed coming to Europe because of the production of the play, and I am only waiting until *As Far as Thought Can Reach* before I sail for Paris. I shall be there a week or so, and then am coming to London. If it will not be one of the intrusions upon privacy which the Anglo-Saxon-Americans have learned from the Irish in their midst, I would like to see you while I am in London to tell you in person about *Back to Methuselah,* to give you some photographs and posters, and to discuss the repertory season we are planning next year.

The second bill included the play *The Tragedy of an Elderly Gentleman,* which contained one of the most long-winded parts ever written, and the strain on the audience listening to the play was excessive. One day a Guild director asked William, our enthusiastic colored doorman, how the play was going. "Fine!" said William. "Less and less people walk out on it every night."

After the opening of the last play of the cycle, I left for Europe, and called on GBS with the intention of securing his permission to cut *An Elderly Gentleman* so that the play would have a chance for a New York run. I was met very cordially by Shaw, and also by Mrs. Shaw, who stayed and chatted with us while we looked over the photographs of the production. "Look, Charlotte," he said to Mrs. Shaw as he examined the pictures of Albert Bruning as the Elderly Gentleman, "they've given the actor a make-up so that he looks like me! Why, the Elderly Gentleman was an old duffer. Why on earth did you suggest me?" "Because he talked on and on and on," I replied. "Besides, he said he could not live in a world without truth, by which we of course assumed you had written yourself into the character."

This was a bad beginning for an interview in which I wished to persuade him to cut the play, but encouraged by Mrs. Shaw, I persevered. "The reason I object to cutting my plays is this," said GBS. "I write a certain amount of deadly serious dialogue, and when I have given the audience as much as they can possibly take, I throw in some humor as a reward. Now when my plays are cut, the actor or other person who does the cutting always takes out the serious dialogue, and leaves the funny parts, so that the whole purpose of the play is defeated. Besides," he said, "you can never trust an actor to cut a play." "But I suggest you cut this yourself," I replied, "and I'll cable the changes to New York." "You shouldn't have given the two plays in one evening," was the retort. "But people can't come in the afternoon," I replied, "and it's so long, they really suffer."

Then GBS began to suffer too. "This goes against all my principles," he said, looking at Mrs. Shaw.

"GBS," she said, "perhaps the Americans don't always know what the Elderly Gentleman is talking about. There's that long piece about John Knox and the Leviathan; hardly any English people know about that either."

I unashamedly and unscrupulously followed Mrs. Shaw's lead and suggested that there was a great deal more in the play that wasn't understood by Americans—or by anybody else either. "Besides," I added, "at least half a dozen times the Elderly Gentleman starts to leave the stage. Each time the audience settles back delighted, but each time he turns around and comes back for another ten minutes of monologue."

"After all," said Mrs. Shaw, "you did intend him to be an old duffer, and it is hard to listen to an old duffer going on and on." GBS squirmed and twisted, but finally gave in. "Very well," he said. "We'll go over it line by line."

"I have some cuts suggested," I said, quickly offering him the printed version on which I had marked my deletions. In a few minutes he grew so interested in cutting the play that he took out at least half as much again as I had originally hoped for. An hour later I left, trying to stop looking too pleased with myself, for I had been told in New York that I would be wasting my time, as no one had ever been able to persuade Shaw to cut one of his plays before. And I doubt very much whether I would have succeeded without the help of Mrs. Shaw.

The play was considerably improved by the cutting, but the run of the cycle was not greatly prolonged as a result, and it closed after nine weeks of playing. I returned to New York in August, and wrote GBS on August 25 as follows:

On arriving here I inquired into what loss had been incurred in respect to *Back to Methuselah,* and found that it had amounted to about $20,000. It was not announced, but the news leaked out as such news sometimes does leak out. Part of this loss was due to the fact that it ran two weeks longer than it should have run; it is not a total loss because most of the materials, etc., which we used can be used over again, and anyway, the Guild is not the least bit worried about it. In having ventured to tackle so big a job we have made a tremendous number of friends and shall have nearly doubled the number of subscribers for the coming season as we had for this season so it will all come back to us eventually.

I wrote him again on September 5:

I find that we lost $20,000 on *Back to Methuselah,* but we shall look for our reward in heaven. Some of it is coming to us in the shape of new subscribers who felt that they could not afford not to belong to an organization that took such chances.

Shaw, however, never quite forgave us for not making a financial success of *Back to Methuselah.* I did my best to take the blame on ourselves, feeling that he should not be discouraged (as if that were possible), and later on, in 1924, I wrote him:

I have been somewhat depressed by your letters, because I think you are angry with the Guild over *Back to Methuselah.* You do not realize that over here it was regarded as a great success, and not as a failure. When you take into consideration that it ran for nine weeks in a small theatre, playing every night, you must appreciate that this was a magnificent achievement. The fact that we lost money was not due to any arrangement of the parts, but because the Garrick Theatre was too small for us to make money out of the play. If we had had a theatre twice the size, there would have been a profit instead of a loss. I hope you will not feel badly anymore about this. I am quite certain that if Goethe had seen *Faust* presented in parts one and two every evening for nine successive weeks, he would have stood on his head in amazement.

Later on I saw Sir Barry Jackson's production at the Birmingham Repertory Theatre, where the plays were done consecutively, and which I did not care for particularly. GBS felt our lack of financial success was due to our producing the three groups with a week between each group. I disagreed but was sharply lectured by him on the subject.

When Lee Shubert, some years later, financed the production of *Jitta's Atonement,* he wrote a letter to Shaw questioning the royalties. Shaw replied to Mr. Shubert that he underestimated the value of Mr. Shaw's name, which had been proved to be worth at least $10,000 a play. He explained this by stating that the Guild had expected to lose $30,000 on *Back to Methuselah,* but had lost only $20,000, thus showing that Shaw's name alone was worth $10,000!

March 22, 1928, found me writing GBS a final letter on how to produce *Back to Methuselah* successfully.

I have requested Boni & Liveright, the publishers, to send you a copy of Eugene O'Neill's *Strange Interlude.* I would be very much interested to know what you think of this play, which has turned out to be of exceptional interest in the theatre. We opened the play about seven weeks ago, and notwithstanding the fact that it lasts for five hours and that the audience has to take dinner in between, it is a great success, both as an acting play and a production; in other words, it is succeeding both artistically and financially. People actually stand up for five hours to watch the play, and one cannot buy seats for love or money.

I am sorry now that we did not have a dinner intermission between each part of *Back to Methuselah.* I think one needs nourishment during these long plays and that they are perfectly all right so far as the public is concerned if you allow people to eat in between. If your new play is going to be a very long one (which I hope it is) please arrange so that we can start at six o'clock and end at eleven, with an hour in between for dinner. This will insure its undoubted success.

I do wish you would start to write your new play this summer, because we would so much rather do a new play than one of the old ones. Don't you think you have done enough for Socialism? Your book will be out of date the minute Socialism is universally adopted by the various governments of the world.

Some thirty-five years later, we became interested in an abridged version of *Back to Methuselah* prepared by Arnold Moss, a well-known actor, who felt the plays could take on new life in shortened form if reduced to a single evening. The Shaw Estate and the British Society of Authors gave their consent, but I am sure that Shaw must have sent a deluge of protests from the other world, for his plays were cut to ribbons. The late Tyrone Power, one of America's most popular motion-picture actors, essayed a group of the roles, supported by Faye Emerson, Valerie Bettis, Arnold Moss and some valiant younger actors, who trouped with the play in an omnibus and trucks, playing to "one-night stands" all over Florida and the Middle West and as far north as Montreal.

Tyrone Power loved to traverse the countryside in the omnibus with the rest of the actors, and his arrival in each town, to sold-out performances, was usually heralded by a corps of motorcycle policemen who came to meet him. I doubt if many in the small-town audiences had ever heard of Bernard Shaw, or would have cared to do so after they had seen the play, but it was a triumph for Tyrone Power, as well as an artistic success, notwithstanding the strain on the actors. Unfortunately, we brought the play into the New York graveyard on January 5, 1958, where it received the usual burial by the critics and lost most of its road profits.

My wife, Armina Marshall, rode in the bus with the actors through Florida, so I decided to emulate her and to experience a trip of this kind at first hand. I joined the company at Albany, New York, where we encountered a heavy snowstorm, so that our bus and trucks arrived two hours late at our next stop, the town of Schenectady. As the audience had been waiting half an hour, I was requested to go on stage and entertain them while waiting for the scenery. I did so by telling some stories of Shaw and the original production of the play. I was relieved that no one walked out of the theatre until the scenery arrived. The play was as well received as usual, for in its abridged form it was enjoyable, and gave the actors an excellent chance to show their versatility by playing different roles during the same evening.

The next morning our omnibus set forth for Montreal, and we passed through miles of icy passes through the Adirondack Mountains. Every time the doors opened for the benefit of Faye Emerson's pet poodles, I shivered with the cold, and by the time we arrived at Montreal I had a high fever. I returned via snow-bound Cleveland, where I met Katharine Hepburn, who was playing in the American Stratford Shakespeare Company's production of *Much Ado About Nothing,* and by the time I reached New York I had a raging attack of pneumonia which kept me in bed for a month. Thus GBS revenged himself on me for our unauthorized cutting of his play. Arnold Moss came off unscathed.

An amusing sidelight on Shaw's perspicacity is revealed in a letter from his secretary, Miss Patch, to us, instructing us to turn down, as a piece of pornography, a license to an enterprising Canadian who wished to produce the first scene of Adam and Eve in the Garden of Eden in a possible nudist version in the city of Toronto.

18th September 1923

In reply to your letter of the 17th August, Mr. Bernard Shaw desires me to say that he shall turn down all applications for licenses to perform the first part of *Methuselah* by itself, as he will conclude that the manager wants a pornographic attraction. Toronto must start with the complete *Methuselah.*

Needless to say, Toronto did not see the pornographic attraction; GBS would permit this only as paprika to spice the entire five-course meal.

As the years have rolled by, it becomes increasingly clear that the basic ideas expounded in *Back to Methuselah* can serve as a basis for a religious faith for intellectuals. Shaw believed in the doctrine of Creative Evolution as expounded by Bergson and others. To this he added his own religious conception of the Life Force which runs through several of his plays and prefaces. Dr. Archibald Henderson, Shaw's official biographer, in a letter to *The New York Times* written just after the death of GBS, remarked of his religion:

In 1921 Shaw set forth a further extension of his philosophical views in the huge work—five plays in one, *Back to Methuselah,* which he sub-entitled "A Metabiological

Pentateuch." Just as Lamarck virtually maintained the living organisms changed because they wanted to, so Shaw believes that there is a purpose in the universe, a will driving toward self-contemplation; to grasp the purpose of life. This purpose, or Life Force, according to Shaw, has blundered along through the centuries, the aeons, making many useless experiments and scattering its forces in many fruitless undertakings. Disease and sin are no less unhappy experiments of the Life Force than are the now extinct megatherium, ichthyosaurus, and diplodocus, scrapped because of their essential brainlessness.

Shaw cherishes the idea of creative evolution, as he once told me, because it gives him something to look forward to, something to hope for. It gives him a deep and satisfying faith in something better and greater, beyond the life-forms already developed. Man he thinks of as only a stage in the scale of evolution; and entertains grave doubts as to man's survival. Shaw is essentially a wishful thinker; he is "on the side of the angels." The Life Force, as he once expressed this mystic hope to me, will continue its efforts to realize itself. After the passage of uncountable aeons it will produce something more complicated than Man: The Superman, the Angels, the Archangels, and last of all the omnipotent and omniscient God.

This ends the saga of *Back to Methuselah* as far as the Theatre Guild and I personally are concerned. It remains to be seen to what extent the play will be performed for the public by adventurous workers in the theatre of the future. The play is as topical as tomorrow's news and will remain so, in my opinion, for a couple of centuries. So here is a challenge which calls for creative imagination on the part of producers who are not afraid to stimulate their audiences with Shaw's excursion into the farthest reaches of thought. And if, as a result of the invention of a new wonder drug, I should happen to live for a thousand years, I shall continue to be grateful to the original actors, producers and artists and to the adventurous Theatre Guild subscription audiences, who made the first production of *Back to Methuselah* possible.

CHAPTER FOUR

Saint Joan–1923

WITH the passage of time and the advent of the United Nations, *Saint Joan* takes on a new importance and a popularity of which Shaw, when he wrote the play, could not possibly have been aware. Although he emphasized the Saint's relationship to the movement of nationalism, he could not have known that over forty years after he had written his play, *Saint Joan* would emerge as the image of a liberator and patron saint and martyr for all the small and large new countries of Africa and Asia which have been coming into being under the aegis of the United Nations. Thus Shaw's play, written to create a heroic religious Saint Joan and to show how mankind has expiated its mistake in burning her at the stake, is also serving to remind future generations that inflicting brutal torture on one's victims has a way of backfiring in the faces of the brutes.

It is generally conceded, after nearly forty years have passed since the writing of *Saint Joan,* that this is Shaw's greatest play. It is furthermore regarded as one of the greatest plays in the history of the theatre. It was first produced by the Theatre Guild and was presented for the first time on any stage at the Garrick Theatre in New York City on December 28, 1923.

The production of the play was accompanied by a good deal of acrimony between the young Theatre Guild and the irate author, who was living over three thousand miles away and was certainly taking a heavy risk in entrusting one of his most important plays to our relatively inexperienced hands. Yet luck was on his side as well as on ours, for despite many disagreements, the production turned out to be one of the best (if not the best) ever to be made of this play, which has since been presented many times and all over the world.

This is the story of the world première of *Saint Joan* as seen through my eyes. It is also a record of the amount of misunderstanding and sheer bungling which can go on in the theatre without destroying the essential values of a great work of art. It is also the story of the futility of the Theatre Guild's efforts to persuade the author to "cut" the play, and includes some comedic aspects of the battle in which we were soundly trounced. This battle still continues.

On my visit to the Shaws in 1922, I had asked whether there was any new play in the offing. "The trouble is, we haven't been able to find a good subject," said Mrs. Shaw. I must have looked astonished, for she continued, "Yes, I sometimes find ideas for plays for the Genius. If we can find a good subject for a play, he usually writes it very quickly."

Some months later, Mrs. Shaw found a good subject. She told me about it later. "I had always admired the character of Saint Joan, so I bought as many books about her as I could find and left them in prominent places all over the house. Whenever the Genius picked up a book on the table or at the side of his bed, it was always on the subject of Saint Joan. One day he came to me and said quite excitedly, 'Charlotte, I have a wonderful idea for a new play! It's to be about Saint Joan!' 'Really,' I replied, 'what a good idea!' " Mrs. Shaw's eyes twinkled as she told me the story.

I first became acquainted with the fact that *Saint Joan* was being written by a letter I received from St. John Ervine in the summer of 1922. I then wrote GBS:

> St. John Ervine has just written me that he has heard you have finished a new play on the subject of Joan of Arc. Provided that this is not the chronicle play in five hundred scenes, I think we shall want to do this, and I hope

you will let us see it. [The chronicle play in five hundred scenes refers to a work mentioned by Shaw in an article he wrote for us in connection with the building of the Guild Theatre. See Addendum A.]

Meanwhile *Back to Methuselah* was to be produced in England by the Birmingham Repertory Theatre, under the management of Sir Barry Jackson. I had written to St. John Ervine suggesting that we visit Birmingham together, and he had agreed to accompany me. Shaw wrote:

Saint Joan is finished except for revising and inserting stage business. It's a star play for one woman and about twenty men. Sybil Thorndike is to play it in London.

Incidentally, I fell on the rocks in Ireland, and cracked a couple of my ribs, besides tearing one of them nearly out of my spine; and though I have kept going I realize that 67 is too old for such games. . . .

Shaw's ribs suggested a "press release," but I was careful to write for permission. This came with the following letter:

Provided you don't suggest to the insurance companies that I am too much disabled, my rib can bear a little publicity.

The scenes in *Joan* can all be reduced to extreme simplicity. A single pillar of the Gordon Craig type will make the cathedral. All the Loire needs is a horizon and a few of Simonson's lanterns. The trial scene is as easy as the cathedral. The others present no difficulty. There should be an interval at the end of the Loire scene and one (very short) after the trial scene, and even that makes an interval too many: the act divisions should be utterly disregarded.

Shaw added:

I enclose particulars as to *Methuselah*. I shall be in Birmingham or the neighborhood for the first set (Oct. 9-12). If you can come, then or later, let me know to this address, and I will secure seats for you for any dates you name. Say how many you will require: I don't know the size of your party.

Early in October, St. John Ervine and his wife Nora accompanied me to Birmingham, where *Back to Methuselah* was produced consecutively for five performances, each afternoon and evening for three days. The effect of seeing all these plays one after the other was murderous, but GBS was triumphant. "This," he said, "is the way you should have done it in New York!" I replied that the title should be changed to *Back and Back and Back to Methuselah.*

One wet afternoon we were all invited for tea at Sir Barry Jackson's home and sat drying ourselves in front of the fire; luckily for Shaw and Sir Barry, it rained so hard all the time the plays were being presented in Birmingham that the theatre was one of the few dry spots where the public could congregate, and the alternatives to seeing the plays were too damp and dreary to contemplate. Shaw, perky as ever in spite of his broken rib, was explaining how none of the respectable medical men in Ireland diagnosed his trouble correctly, and only when he got in touch with an unorthodox individual known as an American doctor was the fact discovered that his ribs were injured. This, GBS hastened to assure me, was not because the doctor was American, but because he was unorthodox.

"Tell us something about *Saint Joan,*" said Ervine. Whereupon Shaw, his tall figure standing before the fireplace, head erect, white beard waving and blue eyes twinkling, launched into the story of Joan and what he had done with it; his conversations with an Irish priest who had been most helpful; and the impact of his own keen mind upon the original source material. For at least two hours St. John, his wife Nora, I and Mrs. Shaw, grouped around the fireplace, listened with rapt attention as GBS told us not only the story of the play, but threw in practically all the contents of the Preface for good measure.

All of us were exhilarated by his lively stories, which happily seemed endless; and while he held forth, Mrs. Shaw, seated on a low chair at one corner of the fireplace, appeared to be engrossed in her knitting, pausing only to smile now and again, like a kindly mother whose grown son was distinguishing himself before an appreciative audience. During one of the lulls in the conversation, which were infrequent and came only when GBS had reached the end of one anecdote and waited for the chorus of "How wonderful!" before going on to the next, Nora Ervine leaned over to Mrs. Shaw, looked at her knitting and asked with some concern, "Whatever are you making, Mrs. Shaw?" "Nothing," replied Mrs. Shaw in a whisper. "Nothing, really. But I've heard the Genius tell these same stories at least a hundred times, and if I didn't have something to do with my hands, I think I'd go stark raving mad!"

One might imagine from this little story that there was not the greatest understanding and sympathy on Mrs. Shaw's part toward her husband. But that would be erroneous. She regarded him with amused admiration and never lost her sense of humor about him. Mrs. Shaw's influence was always directed to the more human, emotional side of GBS's work, and I felt that had it been even stronger, GBS might have written many more plays of the stature of *Saint Joan,* for her warm human quality was a good antidote for his tendency to theorize on political, social and every other subject under the sun. "All Italian woman are stupid," he once remarked in her presence at Stresa. "How can you say that?" she replied. "You know only three or four Italian women, and you can hardly speak enough Italian to carry on an intelligent conversation with any of them." The Genius subsided. He disliked admitting that *Saint Joan* was his best play, for it was not iconoclastic, and GBS had built his reputation on iconoclasm. A year later he was to write me, "Everyone, to my disgust, assures me it is the best play I have ever written."

Some years later, at Stresa, GBS told me that he felt that *Saint Joan* was directly inspired by the Saint herself. "As I wrote," he said, "she guided my hand, and the words came tumbling out at such a speed that my pen rushed across the paper and I could barely write fast enough to put them down." Since GBS wrote *Saint Joan* in Pitman's shorthand, according to his secretary Miss Patch, we must assume that the words came rushing out in torrents—and that the Maid of Orleans was as long-winded as he was. In an editorial written on GBS's death, one of the leading New York newspapers described him as an atheist. I thought of his remarks about *Saint Joan* as I read the editorial. No atheist could have written *Saint Joan,* nor could an atheist have believed it to be divinely inspired. GBS did not believe in the orthodox religions, but he believed in religion, and I offer this story as evidence of his belief in the afterlife, no matter how often on occasion he pretended to be bored by the prospect of spending eternity in heaven with his friends.

During the rain-soaked interludes between the plays at Birmingham, and later in London, GBS discussed some ideas about casting *Saint Joan.* He had recently seen Alla Nazimova in the moving pictures (they were silent in those days) and thought she might be right for the part, despite her accent. I felt, however, that some quality of the character would be lost if it were not played by a young girl. Eva Le Gallienne had been playing the part of Julie in *Liliom* with a great deal of spiritual quality, and I suggested her as the best possibility.

In due course at my hotel in London there arrived a printed paperbacked copy of *Saint Joan* marked in GBS's meticulous handwriting, "Private and Confidential, to Lawrence Langner." I took a measure of the play; it was terribly long. "Another long-winded one," I thought; but soon lost myself in admiration as I read it. I mailed the book to New York and followed soon after. I rushed from the boat to the Garrick Theatre, where the play had been read immediately on receipt by the rest of the Guild Board. Where *Back to Methuselah* found us hesitant, *Saint Joan* galvanized us all into quick action.

Later on, I learned that GBS had dispatched the following cable to the Guild while I was on the ship journeying to New York; where he obtained his information I do not know.

NAZIMOVA IS IN NEWYORK FORAWEEK PLEASETELL LANGNERBY WIRELESSIF YOUKNOWHIS SHIPWHICHI DONTHEWILL UNDERSTAND.

We all seriously considered Shaw's suggestion of using Alla Nazimova but decided against it. On November 12, 1923, I wrote the following to GBS:

I wish to confirm my cablegram of today's date, and to say that with regard to Nazimova, we saw her in a one-act play in which she is appearing this week and are somewhat dubious about her playing the part of Joan. It is not merely a question of age, and I think you will agree with me that age is of great importance, but it is also a question of the moving picture technique. She has been acting in moving pictures for quite a long time, and that always makes it difficult to get out of habits which are all right for the screen but bad for the stage. I think she is a good second choice, but I believe we can do better. I have no doubt we shall cable you in a day or so giving you details.

I have thought over my letter to you of Friday regarding the possible shortening of the play and have come to the conclusion that I did not explain myself very clearly. I think it is premature to talk about the play being too long until we have tried it out in rehearsal. We can send you a cable giving you the running time and then you can tell us what you want us to do. Please understand that we are entirely in your hands in this connection and that under no circumstances would we eliminate as much as one line without your express permission.

If you feel there is any justice in my remarks about the length of the play, perhaps you yourself would, in the meanwhile, examine this from the strictly technical question of production, and see whether anything could be left out without spoiling the play. We want to do everything possible to make the play a success and we have already started to work on the costumes and scenery.

After a debate as to who should play the Saint, which lasted with undiminished violence for many days, the Board finally selected a young actress named Winifred Lenihan for the part —a selection which was excellent, for I have seen five productions of *Saint Joan* in three languages, and I have yet to see a performance to equal hers. This was due to the fact that she possessed in herself the attributes of courage, fervor and youth which the part called for. The keynote of the Guild's production was its essential simplicity. Lee Simonson's scenery and costumes gave it a stark hard masculine quality which I have never seen in any other production, and the English presentation which Shaw raved about, and which I saw later, struck me as very prettified and feminine indeed.

We all felt that the play was far too long and remembering our unhappy experience with *Methuselah,* decided to write Shaw begging him to make some deletions, mentioning the fact that many persons in the audience lived in the suburbs and would miss the last train home if they waited for the end of the play. Shaw's laconic cable in reply was as follows:

THE OLD OLD STORY BEGIN AT EIGHT OR RUN LATER TRAINS AWAIT FINAL REVISION OF PLAY.

As we were all set for rehearsals, Shaw's reference to a final revised version of the script dropped like a bombshell in our midst. Cables passed back and forth, resulting in the demand by Shaw that we stop rehearsals immediately and postpone the opening. We protested by cable that to postpone for a week would cost £400, and requesting GBS to send the revised draft as soon as possible. Shaw's irate reply of December 3rd arrived a week or so after we received the corrected copy.

I enclose a letter just received from my printers. I presume you have had the corrected copy by this time.

The worst part of dealing with you T.G. people is that you are each and all half and half very superior beings and exasperating idiots. When I heard that you were actually rehearsing from a copy which you knew to be an unrevised first proof I tore my hair. I should not have trusted you with it. A man who would play *Methuselah* in three nights is capable of anything. But at least I did tell you very expressly that what you had was not the play in its final form. Only, you never attend to what I say; and if the stoppage of the rehearsals (not that I have any hope that you really stopped them) cost you £400, which is a great nonsense, my only regret is that it did not cost you £4000, an all-too-slender penalty for such criminal recklessness.

I read the play to Sybil Thorndike from the second set of proofs; and the dialogue occupied exactly three hours and three minutes. Since then I have made another and more drastic revision which has, I think, got the last bits of dead wood out of the play, and have certainly saved the odd three minutes. I think therefore it should be possible to begin at 8 and finish at 11:30. The English edition of *Heartbreak House,* uniform with the proofs just sent you, contains 110 pages, including only two specifications of scenery. *Joan* contains seven different scenes. Compare the number of pages and you will see that your estimate of four hours is far over the mark.

Simonson must not make the scenery fantastic. It may be very simple; but it must suggest perfectly natural scenery. Joan was an extremely real person; and the scenery should be keyed to her reality. Simonson must also be limited to three cigarettes a day.

After being called half an exasperating idiot, I dispatched the following cable to GBS. Wishing him a happy Christmas was an afterthought.

REGRET COMPLETELY MISUNDERSTOOD YOU AT BIR-
MINGHAM HAPPY CHRISTMAS.

As can be imagined, I was between two fires: Shaw on the
one hand, and the rest of the Guild Board on the other. But
lest any of my readers should be under the impression that
Shaw had greatly reduced the length of the play, let me add
that he had omitted very little from his first copy. *Saint Joan*
was, and still is, a long, long play. I replied to GBS:

> Your letter of December 3rd has arrived with explo-
> sive effect. I can only plead that I completely misunder-
> stood you at Birmingham. While you told me that the
> printed copy was an unrevised first proof, yet it had al-
> terations in ink and I thought it was in the hands of the
> publishers. You jokingly said it would run about six hours,
> and I am quite sure that if you told me there was any pos-
> sibility of cutting it down or revising it or anything of that
> sort, I completely forgot it. I have certainly paid the pen-
> alty for my mistake, for in addition to being abused by you,
> the entire Theatre Guild has turned on me for doing such
> an obviously idiotic thing as letting them start rehearsals
> on an unfinished manuscript, but I can only repeat that I
> did not know you intended to do any more work on it; and
> that it was not "criminal recklessness." If God makes
> mistakes all the time, surely I can be forgiven for making
> just one.
>
> As to never attending to what you say, I can only say
> that I listened most attentively at Birmingham; in fact,
> you never gave me an opportunity to do anything but lis-
> ten, nor anybody else either. Not that I wanted to do any-
> thing but listen, but if I forgot something of what you said,
> please put it down to torrents of rain in Birmingham, tor-
> rents of conversation in Birmingham, and fifteen waking
> hours out of forty-eight at the theatre, my mental process
> must have been paralyzed.
>
> When I arrived here, the manuscript came a week
> ahead of me. The Theatre Guild is young and impul-
> sive. It was enthusiastic about the manuscript and ex-
> pressed the most abject dejection that you would not revise
> it. I actually told them it was hopeless to ask you. I admit
> that in doing this I was "an exasperating idiot," but that
> is partly your fault; you have trained me for years and

years to believe that a script from GBS could not have a single line changed. If Moses had attacked me for not breaking one of the ten commandments, I could not feel worse about it.

Please accept my apologies for the troubles which were due entirely to this misunderstanding and which is now happily straightened out.

On the same day, I also wrote GBS:

I thought if I wrote you one long letter about *Joan,* you probably would not read it all through, so here is the second on the subject.

Regarding the time, I think we will begin about eight, and may even finish before eleven-thirty, as we have arranged the scenery in such a way that it will not take long to shift. It will not be at all fantastic; it will be simple but it will suggest perfectly natural scenery, particularly the architecture of the time; it will be more or less a background against which the costumes will give a large part of the decoration. There will be about forty-two costumes, allowing for changes, etc., and the production will be fairly expensive although not at all lavish, but simply from the nature of the period.

I have talked over your comments on the characters with Mr. Moeller and he agrees with them thoroughly; the cast which we have assembled corresponds substantially with your suggestions, and we have a very good man for Charles. Joan was a real problem, but I think we have solved it satisfactorily. As to Nazimova: We did not reject your suggestion but went into it very thoroughly. She has had a very peculiar career. She commenced in the Yiddish theatres and built up a really fine artistic reputation which was afterwards capitalized by the moving pictures. Since then she has played largely exotic parts. Nobody in the Guild regarded her as eminently satisfactory, but out of deference to your wishes, we saw her in New York and discussed the part with her. It transpired that she was tied up in a music hall engagement for two months, and we were anxious to open with *Joan* during Christmas week. She has not been in a successful play in New York for the last five years; this does not mean that she is not a good actress; but it does mean that her following is not very large because the movie public is quite different from the theatre-going public; at least that is so in New York.

Miss Winifred Lenihan, whom we finally selected, seems to have most of the qualities of Joan. I think she is almost an ideal Joan, and I am sure that she will be as good a Joan as Sybil Thorndike, whose acting I admire very much. Miss Lenihan has youth, sincerity, a fine spiritual quality, a boyishness and real beauty, and she is one of the up-and-coming young women in our theatre. We are all keyed to high pitch working on the play, and have every reason to believe it will succeed with the public.

On December 11th I also wrote GBS about some more mundane matters, which gives a picture of our efforts to exploit the play to the fullest extent.

I think we have all prayed fervently during the last two weeks, that your invention by which somebody three thousand miles away might be both visible and audible, had been as effective in real life as it was in *Back to Methuselah.* This is just to say that we are working very hard on *Joan,* and that we are going to have a very splendid production and a very excellent young woman in the part. This is Miss Winifred Lenihan who has been making a steady reputation for herself in the theatre over here. I am enclosing some clippings which give you an idea of what the leading dramatic critics think of her.

I know we would like to have anything you can send us to help along the play by way of publicity. While you are largely right in saying that this takes care of itself, the fact remains that we can get every word you say on the subject into the newspapers, and it does attract attention to the play. I understand you lectured in London on the subject of Joan and if you could either let us have the lecture, or a newspaper copy of same, and any suggestions you may make on the business side (because we value your business judgment), we should be very much obliged. And by the way, I should treasure very much a signed photograph. I suppose everybody bothers you for one, but if you would send two, that would be a change in the form of the request. We would hang one in the lobby of the theatre, and I should like to have the other at home.

P.S. The revised draft has just come to hand. Many thanks.

After our first dress rehearsal we decided to make one more attempt to have GBS cut the play, and cabled him as follows:

JOAN OPENS FRIDAY EVENING. CONSENSUS OF OPINION AT FIRST DRESS REHEARSAL FATAL DROP OF INTEREST DURING TENT SCENE AND BEGINNING TRIAL SCENE. WERE YOU HERE SURE YOU WOULD AGREE WITH US. WE WILL NOT DROP ONE LINE WITHOUT YOUR CONSENT BUT FOR GOOD OF PLAY AND TURNING POSSIBLE FINANCIAL LOSS INTO ASSURED ARTISTIC FINANCIAL SUCCESS STRONGLY URGE YOUR CABLING CONSENT OUR EXPENSE FOLLOWING OMISSIONS. . . . OUR DUTY TO GIVE YOU OUR FRANK OPINION. FINAL RESPONSIBILITY YOURS. PLAY MAGNIFICENT.

My readers will note that we suggested Shaw's cabling at our expense, but even with this inducement, he maintained an obdurate silence.

On Friday, December 28th, *Saint Joan,* brilliantly directed by Philip Moeller, made its first appearance on any stage. It was enthusiastically received by its audience. But as usual the critics complained of its length. Also, on the opening night, many of the audience left before the final curtain, which came down at 11:35. While many good things were said about the play, the complaints about its length from the press, coming after the disappointment of *Back to Methuselah,* the failure of which we felt was largely due to its overlength, caused us to cable to Shaw the next day for permission to cut the play. Our cable read as follows:

JOAN OPENED FRIDAY SPLENDID PRAISE FOR LENIHAN MAGNIFICENT CAST AND PRODUCTION PLAY LIKED BUT FEELING UNIVERSAL WITH AUDIENCE IT STILL CONTAINS MUCH REPETITIOUS MATTER MANY LEFT BEFORE END ENTIRE PRESS EMPHASIZES THIS WOOLLCOTT HERALD SAYS CERTAIN SCENES GROW GROGGY FOR WANT OF A BLUE PENCIL CORBIN TIMES SAYS PLAY HAS MANY BACKWATER EDDIES IN WHICH THE DRAMA WAS LOST IN MONOTONOUSLY WHIRLING WORDS BROUN WORLD SAYS IT HAS PARTS WHICH ARE TEDIOUS GOOD

AUDIENCE ASSURED FOR FIRST FOUR WEEKS BY GUILD
SUBSCRIBERS AFTER THAT PLAY WILL FAIL UNLESS
YOU MAKE TEXTUAL OMISSIONS NOW WE STAND TO LOSE
OVER FIFTEEN THOUSAND DOLLARS WE DONT LACK
COURAGE BUT WE CANT AFFORD LOSS FIFTEEN MIN-
UTES OUT OF THE PLAY MEANS POSSIBLE SIX MONTHS
PROFITABLE RUN WE CAN DO THIS WITHOUT SACRIFIC-
ING ANY ESSENTIAL POINT BY OMITTING MINOR REPETI-
TIOUS MATTER WHICH DRAGS IT TAKES INTELLIGENCE
TO RUN OUR SORT OF THEATRE WE URGE YOU TO HAVE
CONFIDENCE IN OUR PRACTICAL JUDGMENT YOU ARE
THREE THOUSAND MILES AWAY.

Alas, we had bitten granite. My own personal cable, equally
unsuccessful, was as follows:

ONE CRITIC COMPARING YOU WITH SHAKESPEARE
SAYS THAT JOAN CANNOT BE SUCCESSFULLY GIVEN
UNTIL AFTER YOUR DEATH BECAUSE IT CAN THEN BE
CUT. SPLENDID OPPORTUNITY TO PROVE AGAIN THAT
YOU ARE GREATER THAN SHAKESPEARE BY CABLING THE
GUILD TO USE ITS DISCRETION IN MAKING SOME OMIS-
SIONS OF UNESSENTIALS. GUILD HAS DONE SPLENDID
WORK. SURE YOU WOULD AGREE IF YOU WERE HERE.

We even persuaded Winifred Lenihan to cable in her own
name, asking him to shorten the play. Her cable read as follows:

AFTER STRIVING FOR WEEKS AND ENTIRE COMPANY
HIGHLY SUCCESSFUL CHAGRINED THAT ALL CRITICS
AND AUDIENCE COMPLAIN OF LENGTH WONT YOU
AGREE TO SOME OMISSIONS FOR SAKE OF COMPANY WHO
HAVE ALL WORKED SO HARD FOR THE SUCCESS OF JOAN.

To the above cable GBS condescended to reply, the only
one he bothered to notice. He cabled her:

THE GUILD IS SENDING ME TELEGRAMS IN YOUR
NAME. PAY NO ATTENTION TO THEM.

By this time, GBS was thoroughly aroused, and wrote us
one of his most scathing letters, addressed to all of us as "My
dear Theatre Guild."

I have had your cables including the one you dictated to poor Winifred. You ought to be ashamed of yourselves for getting a young actress into trouble with an author like that. Anyhow *I* am ashamed of you—thoroughly. Your nerves seem to have reached the Los Angeles level. You get such a magnificent press (considering) that it is extensively reproduced in London; and yet you run screaming to me to say that Messrs. Broun, Corbin & Co. want the play cut, and that you will be ruined if you don't obey. When I urged you to have some consideration for the public in *Methuselah* you insisted on the horror of two plays in a night, sending around buckets of coffee and finishing at two in the morning. Now that you can play in 3½ hours and begin at 7:30 if you like, you want to cut the play and to tell the public that I have cut it, and that you are beaten and that it is now quite like the *Garden of Allah* and *Chu Chin Chou.* And then you ask me to trust your judgment on the ground that you don't trust mine! If Shubert treated me like this I would never speak to him again.

I enclose an article which you can send to the press if business *looks bad*—not otherwise, mind. DON'T edit it and don't rush it to the press with this letter, unless you want a testimonial to your incapacity very badly.

You have wasted a whole morning for me with your panic-stricken nonsense, confound you! What did you do it with—morphia? There must be some dope or other at work.

Out of all patience.

The article, which we did not use, does set out in Shaw's own words his motive for writing the play. It read as follows:

As there seems to be some misunderstanding in the New York press of my intention in writing *Saint Joan,* I had better make myself quite clear. I am supposed to have set myself the task of providing the playgoing public with a pleasant theatrical entertainment whilst keeping the working hours of the professional critics within their customary limits; and it is accordingly suggested that I can improve the play vastly by cutting off a sufficient length from it to enable the curtain to rise by half-past eight and descend finally at ten minutes to eleven. Certainly nothing could be easier. In the popular entertainment business, if your cradle is too short for your baby, you can always cut down your baby to fit the cradle.

But I am not in the popular entertainment business. The sort of entertainment provided by the fate of Joan of Arc seems to be quite sufficiently looked after in the United States by the Ku Klux Klan, and is all the more entertaining for being the real thing instead of a stage show.

As to the grievances of the professional critics, I, as an ex-critic, understand it only too well. It is a hideous experience for a critic, when at half-past ten he has all the material for a good long notice, and is longing to get back to his newspaper office and write it at comparative leisure, to be forced to sit for another hour by that rival artist the author, until all the leisure is gone and nothing but a hurried scramble to feed the clamoring compositors is possible. But the remedy for that is, not to demand that the play shall be mutilated for the convenience of a score or two of gentlemen who see it as their breadwinning job on the first night only, but to combine as other professional men do, and establish the custom of beginning plays of full classical length an hour earlier on the first night.

So much for the negative side of the situation. As to the positive side, I am, like all educated persons, intensely interested, and to some extent conscience stricken, by the great historial case of Joan of Arc. I know that many others share that interest and that compunction, and that they would eagerly take some trouble to have it made clear to them how it all happened. I conceive such a demonstration to be an act of justice for which the spirit of Joan, yet incarnate among us, is still calling. Every step in such a demonstration is intensely interesting to me; and the real protagonists of the drama, the Catholic Church, the Holy Roman Empire, and the nascent Reformation, appeal to my imagination and my intellect with a grip and fascination far beyond those of Dick Dudgeon and General Burgoyne. When in the face of that claim of a great spirit for justice, and of a world situation in which we see whole peoples perishing and dragging us toward the abyss which has swallowed them all for want of any grasp of the political forces that move civilization, I am met with peevish complaints that three hours or so is too long, and with petitions to cut the cackle and come to the burning, and promises that if I adapt the play to the outlook and tastes and capacities of the purblind people who have made the word suburban a derisive epithet, it will run for eighteen months and make a fortune for me and the Theatre Guild, the effect is to make me seem ten feet high and these poor people ten inches, which is bad for my soul, and not particularly healthy for theirs.

In theatres as elsewhere, people must learn to know their places. When a man goes to church and does not like the service nor understand the doctrine, he does not ask to have it changed to suit him: he goes elsewhere until he is suited. When he goes to a classical concert and is bored by Beethoven, he does not scream to the conductor for a fox trot, and suggest that Beethoven should introduce a saxophone solo into the Ninth Symphony; he goes to the nearest hall where a jazz band is at work. I plead for equally reasonable behaviour in the theatre. *Saint Joan* is not for connoisseurs of the police and divorce drama, or of the languors and lilies and roses and raptures of the cinema, and it is not going to be altered to suit them. It is right over their heads; and they must either grow up to it or let it alone. Fortunately for me, it interests and even enthralls serious people who would not enter an ordinary theatre if they were paid to, and draws novices who have never crossed the threshold of a theatre in their lives, and were taught by their parents that it is the threshold of hell. And the class of intelligent and cultivated playgoers whose neglected needs have brought the Theatre Guild into existence, naturally jump at it.

However, even at the risk of a comprehensive insult to the general public of New York, I must add that the limitation of the audience to serious, intelligent, and cultivated Americans means that *Saint Joan* must be regarded for the present as an Exceptional Play for Exceptional People. It has cost a good deal to produce it for them, and is costing a good deal to keep the opportunity open. This will not matter if they seize the opportunity promptly with a sense that if they do not, they will miss it, and discourage the Guild from future public-spirited enterprises of this class.

The solvency of a play depends not only on the number of persons who pay to witness it, but on the length of time over which their attendances are spread. Even a million enthusiasts will not help if they arrive at the rate of ten per week. *Saint Joan's* present prosperity cannot in the nature of things last many months. Those who come early and come often are the pillars of the sort of play that gives you something to take home with you.

As the above is a historical document, I have reprinted it for the light it throws on Shaw's attitude toward the Saint. It should be enforced reading by every dramatic critic who complains of the length of a play, and it should teach all producers to start long plays earlier in the evenings.

Ben Jonson wrote of Shakespeare that he was one of the most long-winded of men. I venture to say the same of Shaw. In later years, I felt a relaxing of the relentless rule regarding cutting. On one occasion Shaw said to me, "If only you would not bother me with asking for permission!"

Despite the length of *Saint Joan,* the large theatregoing public came flocking in to see it. On January 9, 1924, I was writing GBS as follows:

It is extremely annoying to have to admit that you are right. People are coming in droves to see *Saint Joan,* and it is a great success. I have complete confidence in your business judgment. I still hold my own opinions about the length of the play.

Receiving no answer to this letter, I wrote him again ten days later:

I know I am in thorough disgrace at No. 10 Adelphi Terrace, and my name is probably not mentioned without imprecations.

We had a most trying time producing *Joan;* it was a great strain on everybody, and after putting so much time and effort into the thing, not to mention the money involved, and then to see the newspapers attacking it so violently on account of the length, as well as some of the audience leaving the theatre—well if I did act in a manner which now seems to you to be silly, I don't think you would have thought it quite so silly if you had been in my shoes. However, all that is over and done; the fact remains that the Guild has made a magnificent production, and that *Joan* is going over *big* with the public. The ticket sale has been increasing and we think it has settled down for a long run.

We had to invent a very clever method of staging the production to avoid any waits between the Acts, and this has been done extremely ingeniously and without in any way sacrificing the pictorial values of the play, which are very startling and beautiful. I hope you won't object to my dwelling on the pleasant side of the proceedings. *St. Joan* is a great success, and we are all delighted with it. *St. Joan* is one of the finest plays written in the English language and we are very proud to have produced it.

Having heard nothing for some time, I was convinced GBS was too annoyed with me to write. However, his letter dated February 1, 1924, was finally forthcoming. It covered many points concerning the production, including some inevitable complaints of a minor nature. It also contained one paragraph of more than passing personal significance to me:

I am not at all anxious about *Joan;* but I am somewhat concerned about you. You could hardly have been rattled by Heywood Broun and Alan a Dale *et hoc genus omne* if you had not been rattled already. As a matter of fact you were rattled at Birmingham before *Joan* came into operation at all. I sympathized, but did not like to say anything, as it was evidently some private grief that had disconcerted you. What about that pretty lady who called on me and said she was Mrs. Langner, and did not take the smallest interest in the theatre, nor, as far as I could make out, in me? Has she been giving you trouble; or have you been giving it to her? You need not answer this impertinent question: I put it only to show that my recent assumption that you were not *compos mentis* at the theatre was not founded on your panic over *Joan.*

GBS's intuition regarding the pretty lady, my former wife Estelle, who was not interested either in the theatre or in him, was correct. I replied to his questions:

Either you are a mind reader, or St. John Ervine has been talking, because the fact is, that the pretty lady who called on you and did not take the smallest interest in the theatre, nor in you, also took no interest in me, which was very disconcerting as we had been married for eight years and have a little daughter.

GBS also wrote in the same letter on the subject of publicity for *Saint Joan.*

The great press feature of the production was the notice by Pirandello, which you never even mentioned. The N.Y. *Times* has sent it to me specially with an invitation to comment. Perhaps I will; in the meantime let Terry sit tight on that article that I sent her when you had cabled a ghastly failure. She had better send it back to me.

By the way, you must stop your people from giving away my private business letters to the press. It is impossible to correspond on such terms. Nothing requires greater tact and knowledge of what is allowable than giving to the press matter not meant for it; and the silly young folk who become press agents because they are congenital unemployables are the last in the world to be trusted with such delicate business. You must give a flat instruction that nothing that I write, past or present, is to be given to the press without my express permission.

Terry's latest is a request for a new play to open the new theatre next January. She should have saved up *Joan* for it. I have no more *Joans* in me. Are you going to put in a revolving stage? It would have come in very handy for *Joan.*

He also gave me his views on the photographs we sent him.

The pictures have arrived. I had a long letter from Simonson, the Reformed Smoker (or has he reformed?), about it. On the whole there is nothing to complain of, which is a pity, as I complain so well. However lots of things are wrong; so here goes.

In Act I the Steward should be much older than Baudricourt; and both Baudricourt and Poulengy should be in half armor and be obviously soldiers and not merchants. This is important, as it strikes the note of France in war time. As it is, Poulengy's coat should not be belted. Baudricourt should be smart, a *beau sabreur.* The Steward should not be a zany, but a respectable elderly man whom nobody nowadays would dream of assaulting. Otherwise B's handling of him becomes mere knockabout farce.

In the second act Joan's hair should be bobbed; and she should be dressed as a soldier, quite definitely masculine in contrast to her girlish appearance in the first act. And at the end of the act she should be in front of all the rest, in command of the stage in the good old fashioned way from the point of view of the audience, and not beautifully composed in the middle of the picture with all the other people turning their backs to the spectators. Why don't you carry out my directions and get my effects instead of working for pictorial effects? As to the Dauphin I believe his wig is wrong. His portrait shows that his hair was completely concealed by the fashion of the time, giving him a curiously starved and bald appearance that would be very effective on the stage.

The Bishop looks about right for the Inquisitor and the Inquisitor for the Bishop. My effect of a very mild and silvery Inquisitor and a rather stern Bishop has been missed as far as the make-up is concerned. The altar and candles in the middle of the cathedral scene are feebly stagy, and do not give the effect of a corner of a gigantic cathedral as my notion of one big pillar would. And it leads to that upstage effect, with a very feminine operatic-looking Joan in the centre, which I wanted to avoid. The drag toward the conventional is very evident; and is the last word in operatic artificiality (an angry woman tears a thing downward and throws it to the floor); but still, it is all very pretty in the American way, and might have been worse. I am going to see Charles Ricketts' plans and sketches for the London production this afternoon; and it will be interesting to see what he makes of them. I must break off here, but you cannot complain of the shortness of my letter.

Meanwhile, the demand for seats for *Saint Joan* had increased to such an extent that we had to move to another, larger theatre, of which fact I informed GBS; and we requested him to write us some articles and letters that we could use to publicize the play at its new home. This is what I asked for, to which I received no reply.

March 14th, 1924

Saint Joan has now moved into a theatre twice the size (The Empire Theatre), and the business ought to build up much bigger.

You can help tremendously by writing us articles and letters which we can put in the paper to help build up the business from the publicity side. I know that you don't believe in that sort of thing, but when you take into consideration that there are nearly sixty theatres in New York, each one fighting for audiences, you will realize that the Guild is not being merely childish in asking you to help. I have no personal axe to grind in the matter, as whether *Saint Joan* plays for ten weeks or ten months, it will not add a penny to my pocket in any event, but I do feel that for your own sake and the sake of the play, now that we have gone into a theatre with double the capacity, the Guild is not unreasonable in asking you to send articles.

The plans for the new theatre were completed on Saturday and we expect to open next February. We shall have wagon stages which will enable us to shift scenes very quickly. Owing to the very clever scheming of the *Joan* production, the shifts barely took two minutes; in fact, they were miraculously quick. I saw the play again on Thursday. It is very wonderful and very moving. I gather from your letter that the play will soon be produced in London. I wish you every success.

I also sent GBS a copy of a skit I had written on *Joan* which was performed at one of our annual dinners. My last letter from GBS on the subject of *Saint Joan* was dated May 28, 1924.

What an unreasonable chap you are, wanting your letters answered! I never answer letters: if I did I should have no time for anything else.

The skit on *Joan* tempts me to write it up for London. The play has repeated its American success here: it is going like mad; and everyone, to my disgust, assures me it is the best play I have ever written. Sybil Thorndike's acting and Charles Ricketts' stage pictures and costumes have carried everything before them. I am convinced that our production knocks the American one into a cocked hat. Why don't you come over and see it?

The press notices here were just like the American ones: play too long: cut out the epilogue; magnificent play only needing the blue pencil to be a success, etc., etc.

Cardinal Hayes's medal [presented to Winifred Lenihan for her performance] was a Godsend, as a press correspondent named Thomas had just written to the French papers to say that I had "bafouée" Joan. The medal brained him and left him for dead.

I received Terry's demand for articles and so forth with the composure of a man swimming the Niagara rapids and being asked casually for a light. Terry thinks I have nothing else to do but job about as her press agent, and throw in a play occasionally. She should thank God for having done so well.

Who keeps the daughter? Hadn't you better marry Terry until the other lady finds that all husbands are equally dull, and comes back? Meanwhile, why not run her through half a dozen plays like Strindberg?

After the play had run for 214 performances in New York, we decided to send it on tour when the New York engagement was over. We offered the part again to Winifred Lenihan, but unfortunately for her own career and that of the play, she decided to accept another engagement in New York. Like many another young actor or actress both before and after her, she did not realize at the time the value of a so-called "road" following which added so much to the careers of such stars as Helen Hayes, Alfred Lunt, Lynn Fontanne, Jane Cowl and many others. These, when they had a great New York success, almost invariably took it to the hinterland and built a national rather than a New York following. (Today's younger crop of actors also prefer to stay in New York and Hollywood, where they often earn reputations which do not particularly impress the nation's theatregoers.) We reluctantly sent out Julia Arthur, a well-known star, in her place, but she lacked the youth and vitality of Lenihan and the play lost much of its impact.

In the year 1935 our business manager Warren Munsell noted that Katharine Cornell was announcing a New York production of *Saint Joan,* and he wrote GBS reminding him of our agreement that we were to have "the first refusal" of his plays. This was not done obstructively, but merely to know where we stood. The following interchange of letters is amusing. The first is GBS's answer to Mr. Munsell, date 21 June 1935, and the second is from me the following August.

Guilds that deal with me must look for surprises. You have had your fling with Joan and now it is K.C.'s turn. But you have nothing to regret, as I have made a scenario of the play for Elisabeth Bergner; and when this is released there will be the end of the stage version as far as big business is concerned. There is just barely time for a last revival of it next fall.

I cannot reasonably object to a revival of *Brassbound* if Mr. and Mrs. Lunt can be induced to take any real interest in it. But when it was mooted before Mrs. Lunt's feet were cold; and I see no reason for believing that they are any warmer now.

As to any other cast, I reserve judgment. But if you cared to try with Sybil Thorndike and Merivale, that would be all right.

I have just had a flashlight of a very beautiful production of *The Simpleton* from Leipzig, where it has had a success. You threw that play away wickedly in spite of all the pains you took with it. The returns shewed the astonishing fact that not a single person outside your subscription list went to see it. That is a record, isn't it?

Here is my answer to the above letter.

I have been very much tied up at Westport this summer, and did not have time to answer your recent letter which came in the absence of Warren Munsell.

Of course we expect you to do *The Unexpected,* but we do hope that if you are contemplating doing *The Unexpected* again, you will let us have a little warning as we are making plans on the basis of continuing playing your earlier plays, and would be glad to have your suggestions in this regard.

We recently leased *Caesar and Cleopatra* to a summer theatre and Helen Hayes is appearing in the part for a week. We may be able to persuade her to reappear in New York City. Her acting has tremendously improved. . . . In her recent tour over the country, she was playing to an average of thirty-two to nearly forty thousand dollars. I shall be glad to hear from you about this at your convenience.

I have seen many *Saint Joans,* including Ludmilla Pitoëff in Paris, Katharine Cornell in New York and Sybil Thorndike in London. Each possessed some special attributes and some personal problems, but one and all shone in the role, showing that the part itself was the foundation of their success. When it was announced many years later that Gabriel Pascal was to make Shaw pictures in Ireland, GBS told me, "As soon as the news was announced, I was inundated with requests from beautiful Irish girls to play the part of Saint Joan. They seemed to think the only qualification they need is to be Irish." One of the Irish girls who wrote him was the young Irish actress Siobhan McKenna, who had far better qualifications for the role. She since played the part with great success in three countries.

Shaw, in discussing the performances of all the other Joans, referred to a certain continental actress who shall be nameless. He said of her:

> I never liked her in the part. She made the audience weep, but for all the wrong reasons. She played St. Joan like a servant girl who has to go to jail for three months for stealing milk for her illegitimate child. Now that is a tragic situation, I admit, but it is definitely *not* Saint Joan!

And speaking of this lady's success, Shaw quoted another playwright as saying:

> 'Her great acclaim in the part of the Saint was due to the fact that her every gesture and intonation was directly contrary to the spirit and intention of the author.'

The Theatre Guild was ill-advised enough to revive *Saint Joan* in the year 1951 in a production directed by Margaret Webster and starring Uta Hagen. We first suggested to GBS that Katharine Hepburn might appear in this revival, and that since Gabriel Pascal was planning to make a picture with Kate playing the Saint, it would help matters if she first appeared in the stage version. Here is what I wrote on June 26, 1945.

> We would like to do *Saint Joan* with Katharine Hepburn, and I have been corresponding with Gaby Pascal. Pascal has no doubt communicated with you on the subject, and we want you to know that, in our opinion, a stage

production will only enhance the picture. Katharine Hepburn is at the peak of her career and has become a much finer actress. She has the inspirational quality to make a great Saint Joan.

Shaw did not rise to the bait at all. He replied shortly and sharply to the point on July 9.

The lady's age and very striking Dago-American personality are right for *The Millionairess* and wrong for *Joan,* a revival of which must wait until the projected Pascal film has had its fling.

Why GBS characterized Kate's New England personality as Dago-American, I will never know. And neither will she.

Unfortunately, the revival of *Saint Joan* with Uta Hagen lacked the spontaneity which was present in the original production. Our enthusiasms were warmed over, and we were unable to overcome our tendency to make invidious comparisons. One amusing episode occurred when our star, Uta Hagen, repeating Winifred Lenihan's earlier mistake, refused to go on tour after the New York run, and we toyed with the idea of using the talented picture actress Jennifer Jones in her place. Alas, Jennifer, who was pronounced excellent by Margaret Webster who auditioned and rehearsed her in the role, was protected to such an extent by her husband, David Selznick, that we could never get together. I was in Philadelphia while the negotiations were in progress, and almost each day I received a long telegram from David with additional terms. I was touched by his husbandly devotion, but baffled by his telegraphic effusions. One well-remembered afternoon I received a telegram from him so long that the Western Union messenger boy delivered it to me in my hotel room wrapped in a brown paper parcel. I counted twenty-eight pages which ended with the phrase: "If I do not receive an affirmative answer by Sunday, the deal is off." "What a painless method of ending the matter," I thought, after wading through the twenty-eight pages.

The story of *Saint Joan* is not ended. It was recently revived in London (1960) and a spirited controversy raged as to the Epilogue. Why not omit it, was reiterated by important English literary figures. I remembered what Shaw had said to me when I suggested omitting the Epilogue, which seems an obvious cut since it takes place years after the martyrdom of Joan. "The reason for the Epilogue," said GBS, "is to show that the story of Joan did not end with her death. I was writing about Joan the Saint, not plain Joan. I had to include in the play the reversal of the position of the Roman Catholic Church which resulted in her being canonized in the year 1920." But in addition, had the play ended on the actual scene of horror on her death, the audience would have left the theatre with a sense of deep tragedy, which was contrary to Shaw's intention. He wished the play to inspire audiences, not to depress them. And so, in his Epilogue he was able to end on the high beauty of Saint Joan's last uplifting speech, rather than on the horrifying scene of her burning.

I close this chapter by quoting the inscription on the first English edition of the play given to me by GBS after all was forgiven:

To Lawrence Langner of the American Theatre Guild, which first gave this play to the world, from G. Bernard Shaw, 29/11/24.

CHAPTER FIVE

The Devil's Disciple
and Other Plays

BEFORE we produced *Back to Methuselah,* we decided to put on a play that was an old love of ours, *The Devil's Disciple.* Shaw told us that this play was "a star melodrama, and, as such, not so much the Guild's business as, say, [John] Barrymore's." He also stated that Richard Mansfield had "squeezed the last farthing out of the *D. D.,*" an unusual financial error on the part of the Sage of the Adelphi.

The Devil's Disciple is one of Shaw's most popular and endearing plays. While purporting to be about the American Revolution, Shaw actually used the historical facts of the Revolution as a background to display some of his most brilliant verbal fireworks on the subject of puritanism, religion, conventions, English and American stupidity, and the value of British charm as an antidote to the obtuseness of the military. That the intelligent Colonials who fought the British were really dominated by British liberal thought, such as the ideas of Thomas Paine, illuminate how much we Americans owe to the English for supplying us with a clear reason why we were fighting against them, other than the materialistic "no taxation without representation." Shaw seemingly admired neither the

American nor the British side of the dispute, but he favored the British by showing "Gentleman Johnny" Burgoyne to be a most charming Shavian gentleman, a man of wit and character, who was beaten by the Americans mainly because of the traditional British custom of high officials going away to the country for week ends.

The Devil's Disciple does not deal with any of the deep underlying issues between the American colonies and England. Hence it throws no light on the questions raised by the Revolution, and Shaw was correct in regarding it as a "star" melodrama with well-tried theatrical situations. What has given it its enduring quality as a theatre piece is the use of Dick Dudgeon and Burgoyne as mouthpieces for Shaw's diatribes against so-called good people who do evil in the name of God. In opposition to this, Dick Dudgeon does good in the name of the Devil. This so shocked the English critics when the play was first given in London that Shaw was impelled to state that he was by no means the originator of this idea and quoted earlier authorities "from Bunyan to Blake to Buchanan" to prove that his concept was not original. (See his Preface on Diabolonian Ethics.) Largely thanks to the character of Burgoyne, who joins with Dick Dudgeon in Shavian witticisms, the play is worthy of constant revival and retains its freshness despite the fact that it was written over sixty-five years ago.

By this time we of the Guild were beginning to feel our financial as well as our artistic oats, so we sent our London representative, Vaughan Thomas, to see GBS following a letter I wrote him on May 6, 1921:

> I have asked Mr. Vaughan Thomas to call and see you in regard to a production we contemplate making subject to your consent, of *The Devil's Disciple* early next season. We want to play it for the most money there is in it, as we are hoping to purchase a second theatre towards the close of next season, and we have perfected an arrangement with Erlanger, under which plays which are successes in the Garrick Theatre, move out into one of his theatres in the centre of the theatrical district. *Liliom* by Molnar, which we have just put on, is playing to capacity at the Garrick, and we have just signed a lease on the Fulton Theatre where we are moving it on the 23rd of this month, and we expect to play to between $10,000. and

$12,000. a week. *Mr. Pim Passes By* was moved out of
our theatre into one of Erlanger's theatres, the Henry
Miller, and is doing an average of $9,500. a week. *John
Ferguson* is going to be revived at the Garrick on the 23rd
of May, and is expected to play to between $6,000. and
$7,000. a week. All this is to show you that the Theatre
Guild is quite capable of making money. I may add in addition that we are giving a performance of Verhaeren's
The Cloister, which proves we are also capable of losing it
in a good cause.

In casting *The Devil's Disciple,* we have in mind using
either Schildkraut who has made an enormous success in
Liliom, or Frank Reicher, a very successful actor here who
has a distinct following, and will get the last ounce out of
the play. The Barrymores are all engaged for next season,
and even if it were possible to get John Barrymore, I very
strongly doubt the desirability in view of his temperament, as he has been very much spoiled by success. He
left *The Jest* when it was doing splendid business, and he
also left *Richard III,* causing an enormous loss to the producer, although the author did not suffer. However, if he
were to drop out of *The Devil's Disciple* in the same way,
the author would suffer, and I am very anxious to relieve
you of any suffering. I feel sure that the Guild can give
you a better production than any other company in America, and in casting the other parts will get the best stars
available, as we have no objection to featuring people in
this play, since it is put on distinctly to enable us to put on
better plays such as *Back to Methuselah.*

If you have enough confidence in us to let us have the
play, you have the assurance of all of us that we will not
only give you a thoroughly competent cast, but also a
money-making cast. We will sign your usual form contract,
and this letter may be regarded as a definite acceptance on
our part to sign a contract similar to that of *Heartbreak
House.* We are at the present time endeavoring to negoti-
ate an opening for *Heartbreak House* in Chicago next season, and hope to have some news for you in this connection shortly.

The Devil's Disciple opened at The Garrick Theatre on
April 23, 1923, with the well-known English actor Basil Sid-

ney as Dick Dudgeon and Roland Young as Burgoyne. As is always the case, Burgoyne ran away with the play, and Roland Young, an English comedian of the first water, achieved his greatest success in this role, as did Dennis King in a revival years later, when he played the part with Maurice Evans as Dudgeon. On April 27, 1923, I wrote GBS as follows:

> Now that our travail with *The Devil's Disciple* is over, and it seems to be launched with every possibility of success, let me tell you a few things about the performance and what I think of it. Basil Sidney, who plays the lead, is very handsome, and plays with a great deal of vivacity and distinction. On the opening night he was not at his best, but notwithstanding this, the newspaper notices were quite excellent. I have just come from seeing the first matinee, and it is full of women from every suburb of New York, willing to fall a victim to the charms of our particular Disciple, who has a reputation for being a sort of Devil with the women (he is the husband of Doris Keane, of "Romance" fame).
>
> Roland Young, who took the part of Burgoyne, came off with high acting honors. He is an excellent actor for the part and his attack on the lines is so good that we feel we could use him to advantage in some other play of yours at the end of the run of *The Devil's Disciple,* which I am confident will be over, in New York at least, by the summer of 1924. We cannot expect business to continue at top speed during the summer months, so it may be better to keep it in the Garrick Theatre so as to "nurse" it through the summer and get it comfortably settled in a large theatre to run through next winter. We shall afterwards send it on tour throughout the States.
>
> We now have over six thousand subscribers to the Guild plays and those who have seen it are all delighted with *The Devil's Disciple.* I think you would be particularly pleased with the mounting of the play which has been done by Lee Simonson in a most authentic way. Each set is a picture and the atmosphere of the settings is in harmony with the play throughout.
>
> I am anxious to get our collective teeth into *Caesar and Cleopatra* or *Arms and the Man.* Miss Helburn is very keen about *Man and Superman.* Which do you think

would be best? We have good men available for all these parts and should be able to find a place for one of these plays early next season.

You will, I am sure, be interested to hear of the progress of our plans to build a theatre. We floated a bond issue to the extent of £100,000. English money, and gave ourselves four weeks to raise the money. Three weeks and a half have gone by and we are only $50,000. short. We shall get the $50,000. by Sunday and we shall have our own theatre next year. I shall be much interested in having your comments on some of the questions raised by this letter, and remain, with kind regards to yourself and Mrs. Shaw.

The play added to our luster, and on June 6 of the same year I wrote to GBS:

In spite of the hot weather, *The Devil's Disciple* seems to be holding up pretty well and I think it ought to continue through to next Fall on an average business of $4,000 to $5,000 per week after which we expect the business to increase. From now on visitors will begin to come into New York and they keep the theatres busy during the hot season.

Those moguls who wonder what is the matter with the present-day American theatre will open their eyes in astonishment at the summer business of $4,000 to $5,000 per week which was sufficient to pay everyone's salaries and Shaw's royalties in the year 1923.

The Devil's Disciple ran for a period of several months, and we managed to squeeze a few farthings out of it which were overlooked by GBS and Richard Mansfield.

Some years later we were approached by Maurice Evans to co-produce the same play on a partnership basis, but our negotiations fell through and he secured Shaw's permission to go ahead on tour without us. I remember Maurice giving as one of his reasons for this the fact that we were too extravagant in our business affairs. "You see, Lawrence," he said, "I even keep track of every phone call." This was literally true, for like Shaw himself, Maurice had been a bookkeeper in his early days and kept an old-fashioned bookkeeper's desk in his dressing room. More power to him for maintaining a fine reputation for artistic work in the present-day theatre, in which a knowledge of bookkeeping is apt to be even more important than a knowledge of acting, in both of which fields he is a master.

During the third year of our occupancy of the Garrick Theatre, I and other Guild members became acutely aware of the necessity for a permanent home for the Theatre Guild. Alas, I was also acutely unaware, at the time, of the troubles which lie ahead for those who seek to enshrine an ideal into a building— and especially, in our own case, the ideal of a repertory acting company.

I believed that the only kind of art theatre worthy of the name was one where the actors appeared in a repertory of plays, as was the case with the Moscow Art Theatre. In this way, the actors do not become stale by playing the same part every night and they also have the opportunity of playing widely diversified roles. Eva Le Gallienne made a number of gallant attempts to operate this kind of dramatic theatre in New York, but the difficulties and expenses (especially the cost of stagehands) have been so great that so far no repertory company in New York has lasted.

GBS believed in this kind of theatre and encouraged us to build the original Guild Theatre, which was dedicated to repertory. In order that there might be plenty of room for a number of different productions in our repertory, the stage of the theatre was made so large that there was hardly enough space left for the actors' dressing rooms, and certainly not enough room for the audience. We made the ghastly mistake of providing a theatre with all the stage space necessary for a repertory of plays, but without enough seats to provide the income needed to support us. Blame this on our inexperience, but suffice it to say that we had plenty of room for the scenery, but not nearly enough for the actors and audience.

In March, 1922, when we celebrated our fourth birthday, we announced our plans for building the Guild Theatre. It received the hearty acclaim of our friends and supporters, including GBS, and everybody proceeded to work with the greatest enthusiasm on raising the money to build it. Along with the late Maurice Wertheim (one of the Theatre Guild's directors who was also a banker), I was strongly opposed to asking for private subsidy, remembering what had happened to that rich man's plaything, the subsidized Century Theatre, which lasted only three seasons under Winthrop Ames. We raised over a half-million dollars by the sale to the theatregoing public of second-mortgage bonds at a high rate of interest. All the interest due on these bonds was ultimately paid, despite the real-estate slump caused by the depression of the thirties which wiped out the second-mortgage bonds on all the other New York theatres and eventually cost our own kindly bondholders a considerable part of their equities in the Guild Theatre bonds. Thus the generosity of our friends, as well as the depression which took place later, resulted in our unwittingly handicapping our fortunes early in our career; and if we succeeded in maintaining the artistic standards we set for ourselves, it was in spite of the burden of the Guild Theatre rather than because of it. There was a value in having a home, however, no matter how much of a misfit it turned out to be, and I firmly believe this home kept us together in the same way that a Southern family is often kept together in an ancestral mansion from which it is too poor to move.

At the time of the opening of the Guild Theatre, our enthusiasm for its possibilities was tremendous, and my colleagues and I enjoyed the genuine pleasure of seeing before our eyes a magnificent building planned for our own kind of artistic theatre and in which we hoped that all our dreams were to be realized. The theatre in which many of our finest plays were given was finally taken over by our bondholders after twenty-five years of operation, of which only two seasons were profitable. They in turn disposed of it to ANTA (The American National Theatre and Academy), which increased its seating capacity and has been operating it as a commercial theatre on a tax-free basis, which has made the burden of carrying it far less than ours. One of ANTA's first moves in renovating the building was to rename it and to obliterate all traces of the Theatre Guild's and the New York public's having either built it or occupied it or such masterpieces as O'Neill's *Mourning Becomes Electra* having opened there. Perhaps some future recognition of these facts will take place, especially since, when the theatre was in difficulties later on, it was saved for ANTA by my arranging with Robert Dowling and Roger L. Stevens for its partial occupancy by the American Academy of Dramatic Arts (of which I was president at the time), which resulted in ANTA not paying taxes on the building for several years and also gave them a rental income of over thirty thousand dollars a year which still continues and has reached an amount of over three hundred thousand dollars. But all this was in the far future when we were working like beavers to build the Guild Theatre in 1923.

Since we were asking all our friends to make contributions toward the building and were heavily involved financially ourselves, we asked GBS to invest in the theatre, which he wisely refused. However, he decided to write an article for us which we could sell, and we were then to use this money toward the costs of the building. He explained his idea in a postcard dated April 9, 1923.

> I have written an article on the need for a new theatre, and am sending it to London today to be typed from my shorthand. You can, if you like, sell the American serial rights for a substantial sum and take it as my subscription to the theatre fund. That would not prevent you from using it later on (when the magazines have had their market) as a supplement to your appeal for subscriptions.
>
> I will give further instruction as to how to sell the article when I send you the text of it.
>
> G. Bernard Shaw

We sold the article, which was entitled "Wanted: A New Sort of Theatre," to *Theatre* magazine, which printed it in their issue of May, 1925. Shaw had added "For an Old Sort of Play" in his original title. I recommend the article to the attention of all those engaged in theatre building today, so farseeing is it in its demands for a theatre in which plays with dozens and dozens of scenes could be produced. It was a forerunner of the so-called arena theatres, and had we been smart enough to follow Shaw's ideas, the Guild Theatre would have revolutionized the art of theatre building, a task which has now fallen into the hands of another Irish-English theatre genius, Sir Tyrone Guthrie. Because of the modern applicability of Shaw's ideas on theatre buildings, it is reprinted here *in toto* in the Addenda, together with his instructions on how to sell it.

On June 6, 1923, I wrote to GBS about his article:

> I was tremendously interested in your article about the theatre; I quite agree with you, and we are going into this new theatre with our eyes very wide open. St. John Ervine says that he wants to start a similar movement in London, and I have decided that while I am in London I will show

them how we conducted the campaign and an absolutely sure way of raising money; that is, as sure as anything is sure in this uncertain world. We are going to launch an auxiliary campaign in a couple of months and have decided that we shall use your article as the principal propaganda, because the magazines thought the article too much like propaganda and would not pay a very high price. We will therefore get the most out of it by using it for propaganda.

I would like to suggest that, even at this late date, our "plan" might be used to build the British National Theatre which has moved so slowly, and some other theatre buildings in this country.

As the Guild Theatre took shape in a pseudo-Italian style of architecture which was fashionable at the time, we decided to ask Bernard Shaw to open the theatre. Maurice Wertheim invited him to stay at his estate, which I described as "one of the most beautiful places near New York." I approached him while I was in London, but he refused. I thought Mrs. Shaw might be more amenable, so I wrote her as beguilingly as I could, but my blandishments were of no avail. I received a picture postcard from Madeira showing a chromo of Reid's Palace Hotel, and the following in Shaw's neat handwriting on the back:

January 5, 1925

This also is one of the most beautiful places near New York: flowers, sunshine, bathing, and no theatres to open. I have written to Mr. Wertheim to acknowledge his very handsome invitation. I may be the means of shutting the new theatre some day; but as to opening it, I leave that to the President; it is his job, not mine. We expect to be here until the middle of February.

Shaw also sent us another postcard saying:

You can open the new theatre without sending to England for a crowbar. Anyhow, I won't.

Eventually, President Coolidge opened the Guild Theatre by pushing an electric button in Washington, and, blessed in this way by the Apostle of Taciturnity, we presented Shaw's brilliant comedy, *Caesar and Cleopatra,* in which Helen Hayes and Lionel Atwill played the title roles, while Philip Moeller directed the play.

The year before, in order to raise money to purchase two beautiful tapestries to decorate the walls of the theatre, we gave a subscription ball at the Hotel Commodore which we called "The Tapestry Ball." Our efforts were successful, and on the opening of the new theatre, the tapestries were hanging on the walls of the auditorium. (They have now been given by us to the Shakespeare Festival Theatre at Stratford, Connecticut.)

The opening night of Shaw's *Caesar and Cleopatra* was a brilliant affair. Under other circumstances, the play and performance would have merited high praise, for Helen Hayes was delightful as the child Cleopatra, Atwill was satisfyingly romantic as Caesar and Helen Westley incredibly magnificent in the role of Ftatateeta. But the critics, who had so often been our good friends, after noting the palatial appointments of our new home, began to fear that our new theatre would go to our heads. The critic Alexander Woollcott coined the phrase, apropos of the tapestries hanging in the auditorium, "The Gobelins will get you if you don't watch out!"

When I was discussing the play later with GBS, he remarked that the best Caesar was Forbes-Robertson, who had opened the Shubert Theatre with the same play. "Unfortunately," said GBS, "I gave Forbes-Robertson the business of eating dates during an important scene, not knowing that he had false teeth. On the opening night his teeth stuck together, so that he became speechless and had to rush off stage to take them out and replace them again."

Helen Hayes, in my opinion, was one of the best young Cleopatras I have ever seen. She was a Shavian kitten, not a sexy vampire—which is what deluded audiences always look for whenever the part of Cleopatra is played in the theatre. In this way they overlook the fact that Cleopatra was a superb strategist and politician. In both *Antony and Cleopatra* and *Caesar and Cleopatra* it is her development as a woman which is stressed by Shakespeare and Shaw, and not the sexual performances which the public for generations seemingly longs for.

Notwithstanding our bad luck with *Caesar and Cleopatra* (it ran only six weeks), we returned to the old adage I had coined, "When in doubt, play Shaw." In the same year we launched *Arms and the Man* (September 14, 1925) at the Garrick Theatre and a double bill, *The Man of Destiny* and *An-*

drocles and the Lion, at the Guild Theatre (November 23, 1925).

When we first wanted to produce *Arms and the Man,* we approached GBS on the subject and received the following on a postcard from Madeira under date of May, 1925:

> *Arms and the Man* is all nonsense: why not do *East Lynne* or *Charlie's Aunt?* Leave it to Lorraine [an English actor of Shaw comedies] if he wants it.

Shaw's habit of deprecating his earlier plays should not fool people today. Many of these plays were better constructed and more actable than his later more didactic plays. They also contained some of his most original characters, such as Bluntschli and Sergius. His satire on the military mind in *Arms and the Man* will be popular so long as military minds continue to be regarded as a necessity by mankind (How long, O Lord, how long!).

Despite Shaw's warning, *Arms and the Man* was put in rehearsal with Alfred Lunt in the role of Bluntschli and Lynn Fontanne as Raina. They added to their rapidly growing laurels in this play, in which Petkoff was played by Ernest Cossart and Nicola by Henry Travers. One of Alfred Lunt's unforgettable scenes of acting took place in Act I where he enters Raina's bedroom and fights against falling asleep from sheer fatigue. Alfred pointed out to me years later that he liked to find a place in every play where he could win the sympathy of the audience. He certainly found it in this scene. This play remains one of the most successful in the Shaw repertory, and it was produced again with great success at our theatre at Westport in the year 1936 with José Ferrer, Claudia Morgan and Kent Smith in the leading roles. It had also been made into the successful operetta, *The Chocolate Soldier,* an experience which infuriated Shaw.

On October 19, 1925, I wrote GBS:

> *Arms and the Man* is a great success, and we are quite ready to do the next play of the Shaw cycle. By the time these lines reach you, we shall probably have made a decision, and be in rehearsal.
>
> The Guild is prospering beyond belief; the number of paid subscriptions for the six plays now amounts to over 17,000 and it is expected to go up to 20,000, at which point we shall have reached the limits of human endurance.

Anyone who loves animals must necessarily admire *Androcles and the Lion,* which reflects Shaw's broad Christian sympathy toward animals as well as humans. His Preface to this play, which should be required reading for every minister of the Gospel, is still vitally alive today with his reverence for the teachings of Christ. ". . . I am ready to admit," Shaw wrote "that after contemplating the world and human nature for nearly sixty years, I see no way out of the world's misery but the way which would have been found by Christ's will if he had undertaken the work of a modern practical statesman."

Shaw was himself not especially noted for turning the other cheek. But his attitude toward the people he loved was colored by his attitude toward animals. It was no health fad which made him a vegetarian, but a refusal to eat the flesh of a fellow creature which suffered in dying. His inherent personal kindness, of which many examples will be found throughout this book, suffused his play *Androcles and the Lion* and made it one which will live for many years to come. And almost every revival of the play since it was first written has found new audiences among new younger generations of theatregoers.

Our production turned out to be a charming effort, with Henry Travers as the humble Androcles and Romney Brent as the affectionate Lion. Covarrubias, the brilliant Mexican artist, designed the decor, which was unquestionably more Aztec than African. On the same bill Edward G. Robinson played the part of the young Napoleon in *The Man of Destiny,* with the brilliant actress Claire Eames playing the role of Lavinia. I reported to GBS on the subject in my letter of November 30:

> *Androcles and the Lion* has turned out to be a great success, and I think you would very much enjoy the production, which is very imaginative and amusing. It seems to be going well with the audiences, and I should not be surprised if it ran for several months.
>
> *Arms and the Man* is still going strong, and will be moving back to the Garrick Theatre this week.
>
> You will note that all our plays play to very much higher business during the first five weeks than thereafter. This is because of the large number of subscribers who buy tickets in advance to all of our plays.

Shaw's attitude to these productions was expressed in a letter to Terry Helburn:

They tell me that *Androcles* is first rate, and *The Man of Destiny* quite unbearable.

I have seen a photograph of Raina and Bluntschli in which he is holding her in his arms in the bedroom scene. She would have screamed the house down and had him shot like a mad dog.

Your producer had no *dull*icacy.

Yah!

The growth of our subscription audience was largely due to the great following Shaw's plays were building up in this country. With Shaw represented in New York by three productions during the year 1925, we were well on our way with the alliance with him which continued to the end of his life.

When I was in London in the summer of 1922, Shaw told me of the unhappy plight of his Austrian translator, Siegfried Trebitsch, now ruined by the war, who had written a drama called *Jitta's Atonement*. To earn some money for him, Shaw had translated it into English. "But how could you translate it when you don't know German?" I asked. "I have a smattering," he replied. "Besides," he added, with a twinkle, "translating isn't just a matter of knowing the language. The original play was a tragedy—which was all right for Austria where they like tragic endings—but it would never go that way in England and America, so I turned it into a comedy!" Shaw then offered this play to the Guild.

On September 5, 1922, on arrival in New York I wrote GBS as follows:

> I read *Jitta's Atonement,* and liked it. I passed it on to the other members of the Committee but as two of them have been away in Europe and only just returned, it has not been possible to get a decision. I have asked them to take the matter up at the next meeting and I shall be able to write you at that time. Meanwhile there is the question of getting the right actress for the part; not an easy matter as the part must be cast absolutely correctly.

While *Jitta's Atonement* was being considered, Bertha Kalich, a star of the Yiddish Theatre, approached us for the American rights. We acquiesced, and Shaw wrote me on September 30, 1922:

The Guild has cabled to me to give *Jitta* to Madame Kalich, probably blessing her for having extricated it from a difficult situation. But I am not at all happy about it. She seems the right woman for it, and she is very keen on it; but from what she has said to me I suspect that if the production is left in her hands she will suppress the comedy side of my version, and revert to the unrelieved gloom of the original; and I don't think this will succeed in America, because it means that the last two acts will merely wallow gloomily in the memories of the first. What I want is a management who will engage Madame Kalich with two first rate comedians for the widow and Jitta's husband, and will see that it gets full value for their salaries, and that their parts, and the part of the play that belongs to them, are not sacrificed to Jitta's heroics. Also, I believe that if she takes a theatre from Woods or Shubert on sharing terms, they will leave her with a sense of paying impossible royalties, as at 50-50 my percentages will be double what they really are on the whole business.

I saw your press communication about the play; but I do not want it suggested that it is 95% Shaw and 5% Trebitsch. Novelty is always valuable; and novelty is the one quality that I have lost hopelessly with the affirmation of my reputation. The line to take is to boom Trebitsch in New York (steps are being taken to that end on this side), and to suggest that as what has been lacking in my plays is HEART, the combination of the emotional Trebitsch with the intellectual Shaw is ideal, and will make the most dramatic event of the season.

To the above I replied as follows on October 16, 1922:

I had the pleasure of meeting this lady before your letter arrived; she spoke to me of having met you in England, and made a proposition that the Theatre Guild manage her in *Jitta's Atonement.* We are, however, tied up at the present time, owing to the fact that we let our last producer go, expecting to replace him by Mr. Kommisarjevsky, who has not yet arrived. Miss Kalich now tells me she has made arrangements with another management, and I have told her I shall be very glad myself to go to some of the rehearsals and assist in any way I can in the production. I may add that Madame Kalich is a very

competent person, quite capable of handling the play on
a businesslike basis and getting a theatre on good terms.
It is always the custom, whenever a play is produced in
America on sharing terms, to arrange the terms so that
the company pays the royalty while the theatre owner
does not. I imagine that this has happened in all your
plays where the management of the play did not actually
own or lease the theatre.

Alas, *Jitta's Atonement* did not succeed even as a comedy,
but the play stands as evidence of the kindness and loyalty of
Shaw to his friends when in trouble, financial and otherwise.
The famous French actor Firmin Gémier once told me that
Shaw had been so badly translated into French by his authorized
translators that his plays were seldom given in France, but his
loyalty to these translators was so great that it was impossible
to have better versions made by other translators.

Shaw's kindness to Trebitsch was in my mind when, about
this time, I answered his enquiry as to my play *Moses,* which he
had read and liked.

You ask whether the Theatre Guild is going to do
Moses. Was there ever a prophet in his own country? If
Trebitsch is hard up, perhaps I might pay him to translate it into German, secure its production in Berlin, and
then America would want it.

I regarded *Moses* as my most important play. It was later
published by Boni & Liveright in New York, and Gollancz in
London. When it was rejected for production by my confreres
in the Theatre Guild, I almost dropped out of the organization
I had founded to devote myself to playwriting. I sent a copy of
the play to GBS for his comments, and because of their amusing
nature, I include below his letter to me from Ireland of 19
August 1922.

I have read the play right through without difficulty or
an oppressive sense of duty.

It achieves its purpose completely; and as the family
picture—the two brothers and the sister—comes out alive
with the figures individual and the characters natural and
entertaining, it must be allowed that it achieves its purpose dramatically as well.

I don't think it will suggest anti-Semitism; the characters are too human. All races and nations are divided like that and go on like that.

The main difficulty is that you are telling a story which is already known to the world in a version so impressive and so splendid in its literary execution that it is impossible to take it down from the supernatural plane without anti-climax. It is as if Cervantes had had to write Don Quixote without making him comic. However, after the first shock of the cold water I got over this.

I have scrawled some violent protests against your dragging the stage into your descriptions of the scenery. I have shown that this can be dispensed with. You will find no allusion to the boards in my plays, nor any Cs or RC nor LCs nor any other technicalities; yet my directions are complete working directions for the producer.

And in the name of decaying Latinity, I repudiate the verb "to exit." If, like the Elizabethans, you like to give your stage directions in Latin, at least give them in grammatical Latin—exit Moses, exeunt Aaron and Miriam—but don't say Moses exits, or, worse still, they exit. Exit means he goes or she goes, or it goes. Exeunt means they go. Even I remember that much of my school Latin.

I write in haste, packing for my return to England.

To this I replied on September 5:

. . . I have taken most of your suggestions, especially with reference to the verb "to exit." As both the English language and the French language were formed from bad use of Latin, I suppose I could offer as an excuse the fact that in America the word "exit" is actually used as a verb. The stage manager says:—

I exit	We exit
Thou exiteth	You exit
He, she or it exits	They exit

I quite agree with you, it is very ugly, and should be stopped.

One of the interesting facets in Shaw's character was his keen interest in boxing and prize fighting. I have already referred to his correspondence on the Dempsey-Carpentier prize fight. Gene Tunney, America's World Champion boxer for

many years, admired Shaw, and called to see me in the autumn
of 1926 about the possibility of making a motion picture based
on Shaw's prize-fighting novel *Cashel Byron's Profession.* I
brought the two of them together, and they became fast
friends for the rest of Shaw's life.

After Gene Tunney's visit to my office, I wrote the following to GBS on October 15, 1926:

> Dear GBS
>   I cabled you this afternoon about Gene Tunney. He
> came up to the Guild office this afternoon and had a long
> chat with me about the possibility of doing *Cashel Byron's
> Profession.* Under the influence of his very charming per-
> sonality, and also because I was impressed with the pos-
> sibility of his doing a good job of the play, I sent you a ca-
> ble, and by the time this letter reaches you it will no doubt
> be an old story.
>   I am extremely favorably impressed with the character
> of the boy [Tunney] and his ability to play the part. He
> has none of the characteristics of a prize fighter other
> than a magnificent physique, which strikes you the mo-
> ment you see him, but there is nothing brutal or animal
> about him, like Dempsey. In fact, as everyone who saw
> the fight testifies, his performance was a fulfillment of
> your own prophecy, made to me several years ago, that
> Dempsey would some day be beaten by a boxer.
>   Gene Tunney gives the impression of a handsome
> young man who is scientific to the last degree. But, sur-
> prising fact, he noticed a picture of John Masefield up on
> the wall and told the entire Theatre Guild, to their amaze-
> ment, that he had read many of his works and knew he
> worked in a saloon down in this part of town when
> Masefield was a young man; in fact, though it sounded
> like a fairy tale, one can almost envisage Tunney as a lit-
> erary connoisseur who wins world's championships to pay
> for his library.

At the end of our 1927-1928 season I wrote to Shaw telling
him of our plan to develop our subscription system all over the
United States. My letter of May 10, 1928, is interesting as
showing the way our subscription was built up, based to a substantial extent on Shaw's popularity.

I have just come back from a trip to the leading cities outside New York, where we are arranging to start Theatre Guild memberships similar to our membership in New York, which has now reached the figure of twenty-five thousand subscriptions. We expect to have members subscribe to the Guild plays in all the leading cities of the United States, and after the plays have been played in New York, they will play in other cities to an organized audience which will have bought the tickets in advance. This is likely to work up into a very wonderful thing for all concerned, although it is going to take a great deal of work to put it over.

During my visits to these cities, I delivered a lecture on the subject of "GBS and the Theatre Guild." It went very well indeed, as you are unquestionably the darling of all women from twenty to forty-five throughout the United States. It is well for you that you do not come over here, as I believe you would be literally hugged to death. Indeed, I have considerable doubts about the safety of my own person, merely because I happen to know you.

During the course of my lectures I found I was constantly being asked about Mrs. Shaw, so that while my lecture started as one about "GBS," it finally ended up as one on "Mr. and Mrs. Shaw," as all the women seemed to be exceptionally curious to know how Mrs. Shaw manages to put up with you.

I am very anxious to see your new book. I hope it will be out before long. Have you found a subject for a play yet? I know how difficult it is for you to find a character sufficiently noble to interest you, but my suggestions about Voltaire and Socrates having been turned down, I have another suggestion to offer: Why not write a play about yourself?

On Shaw's seventieth birthday in July, 1926, I could not resist "pulling his leg" on the subject of his age and his royalties:

I see from the newspapers that you will reach the age of seventy on July 26th, and I hope this letter arrives in time for me to wish you many happy returns of the day. But I cannot understand all this pother in the newspapers about your birthday. It gives the impression that you are getting to be an old man, which of course is ridiculous.

One paper here says that you are going to do a play
about Queen Elizabeth. I hope this will be followed by additional plays, one for each member of the British Royal
Family from that time down to the present. We will be
very happy to do them, one by one, in a manner as ama-
teurish as possible, as I understand from St. John Ervine
that you have reduced your rates to amateurs.

I am very sorry that neither my wife (Estelle) nor myself (we are still married) will be in London this summer,
as we should be so happy to see you and Mrs. Shaw again;
but perhaps you will be glad to see some of the other Theatre Guild directors, who don't know you so well and
who will therefore be more afraid of you than I am.

I hope that Mrs. Shaw is well and that you are not working too hard.

Another American newspaper writer who evinced a great desire to meet Shaw when I was in London one summer was the
late Franklin P. Adams (FPA) who conducted one of the most
brilliant newspaper columns of his day under the name of "The
Conning Tower." I invited him and his wife, Esther, to have
tea with GBS in a service flat we had rented in Duke Street,
St. James. Shaw arrived wearing his usual "plus fours," and his
flow of witty stories actually silenced the usually loquacious
FPA. Just as Shaw was leaving, he turned to me and remarked,
"I'm surprised to find you living in this building. This is the
place where Isadora Duncan used to live, and I was invited to
visit her here and father one of her children." He then told us
the oft-repeated story of how Isadora wanted to have different
children by a number of famous men, and had invited him to
join the group, with the remark that the resulting child would
be wonderful if it had her body and Shaw's brain. "But imagine how terrible the result would be," replied Shaw, "if it had
my body and your brain!" With that story he made an effective exit, leaving us speechless.

CHAPTER SIX

When in Doubt, Play Shaw

S H A W ' S *Pygmalion* is his most popular play. It has been given by countless amateur and professional companies all over the world and translated into many languages. Since its original production in English at His Majesty's Theatre, London, in 1914 with Mrs. Pat Campbell in the role of Liza and Beerbohm Tree as Professor Higgins, it has continued to make theatrical history in its original play form; also as one of the best motion pictures ever made; and as a basis for one of the world's most successful musicals. And the popularity of the play increases with the passage of time. Shaw, as usual with his best plays, grumbled about its popularity.

We first produced *Pygmalion* on November 15, 1926, with Lynn Fontanne playing the part of Eliza Doolittle, Reginald Mason as Professor Higgins, and Henry Travers as Alfred Doolittle. The outstanding feature of this production was the remarkable portrayal of Liza by Lynn Fontanne. Looking like a replica of Hogarth's "The Shrimp Girl" in the British National Gallery, Lynn played the role with the comic relish of a true Londoner. She reached down into the depths of her childhood memories of the London coster girls, and she lived the part. I have seen the role of Liza played on many occasions by actresses both here and in London, but I can write truthfully that Lynn excelled all of them, including Mrs. Pat Campbell, whom I saw in the original London presentation.

The brief report I wrote GBS a few days after the opening reads:

> This is just a line to tell you that *Pygmalion* has gotten over very well, and it looks as though it will have a very good run indeed. Last night there was just a handful of empty seats in the house, and it looks like a complete sell-out so far as anyone can prognosticate. But better than all this, the play comes out as fresh and amusing as the day after it was written, and the audience enjoys it hugely. I will send you some photographs of the sets, the first act being particularly successful and ingenious.
>
> You will undoubtedly receive a copy of the press notices, and you will find that some of them have referred to our ending being different from the ending of Mrs. Pat Campbell's production, and that other changes have been made. During rehearsal these changes made by Mrs. Pat Campbell were brought up, which resulted in our cabling you, and I want to state, on behalf of everybody in the Guild, that the play as it was played in our theatre when the play opened and as it is now being played is word for word exactly the same as the play in the printed form, without there being one cut, change or alteration of any sort, except that Miss Westley refers to her car, instead of her carriage, as in the printed text. This is purely an alteration due to the fact that the play is being done in the costumes of today.
>
> I may add that the Director of the play, during rehearsal, came to us with a request to make cuts in the last act, and we told him that under no circumstances was a single cut to be made; I mention this because he has said he would write to you and ask whether you are holding us down to such a condition. The gentleman in question is Mr. Dudley Digges.
>
> May I take this opportunity of congratulating you upon the Nobel Prize? It seems to me you should have received it years ago.

If I sounded as though I was placating GBS, this is an accurate appraisal of my attitude. There had been so much talk and correspondence about "cutting" his other plays, such as *St. Joan,* that I blatantly took his side in this instance. As to the Nobel Prize bestowed on GBS, I felt it was a fine gesture toward the theatre, and I felt even more grateful when some years later our own Eugene O'Neill received the same award.

The play, which combines the ancient legend of Pygmalion and Galatea with Cinderella, was, according to its Preface, written by Shaw in part to make "the public aware that there are such people as phoneticians, and that they are among the most important people in England at present." And he adds that if the play does this, "it will serve its turn." He goes on to boast that *Pygmalion* "has been an extremely successful play. . . . It is so intensely and deliberately didactic, and its subject is esteemed so dry, that I delight in throwing it at the heads of the wiseacres who repeat the parrot cry that art should never be didactic. It goes to prove my contention that art should never be anything else."

However, it was neither didactics nor phonetics but the elements of the Cinderella story coupled with the frustrated love story between Liza and Professor Higgins (which Shaw disdained to bring to fruition) which account for the popularity of *Pygmalion.* By no means an original story, Shaw nevertheless conceived it in its entirety. The idea of two men taking a gypsy girl, teaching her to speak in accents of the upper classes and their success in passing her off in society as a lady, and with an incident in which a party was given from which she flounced out using rude language, is contained in Chapter 87 of Tobias Smollett's *Peregrine Pickle.* When I once pointed this out to GBS, he told me that I was the hundredth person who had drawn his attention to this, but that he had nevertheless conceived the idea independently. I had no reason to doubt this, because his imaginative powers were certainly greater than those of Smollett. Besides, had he been so indebted, he would have said so, as indeed he did very straightforwardly when he stated in his Preface on Diabolism that the idea of a disciple of the Devil had been used in literature long before he wrote his play on that subject. I dwell on this because I want to emphasize the relative unimportance of the sources of plays as compared with their treatment by the author. Shakespeare appropriated many of his plots, and his plays are no less important because they are based on oft-told stories. Hence it is Shaw's original treatment of the well-seasoned story elements of *Pyg-*

malion which has made this probably his most popular play.

When Shaw died he left the major part of his large fortune to be used by the Public Trustee to carry out his theories of phonetics, something he never attempted in his own lifetime. But I will deal with his strange obsession with this subject, and his failure to accomplish anything in this field during his own life, in discussing his last will and testament in Chapter 16.

While *Pygmalion* was on the boards in New York, someone wrote me a letter complaining of the use of the expression "not bloody likely" in Act 3, which he claimed was not understood in this country. I sent the letter to Shaw, and he replied on March 23, 1926.

> The man is a fool. America knows the word as well as England; and the effect will be precisely the same. Also, it is not of the smallest importance—just a passing laugh and not in the least the climax of the play.
>
> Hope to see you next year, with a good play in your pocket. I have been knocked out for a month by what they call influenza—pyrexia and nothing else.

Pygmalion was given by the Theatre Guild's first successful Repertory Company and played in New York throughout the season of 1926-1927 in a program of plays which included *Juarez and Maximilian, Ned McCobb's Daughter, The Silver Cord, The Brothers Karamazov, Right You Are If You Think You Are* and *The Second Man.*

In the fall of 1927 we brought our Repertory Company headed by Alfred Lunt and Lynn Fontanne to Chicago in a group of plays which included Shaw's *Arms and the Man* and Molnar's *The Guardsman,* to which we added our opening production of Shaw's *The Doctor's Dilemma.*

This was an historic event for the Theatre Guild and the American theatre in general, for it was the beginning of the Theatre Guild subscription system which has been in existence in one form or another ever since and has contributed to the nationwide support of plays on tour for the past thirty-five years. Indeed, but for this system, combined with The American Theatre Society and the Council of the Living Theatre, our country would be a theatrical desert except for the few larger cities. It is not generally known that Shaw was indelibly connected with the early beginnings of this system, made up of what he called his congregations in various cities.

One day in the winter of 1926, a Chicago public-utilities magnate named Samuel Insull dropped in at the office of the Theatre Guild and unintentionally influenced our entire future, for it was he who was responsible for our going to Chicago. Mr. Insull called on our business manager, Warren Munsell, and informed him that his wife was acting in a Chicago theatre venture in which he was interested. He suggested that if the Theatre Guild Acting Company came to Chicago the following fall, he would underwrite it on a subscription basis; the first four plays were to be produced by the Guild, the last two by the local Chicago company.

While we sporadically sent out touring companies, this was the first time a subscription series had been proposed out of town, and Samuel Insull was willing to back his faith in us with his money. A few months later I met him in Chicago; he was a pleasant vigorous man of affairs, small in stature but large in vision, who, like the late Otto Kahn of New York City, thought it was his public responsibility to subsidize the performing arts. Few such benefactors exist today. They have been taxed out of existence, and replaced by millionaires who boast of how much money they have taken out of the theatres.

Insull told me that as a young man he lived in England, representing the Edison Company, and that a tall lanky young Irishman named Bernard Shaw worked for him as an electrician; he knew very little about electricity and caused so much trouble that he was soon fired from his job. I checked this story later with GBS, who told me it was correct, even admitting that he knew very little about electricity. Samuel Insull introduced me to his attractive wife, who belonged to that familiar feminine order which will move mountains in order to act in the theatre. Indeed, it was she who primarily moved us out to Chicago.

The Chicago engagement was so popular that the shrewd Mr. Insull actually received a profit from our engagement— ". . . the first time I ever made a profit in the theatre or opera in my life!" he told me smilingly. Insull's memory was sullied by his losses for investors in his business enterprise in the 1929 crash, but I shall never cease to be grateful for his enthusiasm which helped to bring the Theatre Guild into a far larger field of activity than it might have had otherwise.

Our first Chicago season was further made memorable by our opening *The Doctor's Dilemma* there, with Alfred and Lynn and the rest of our Acting Company which we later brought back to New York. On November 18, 1927, I wrote GBS as follows:

> I went up to Chicago to attend rehearsals of *The Doctor's Dilemma.* It has the most wonderful cast of any play I have ever seen. It acted like a streak and went over beautifully, as you have no doubt noted by this time. We went down to Baltimore and saw the opening there, too, and it went over equally well, with the audience largely made up of doctors from the Johns Hopkins University. It opens in New York Monday night, and I do not doubt but that it will be as big a success as *Pygmalion* was last year, though considerably more expensive for us to run, owing to the large cast.

The outstanding feature of the Theatre Guild's production was Alfred Lunt's extraordinary performance as Dubedat, which he played with such charming rascality, such endearing tenderness and such poetic anguish that his death scene nightly drew tears from the audience. Lynn Fontanne was both touching and decisive in the role of Mrs. Dubedat, while Baliol Holloway as Sir Colenso, Ernest Cossart as "B.B.," and Henry Travers as little Dr. Blenkinsop, added luster to themselves and the reputation of our Acting Company. Dudley Digges not only staged the play but also played Sir Patrick Cullen.

Shaw, throughout his long life, fulminated against the medical profession. His main thesis in *The Doctor's Dilemma* was that under our society we provide for a supply of bread by giving bakers a pecuniary interest in baking for us, and we give a surgeon a pecuniary interest in operating on us. "I cannot knock my shins severely," he says in his Preface on Doctors, "without forcing on some surgeon the difficult question, 'Could I not make a better use of a pocketful of guineas than this man is making of his leg? Could he not write as well—or even better—on one leg than on two?'" And he goes on relentlessly to point out that the worse the doctor pronounces the sickness, the greater the fee. This situation, and many others, will not be remedied according to Shaw until, under Socialism, "the medical profession becomes a body of men trained and paid by the country to keep the country in health" instead of what it is at present, "a conspiracy to exploit popular credulity and human suffering."

Shaw's Preface written early in this century did much to change British thinking on the subject of public medical services so that, under the National Health Service Act of 1946, the British public is now entitled to free medical attention, as is the case with many countries on the Continent. Whatever may be the present defects of the system, these are subject to continuous improvement. Shaw would undoubtedly agree that it is a national disgrace that the American medical profession has been able, by efficient lobbying in Congress, to prevent the enactment of some kind of similar legislation in the USA; the health-service plan, by the way, does not affect the right of wealthy patients to obtain (and pay for) their preferred medical advisers or practitioners.

The Doctor's Dilemma is still a popular play today, not because of its polemics against doctors, many of which are still valid, but because of the dramatic situation created by the question of whether a brilliant but unscrupulous artist, Dubedat, or a scrupulous but mediocre medical practitioner, Dr. Blenkinsop, shall live or die. In raising this question (said to have been suggested by Mrs. Shaw), GBS was able to oppose conflicting opinions on the worth or worthlessness of art, the relative importance or unimportance of honesty, the value of lives lived selflessly or selfishly and a host of other issues not especially germane to the problems of the medical profession. In the character of Dubedat, Shaw gave us an unforgettable portrait of an artist, and his death speech has become as immortal as any speech of Shakespeare's. The poet Shaw never spoke more profoundly than in these few words forming a simple sentence: "I believe in Michael Angelo, Velasquez, and Rembrandt; in the might of design, the mystery of color, the redemption of all things by Beauty everlasting, and the message of Art that has made these hands blessed. Amen. Amen."

During Shaw's lifetime, he lived to see the full or partial conquest of some of the major diseases of humanity such as tuberculosis, diphtheria, influenza, virus pneumonia, polio, peritonitis, cholera, typhus, typhoid, malaria, yellow fever, leprosy and others, as a result of the combination of chemical research and medical research. Yet we have arrived at no medical millennium. Some basically wrong practices at which Shaw railed still exist in the United States.

On December 7, 1927, I wrote Shaw:

> *The Doctor's Dilemma* continues to break all records.
> I wish you could see a performance of it as you would un-
> doubtedly have a good word for the way the Guild has
> cast it.

To this I received no reply. The success of this play was undoubtedly an old story to him. Nevertheless, he was sufficiently
interested to write us the following caustic criticism of our use
of a marionette in Dubedat's death scene.

> I have been for some time forgetting to make a criti-
> cism of *The Doctor's Dilemma* production. One of my
> directions is that there should be a lay figure on the stage.
> The effect aimed at is the contrast between this ludicrous
> and visibly unreal simulacrum of a human creature and
> the living figures on stage; a contrast which becomes
> poignant and acquires a ghastly irony in the death scene,
> where Dubedat himself becomes a lay figure.
>
> Now your producer has taken extraordinary pains to
> defeat this impression, and introduce a formidable and
> disastrous rival to the living actors by procuring, not a
> typical lay figure, but a marionette with all a marionette's
> intensity and persistency of expression; so that when I saw
> the photographs I immediately said, "Who on earth is
> that?," not only mistaking the simulacrum for a reality,
> but for a leading personality. It is as if I had prescribed a
> turnip ghost and you had given me the Ghost in Hamlet
> instead.
>
> A good marionette (and yours is a very good one) can
> play any real actor off the stage.
>
> Sell him by auction with this letter attached for the
> benefit of the Guild; and make a note for reference in fu-
> ture productions.

I continued to report to Shaw on the progress of *The Doctor's Dilemma,* writing him: "It is, of course, old history for
me to tell you that *The Doctor's Dilemma* has been a very great
success and has aroused the most delighted comment throughout the season." But on February 29, 1928, I wrote as follows:

> Apropos of bad theatrical conditions, *The Doctor's
> Dilemma* has begun to show a very considerable decline,

and we have had to place the tickets in that institution known as Leblang's, where orchestra seats are sold at half the usual rates. Owing to the very expensive company which we are using in the play, we are running at a loss, and shall have to close it shortly. We are, however, doing very well with *Arms and the Man* on the road, and we are making plans for next season which will result in considerably greater road possibilities for your plays. We are forming Theatre Guild memberships in ten of the large cities of the United States. These cities are overwhelmingly interested in your work, and we will have subscription audiences in these cities the same as we have in New York City.

Arms and the Man will play for two weeks in Chicago in the Fall, as well as in the majority of these ten cities, and will no doubt do a very large business, as our best actors, Alfred Lunt and Lynn Fontanne, will be playing in it.

Finally on March 28 I reported that "We are sorry that *The Doctor's Dilemma* is closing next week, but the theatrical business is generally bad right now." The play ran for an entire season in New York and was regarded as one of the Theatre Guild's outstanding productions.

Our next Shaw play, *Major Barbara,* was about the Salvation Army lassie, Barbara, who reminds us of the heroine of the famous musical *The Belle of New York* at the turn of the century, as well as other ministering theatrical angels who display their charms and Christianity under the banner of charity. It opened at the Guild Theatre on November 20, 1928, with the crusading Winifred Lenihan in the part of the proselytizing Major, Dudley Digges as the munitions manufacturer Andrew Undershaft, Helen Westley as Lady Britomart and Percy Waram as Bill Walker.

Shaw wrote Theresa Helburn some notes about the casting of the play as follows:

> I do not suppose there is much danger of Winifred Lenihan making Barbara a low-spirited person with large eyes, looking like a picture on the cover of The Maiden's Prayer, though that is the traditional stage view of a religious part.
>
> Bear in mind that Lady Britomart has a most important part, and requires a first-rate robust comedian and

grande dame to play it; for the clue to a great deal of
Barbara is that she is her mother's daughter, and that she
bullies and bustles the Salvation Army about just as Lady
Britomart bullies and bustles her family at home. Barbara
is full of life and vigor, and unconsciously very imperi-
ous.

Cusins is easy for any clever actor who has never seen
the original (Professor Gilbert Murray). The next best
model is perhaps Harold Lloyd.

Do not let Mr. Waram make the mistake of making up
like a thug as Bill Walker. In appearance he is just an ordinary workman excited by drink and a sense of injury,
not in the least like a murderer in a nightmare or a melodrama. He should be clean and good-looking enough to
make the scene in which Barbara breaks down his bru-
tality—which is a sort of very moving love scene—look
natural, which it will not if Bill is disgusting physically
and sanitorily.

The most effective dress for Lady Britomart is a Queen
Mary or Queen Alexandra dress, long and purposely a
generation out of date.

Directed by Philip Moeller, the play succeeded in putting
GBS's messages across on the subject of Christianity and economics, a peculiar mixture which has usually left a confusing
impression on its audiences.

Using Barbara as the proponent of private charity, Shaw
proceeds to demolish her happiness in the work of the Salvation Army by showing that the munitions manufacturer Andrew Undershaft is doing a better job for his workers than any
organized "charity." Undershaft has built a model "garden
city" type of town with desirable clean white houses for the
workers in his munitions plants, and he propounds his philosophy of abolishing poverty (thus abolishing the need for charity) in answer to his son Stephen's reservation, "I cannot help
thinking that all this provision for every want of your work-
men may sap their independence and weaken their sense of
responsibility."

Unfortunately audiences sometimes left the theatre with the
feeling that Shaw was advocating the manufacture of munitions as a desirable means of improving the economic conditions of the workers, which was the last thing he intended.

Shaw's position would have been much clearer had he used as his industrialist a figure such as Cadbury in England or Hershey in America, both of whom built model towns for their chocolate workers, probably on the theory that confectionery makers must employ clean workers, and clean workers must live in clean houses.

The play is still topical because unhappily, in the half century which has elapsed since the writing of *Major Barbara,* the conflict between Christianity and armaments is still unresolved. It would now appear that the manufacture of munitions actually has a great deal more to do with the economy of the world than we dare to admit. Indeed, we of the West cannot stop manufacturing munitions as long as the present international threat to peace continues, and the Communists take the same attitude. As the proponents of both forms of society are always explaining, were we ever able to achieve bilateral disarmament, we could release a tremendous amount of manpower and equipment for school buildings, homes, roads and needed consumer goods which would be available to all mankind.

As for abolishing poverty, "as the one thing we will not tolerate," nothing was easier for the Shavian mind in the year 1906. He gave his own answer to some phases of the industrial problems of our times in his Preface to *Major Barbara,* from which I quote the following:

> . . . there are two measures just sprouting in the political soil, which may conceivably grow to something valuable. One is the institution of a Legal Minimum Wage. The other, Old Age Pensions. But there is a better plan than either of these. Some time ago I mentioned the subject of Universal Old Age Pensions to my fellow Socialist Cobden-Sanderson, famous as an artist-craftsman in bookbinding and printing. "Why not Universal Pensions for Life?" said Cobden-Sanderson. In saying this, he solved the industrial problem at a stroke. At present we say callously to each citizen "If you want money, earn it" as if his having or not having it were a matter that concerned himself alone. We do not even secure for him the opportunity of earning it: on the contrary, we allow our industry to be organized in open dependence on the maintenance of "a reserve army of unemployed" for the sake of "elasticity." The sensible

course would be Cobden-Sanderson's: that is, to give every man enough to live well on, so as to guarantee the community against the possibility of a case of the malignant disease of poverty, and then (necessarily) to see that he earned it.

Well, we have had legal minimum wages almost everywhere for years, and we have also had old-age pensions. Both have their excellent points. We also have social security and unemployment insurance. But that final idea, "Universal Pensions for Life" and "then (necessarily) to see that he earned it"—at the point of a bayonet without a doubt—that has not yet been tried anywhere.

As of the year 1961, neither the so-called Capitalist societies nor the Communists have conquered what Shaw called "the crime of poverty." There is undoubtedly less poverty at present in West Germany under the welfare state into which capitalism has evolved than in East Germany under Communism into which Marxism has evolved. Ironically, both the welfare state and modern Communism owe a great deal to the Fabians and to Shaw for some of the more practical of their ideas—indeed, he may yet end up as a hero on both sides of the Iron Curtain. And whatever one may feel as to the practicality of his ideas for abolishing poverty, there is no doubt that the entire world is now engaging in a quest for a solution to the problems raised by *Major Barbara,* not only in the countries of the Eastern and Western groups of nations, but also in the economically backward and poverty-stricken countries of Asia, Africa and Latin America. And because *Major Barbara* deals with this unresolved subject on a high level of thought, it should always be regarded as one of Shaw's plays which will bear constant revival by the generations to come.

After *Major Barbara* opened in New York, I dutifully reported to GBS on its reception by the press and public, and I also complained that he had not written to me for over a year and gave him some incidental information about our activities:

> *Major Barbara* opened on Monday, and got over very well. You will get a general idea of how the play was received from the enclosed notices. Most of the acting was very good, especially that of Mr. Dudley Digges, who has appeared in a number of your plays. Ervine did not get to

see it, as—due to some stupid convention of the newspaper world—a new play by Somerset Maugham was opening on the same night. We quote one of your characters in *Major Barbara*. "There is a great deal of posh about dramatic critics," and they picked out a shilling shocker, and left *Major Barbara* to the second string critics. These, however, did remarkably well by the play, and the audience liked it immensely.

Will you please hurry up and write the Guild a new play? We have now given eleven, and there are only six or seven left, before we begin to start all over again. The Guild refuses to take as an excuse that you cannot be expected to write another play at your age, and so forth. According to *Back to Methuselah,* you should live to be at least one hundred and fifty and write at least twenty-five more plays. In all seriousness, are you going to write a new play soon? You know that we would love to give it.

Arms and the Man is doing astonishingly well out-of-town, and so is *The Doctor's Dilemma. Strange Interlude* is the world's eleventh wonder, having played to capacity since last January, with people standing up night after night for six hours. Petitions are coming in from cities all over the country asking us to send the company. We may bring it to London.

The Guild makes its first London production in March or April with an all-Negro play called *Porgy.* I hope to be able to come over with it.

It is almost a year since you have written to me. Did you like the Riviera?

Major Barbara ran for eleven weeks in New York but was not presented on tour. The year 1928 found us having completed the presentation of eleven plays by GBS in our first ten years (counting *Back to Methuselah* as a single play).

In the latter part of 1927, H. G. Wells made a savage attack on Shaw and all he stood for in *The New York Times.* It thoroughly irritated me, and I immediately wrote to GBS on December 7, 1927:

I was perfectly furious when I read the ridiculous attack made at you by Wells. What is the matter with him? On the basis of Wells' article, if we had to decide on the relative merits of H. G. Wells, Bernard Shaw and Beecham, the inventor of Beecham's Pills, we would certainly have to decide that Beecham had been the greatest benefactor to humanity. Wells' comparison is a ridiculous one. The men of science have taught us how to make aeroplanes, chemicals, and every kind of electrical contraption, and the main use we seem to have put these devices is to use them to kill one another. As between the man who adds to the sum of human knowledge and the man who shows how that knowledge should be used to best advantage, I believe the latter person is the most important, and it seems to me that you clearly are in that position.

The New York Times told me that you are going to answer Wells' article, and I hope that you will do it very thoroughly. With kind regards to Mrs. Shaw, and best wishes for the holidays.

To this Shaw's secretary Miss Patch replied on December 20, 1927, as follows:

Mr. Shaw wishes me to let you know that he is not going to answer Wells's article. They are very good friends, and it is quite understood that Mr. Wells may blow off steam like that whenever he feels like bursting.

This answer reveals a lot about the attitude of the two men toward one another. They enjoyed sounding off against each other, which is one way literary men keep their names before the public in England. Our own writers have much to learn on this subject.

After the Theatre Guild had achieved the age of ten, Walter Pritchard Eaton, then teaching playwriting at Yale University as the successor to George Pierce Baker, was commissioned by a publisher to write a book entitled *The Theatre Guild, the First Ten Years.*

Someone suggested that GBS might be willing to write an introduction for it, and I was elected to ask him to do so. I met with complete failure despite my attempt to cajole him. The answer was a printed postcard which he evidently used for all such requests (of which, he told me later, he received hundreds) with a few words added below under the date 14/9/25:

Mr. Bernard Shaw is often asked to secure the acceptance of unpublished works by contributing prefaces to them.

Sometimes the applicants add that a few words will be sufficient. This obliges him to call attention to the fact that his prefaces owe their value in the literary market to the established expectation of book purchasers that they will prove substantial and important works in themselves. The disappointment of this expectation in a single instance would destroy their value. A request for a preface by him is therefore a request for a gift of some months of hard professional work. When this is appreciated it will be seen that even with the best disposition towards his correspondents it is not possible for Mr. Shaw to oblige them in this particular manner.

This is what he wrote in ink below:

This puts the kibosh (whatever that may be) on your preface suggestion. Will a picture of the bust do? I am just off to the Riviera where perhaps at last I shall have time to answer you about *Strange Interlude* and other things.

Not to be deterred, I wrote him the following on August 31, 1928:

Regarding your printed postcard and remarks regarding the introduction to our Birthday Book, you are under a misapprehension as to what we want. We do not want any preface, especially one which would take you months to write. You will agree with me that this puts quite a different complexion on the case, as of course a birthday greeting should not take more than ten minutes to write, at the outside.

Knowing how busy you are, it occurred to me that I might save you considerable time by writing the birthday greeting myself, leaving it to you to fill in the blank spaces. I am enclosing one such a greeting on the sheet attached hereto, and hope you will fill it in and return.

This was the enclosure:

PROPOSAL FOR A FORM OF BIRTHDAY GREETING
(And not to be considered as a preface)
by BERNARD SHAW

That the Theatre Guild has survived for ten years as an art theatre surprises everybody else in the world but me. It is obvious that they owe their success entirely to the fact that they produce one or more of my plays each year, and . . .

Another factor which has contributed to the Guild's success is the fact that during these ten years they have never once produced a play by Shakespeare. This shows that I have always been right about . . . .

All the plays I now write are written especially for the Theatre Guild. Indeed, the fact that the Guild produces my plays is the one thing that makes life worth living for me, and compensates for . . . .

In particular they never pester me for photographs, articles, busts and other relics, as is customary with other producers of my plays, and in general . . . .

So long as the Guild continues to present my plays, they will . . .

(signed) G. Bernard Shaw

I should have known better!

The episode ended with the following letter from Miss Patch under date of 12th September 1928:

Mr. Shaw has asked me to tell you that as regards the Birthday Book he is inexorable, and adds that the world is sick of these follies.

Finis!

Lynn Fontanne as Eliza Doolittle in the Theatre Guild production of *Pygmalion*, presented November 15, 1926

Reginald Mason as Professor Higgins *(above)* and Henry Travers as Doolittle in scenes with Miss Fontanne from *Pygmalion*

Alfred Lunt as Louis Dubedat in *The Doctor's Dilemma,* which opened in New York in November, 1927

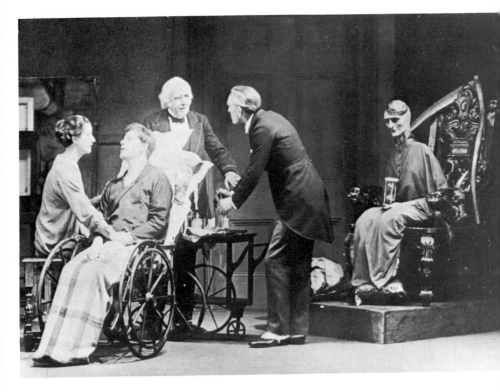

A scene from *The Doctor's Dilemma,* showing Lynn Fontanne, Ernest Cossart, Dudley Digges, Earle Larimore and Baliol Holloway. Shaw objected to the use of the well made marionette *(at right)* preferring "a visibly unreal simulacrum of a human creature"

Winifred Lenihan as Barbara, with Dudley Digges as Andrew Undershaft, in the Guild production of *Major Barbara* in 1928

A portrait of Percy Waram as Bill Walker in *Major Barbara,* and *(below)* another scene from the play, with Miss Lenihan, Mr. Waram and Elliot Cabot as Cusins

Philip Moeller rehearses Eva Leonard-Boyne, Tom Powers and Helen Westley in a scene from *The Apple Cart,* preparatory to its opening in February, 1930

Tom Powers as King Magnus and Violet Kemble-Cooper as Orinthia in the boudoir scene of *The Apple Cart (above)*

Mr. Moeller calls together a distinguished company to begin rehearsals of *The Apple Cart.* Left to right: Mr. Moeller, Cheryl Crawford, casting director, Claude Rains, Frederick Truesdale, Miss Leonard-Boyne, Mr. Powers, Jane Wheatley, Hannah Clark and Ernest Cossart, among others

The Theatre Guild board of directors in 1923. Left to right: Lawrence Langner, Philip Moeller, Theresa Helburn, Maurice Wertheim, Helen Westley and Lee Simonson

Lawrence Langner and Theresa Helburn when the Theatre Guild was relatively young

Snapshots by the author. George Bernard Shaw at Stresa in 1929; *below,* with Armina Marshall

The cast of *Getting Married,* produced by the Guild in 1931. Performers included Hugh Sinclair, Peggy Wood, Margaret Wycherly, Dorothy Gish, Henry Travers, Reginald Mason, Irby Marshall and Romney Brent
A scene *(below)* from *Getting Married*

Theresa Helburn's imaginative casting put Beatrice Lillie, shown here with Hope Williams, in *Too Good to be True,* presented April 1, 1932

Romney Brent and Alla Nazimova in *The Simpleton of the Unexpected Isles,* February 18, 1935 *(above)*

A scene from *The Simpleton of the Unexpected Isles.* Shaw specified East Indian rather than Polynesian costumes

You Never Can Tell, which opened March 16, 1948, was the last Shaw play presented by the Theatre Guild during his lifetime. The cast included *(left to right)* Faith Brook, Tom Helmore, Frieda Inescort, Leo G. Carroll, Pat Kirkland, Walter Budd, Scott Douglas and Nigel Stock

Cyril Ritchard in *The Millionairess*

Katharine Hepburn, who was Shaw's original choice to play *The Million-airess,* and refused in 1937, then justified Shaw's judgment by her 1952 performance

CHAPTER SEVEN

With Shaw in Stresa
and Elsewhere

DURING the years we were producing Shaw's plays, Terry Helburn, Armina Marshall, who had now become my wife, and I made many visits to Shaw, both in London and elsewhere. These visits served as a refreshment of our spirits, for we never failed to return to New York stimulated by our contact with his iridescent personality. I often made notes of our conversations which reinforced my memory, as a result of which I have been able to quote Shaw *verbatim* in a number of these chapters. These visits also enabled us to observe the relationship between GBS and Charlotte Shaw as much as was possible under these circumstances; and as we grew to know them better, we never ceased to be astonished by GBS's old-fashioned manners in relation to Charlotte and her humorous acceptance of his bubbling flights of rhetoric, to which she often added a gentle pinprick of feminine common sense when he stretched his imagination beyond the bounds of actuality. One of our most entertaining visits with the Shaws took place in the summer of 1927, after I wrote GBS that we would be visiting my sister Gladys at Milan. He thereupon invited us also to visit him and Mrs. Shaw at Stresa on Lake Maggiore.

About the middle of August we arrived at Stresa and put up at Shaw's hotel, the Regina Palace, an ornate buff-colored barrackslike structure overlooking the lake. GBS had reserved our room for us and greeted us on arrival. "You must stay here for a few days," he said, and added, "but Americans are not very welcome here, on account of the Sacco-Vanzetti case."

It was ironic that in Italy, where my brother-in-law in Milan a few days earlier had solemnly stopped me in a café from making a derogatory remark about Mussolini for which I might have been arrested if overheard ("We call him Mr. Smith," he added), the populace should be in a state of tremendous tension over whether Sacco and Vanzetti would receive the death penalty. Perhaps this was because they were inured to injustice in their own country but could not bear to believe that the same thing could happen in democratic America.

After settling comfortably in our room for the night, we were awakened at what seemed to be an unearthly hour by a loud knocking at our door.

"Come along, wake up!" cried Shaw from outside. "It's seven o'clock, and if you want to come swimming with me, you'll have to hurry up! See you at breakfast!"

"Do you want to get up this early?" I remarked drowsily to Armina.

"Of course," she cried, leaping from her bed like a gazelle. "How often will you have an opportunity of swimming with GBS?"

I was stumped. First of all, I don't swim very well—about fifty strokes and I am winded. Secondly, it had been blowing quite hard the night before, and I was sure the lake would be full of waves, which have an irritating habit of getting into my eyes, ears and mouth.

"Up you get," she cried. "You can't keep Shaw waiting for you!"

So I got up, protesting mildly, and down we went for breakfast. GBS was waiting for us. It was his custom each morning to cross the lake in a motorboat, then moor this boat off the estate of Albert Coates, the English conductor, swim for the shore and end up with a sun bath on a grassy meadow which sloped down to the beach. We boarded the motorboat dressed in our bathing suits, crossed over toward the other side of the lake and at what seemed to me to be an enormous distance from the shore, GBS dived in off the side of the boat. As his head and shoulders emerged from the lake and he shook the water out of his white hair and beard, the sun caught his pink cheeks and blue eyes and he looked for all the world like Father Neptune emerging from the waves.

"Come on in, it's fine!" he shouted.

Armina, like most California-bred girls, was something of a mermaid, and in she dived, showing off with a very effective scissors stroke. I cautiously lowered myself down the side of the boat, looking nervously at the shore which seemed to be miles away. I suppose the motorboat will keep moving slowly behind us, I thought, throwing discretion to the winds and timidly striking out in the direction of Father Neptune and the Mermaid. I kept going for a while, as the waves waved wildly, and the other swimmers swam rapidly ahead of me toward the shore. I looked back to reassure myself that the motorboat was following me. It was not. The Italian boatman had stopped his engine and was settling down to a comfortable nap. I was torn between the choice of drowning or calling for help. I called for help. The motorboat with the boatman started up, GBS and Armina swam back, and between the three of them I was heaved out of the water and ignominiously ferried to the shore.

Some years later, when recounting this incident, GBS remarked that it was the greatest compliment ever paid him. "Lawrence Langner," he said, with a twinkle in his eye, "followed me to such an extent that when I jumped into Lake Maggiore, he jumped in after me without being able to swim a stroke, evidently thinking that my mere presence would save him from drowning."

Arriving at Villa Intragnola, the estate of Albert Coates, GBS disappeared behind some convenient bushes and returned a few moments later wearing what seemed to be an old pair of white underdrawers. By this time a young lady had appeared on the scene. She was Sylvia Ray, Mr. Coates' secretary, and she was in the habit of joining GBS for his morning sun baths. The three of us grouped ourselves appreciatively on the grass while Shaw expounded his views on one subject and another.

Not unnaturally, since the aging philosopher was in a state of next-to-nudity, the question of modesty came up for discussion, since the Pope had recently forbidden all Italian women to enter churches in dresses without sleeves and skirts which did not cover the ankles.

"What on earth do priests know about morality!" Shaw

asked impatiently. "The trouble with these men who try to ad-
judicate upon what is moral or immoral is that they really know
nothing about the subject. Any man who attempts to decide that
one style of clothing is seductive while another style of clothing
is not must know something about the art of being seductive,
and priests who rail about the theme of women's costumes
are obviously the very last persons to be in a position to express
an opinion on the subject. I remember in my young days when
women dressed in accordance with the dictates of the clergy,
they were literally swathed in clothing so that they resembled
feather mattresses more than anything else, and I may add the
women who wore these clothes looked considerably more seductive than the half-clad girls of today. There are really only
two competent judges of what is seductive in women's clothing,
and they are the women who make it their business to be seductive because they study it and playwrights like myself, because it
is our business to know what women must wear in order to be
seductive."

I had myself been giving considerable thought to the subject
of the effect of clothing on morality and had in mind writing a play on Lady Godiva, the purpose of which was to demonstrate that by the combination of clothing and religion man
could regard himself as related to the gods and partly because
of this had been able to develop what we loosely term "civilization." This conversation which I noted down at the time stimulated me greatly in writing my play. Later on I decided to devote several years to research on the subject, the result of which
was my book *The Importance of Wearing Clothes,* as well as
my play *Lady Godiva* produced at Westport and London.

Shaw went on to say the clergy, and playwrights too, might
turn their attention from women's clothes to an abuse of marriage which he noticed had been growing recently: "That is,
the selling of husbands by their wives to wealthy women who,
in return for the husbands, paid handsome sums by way of
damages for alienation of affection. This new trade in husbands
is gaining considerable headway."

"How do you spend your time here?" I asked.

"Every afternoon," he informed me, "I go to Prince Paul
Troubetzkoy's studio to sit for a statue of myself. It's very tiring
but I have to do it."

"Why?" I asked.

"Well," he replied, "the Prince's wife died last spring, and he was very upset over losing her, so in order to get his mind off his troubles, I decided to commission him to make a statue of me. Not that the statue isn't very good," he added. I was impressed by this example of GBS's personal kindness.

Later we met the Prince, a tall, distinguished Russian who seemed very sad and serious. He was an old friend of Shaw's and had done a very fine head of him some twenty years earlier. The Prince dined with the Shaws and us at the hotel. He was an ardent vegetarian and joined Shaw in his choice of soup and greens. Most vegetarians I have met have a habit of proselytizing, and the Prince was no exception.

"If you are guest of my house," he said solemnly at dinner, in rounded Russian accents, "and you wish to eat lamb chops, I gave you big knife and take you into garden and show you little lamb, and you can assassinate him!"

As I had no desire to assassinate a little lamb with a big knife, I was glad I was not a guest in his house. Still, I felt I should defend my taste in lamb chops, so I ventured to remark that but for our habit of eating lambs, they would probably have no existence whatever and I instanced the fact that up to the time of their deaths domestic animals were fed, cared for and relieved of all anxiety by their owners, who even supplied them with mates in order that succeeding generations of lamb chops might be perpetuated.

"I violently object," said Shaw, "to being a procurer for domestic animals. But," he added, "unlike the Prince, I don't advocate vegetarianism for anyone but myself. You see, I'm really a sort of saint!"

In objecting to being a procurer for animals, Shaw was seconding Shakespeare's humorous attitude on the subject, as expressed by Touchstone to the Shepherd in *As You Like It*. "This is another simple sin in you, to bring the rams and ewes together and to offer to get your living by the copulation of cattle: to be a bawd to a bell wether, and to betray a she-lamb of a twelve month to a crooked-pated, old, cuckoldly ram, out of all reasonable match." We know little about Shakespeare, but his writings clearly show that, unlike Shaw, he was no vegetarian.

"I tried vegetarianism, but had to give it up a long time ago," said Mrs. Shaw quietly across the table to Armina. And then she whispered, "It's very bad for the teeth." I glanced sidewise in the direction of Mr. Shaw's teeth, but saw no evidence of any disastrous results. "Can anything about GBS be false?" I asked myself, but I feared to carry the inquiry any further.

Years later I learned that a certain General Kwei was brought by a Mr. Hsiung to see GBS. The General started to voice his admiration for Shaw, for his impressive beard, his sparkling eyes, prominent forehead, his nose and mouth and even his teeth. That was going a little too far, and Shaw stopped him by saying, "Do you really admire my teeth? Well, you can do so at closer quarters," and he took them out of his mouth and offered them on his palm to Kwei. So there *was* something false about Shaw after all!

Prince Troubetzkoy invited us to his studio, not to partake of lamb chops, but to see the statue for which GBS was posing, and one fine afternoon we accompanied him and Mrs. Shaw down the lake on a small steamboat to the little village where the Prince made his home. I brought my 16mm movie camera along with me and had a field day taking pictures of GBS posing for his statue. Then I asked him and Mrs. Shaw to allow me to take a picture of them walking together, and they both kindly obliged. As they approached the camera, GBS suddenly embraced Mrs. Shaw and kissed her. Mrs. Shaw, taken by surprise, remarked, "What on earth did you do that for?" "Don't you know that every movie ends up in a clinch!" was the reply. And thus I came into possession of the only picture extant of Mr. Shaw kissing his wife!

We took our departure soon after, but before leaving I asked GBS whether I could not obtain a duplicate of the early Troubetzkoy bust to place in the lobby of the Theatre Guild.

"I have two already," was the reply, "but there's no sense in my giving you one, because in a year or so, if you go on producing my plays, you'll ultimately become bankrupt, the Guild Theatre will fall into the hands of the Shuberts, and my bust will be your only asset!" However, Mrs. Shaw said she thought something might be arranged.

A month or so later I heard from Mrs. Shaw in reply to a suggestion that we might consider purchasing the bust:

> Now about the bust. You speak of purchasing—but, you know, at Stresa we had an idea of letting you have one of the two we had here! Of course, if there is any probability of the Theatre Guild buying it would not be right for us to come between Prince Troubetzkoy and a sale! If that

was to come about you would have to write to him and ask him his price (Prince Paul Troubetzkoy, Villa Cabranca, Suna, Lago Maggiore, Italy). But the other idea is this: GBS does not want to give the bust unconditionally to the Theatre Guild. He says (ironically) "you never know what will happen in the theatre—they may come to grips or . . . something may happen." I tell you what he suggests. He might lend the bust to you, and give you a free hand to do what you like with it; show it to whom you like, or make what arrangements you think best: with the private arrangement between you and him that you put it up in the theatre as long as the theatre is in a satisfactory state. If it should ever happen that you wished to withdraw it from there—then you could arrange with us as to its future disposition: but you could have full power to withdraw it at any time, on your own private judgment.

The bust of Shaw arrived in due course and was placed in the lobby of the Guild Theatre. The bronze of the bust had since turned green, either out of deference to the Emerald Isle or to show Shaw's passionate addiction to vegetables. The bust was originally made when Shaw's hair and beard were a flaming red, and great clouds of flame and smoke proceeded from his mouth as he expressed his explosive views to a startled Victorian world.

In November of 1928 I wrote GBS:

Your statue looks very well indeed in the Guild Theatre lobby. Unfortunately, however, a vendor of cigarettes has placed his stand underneath it so that you look for all the world like the patron saint of nicotine. I think we shall have to hang a card around the neck of the statue bearing the words, "Mr. Shaw does not recommend these cigarettes."

Upon our leaving the Guild Theatre (the mortgage on which was then owned by the Shuberts, as Shaw prophesied years before) we took the statue with us. Later on it ornamented the entrance hall of the Theatre Guild building at 25 West 53rd Street, New York, and was placed in front of the elevator; it wore an expression which suggested to the passer-by that it is healthier to walk upstairs than to ride. After GBS's death, I learned that he stated in his will that we might keep the statue so long as we existed, but since the Theatre Guild is not a "permanent" institution, upon our passing out of existence, the bust is to be given to the Metropolitan Museum in New York. Every time I see it now, I say to myself, "Well, Shaw, we're still here!"

While in London in the year 1929, we took GBS to see *Caprice,* and he was delighted with it and with the performance of the Lunts. As we stood on the pavement with Carl Van Vechten after the play was over, waiting for a taxi, GBS expounded his views on the play and performances, to the edification of a throng of admiring onlookers who gathered around us. As he continued to speak, the crowd continued to grow, and GBS watched it out of the corners of his eyes. When the number approached that which usually attends upon Royalty or movie stars, GBS said, "Look here, I've got to move on"—and move on he did, after smiling and bowing to the appreciative onlookers.

I heard late in 1932 that Mr. and Mrs. Shaw were taking a trip around the world on the S.S. *Empress of Britain* and would visit New York under the auspices of a little-known organization, the Academy of Political Science. I wrote an article for our Theatre Guild magazine in which I stated:

I am intensely disappointed to hear that Mr. Bernard Shaw is coming to America. For the past ten years I have repeatedly suggested that he ought to come over here for a visit, only to be met with a statement that under no circumstances would he ever come. I feel that he has really broken his word to America.

As I have always known Mr. Shaw to be a man of the highest integrity, I am inclined to think that Mr. Shaw probably feels that he has not broken his promise, for the America to which this promise was made no longer exists. It was an America of easy money, of smug self-satisfaction, of rampant materialism. Four years of depression find an entirely different America, and one which is looking for both spiritual and material guidance. Perhaps Mr. Shaw, realizing that America is in a chastened mood, feels that he can withdraw his promise.

I once suggested, as a reason for Shaw's visiting America, that in this way he would learn what Europe would be like twenty years hence, to which Shaw characteristically replied, "God forbid!"

It will be remarked that Shaw does not intend to stay very long in New York. According to reports, twenty-four hours is thought to be the maximum, but GBS is returning from a trip around the world, and I am sure that he will want to talk for at least fifty consecutive hours upon his arrival here. He probably has the material for another twenty plays, several of which he has no doubt started on the boat, and I am looking forward impatiently to reading at least three new scripts on his arrival.

On March 28, 1933, I wrote GBS:

This is just a line to welcome you to New York. Armina wrote a letter to you which she thought would probably get to your boat in Egypt, telling you that we would love to have you stay at our home when you are here, and Maurice Wertheim also offered to put his country place at your disposal. We have not heard from you, and therefore assume that our letter did not reach you.

The Academy of Political Science seems to have taken complete charge of you, and I have a feeling that we will be fortunate if we get a glimpse of you from a seat in the last row of the Metropolitan Opera House.

I know that the Theatre Guild is very anxious to have a small and intimate luncheon in your honour, and I also know that if you are not completely inundated, Armina and I would consider it a great privilege if you would either lunch or dine with us, but we know that everyone is going to press you, and we want to make things easier for you, and not harder.

In addition to my personal invitation to the Shaws, Terry also wrote him asking whether we could put on a theatrical performance to make his stay in New York more "eventful." In his reply written at sea "on the *Empress of Britain,* Meridian Day between 13-14 March 1933 on the Pacific," he held forth as follows:

My dear Terry (which I still maintain should be Tessie)
It is odd that in spite of the blazing publicity of this tour round the world I cannot knock into people's heads the fact that I am *not* going to spend a month in New York and address large audiences every night after days spent in being lionized to death. The ship is timed to land

me in New York at noon on the 11th of April. After letting the press do its worst I have to convince the authorities that I am eligible for admission to New England. When I carry that point I have to address as many Americans as the Metropolitan Opera House will hold for about an hour for the pecuniary benefit of the Academy of Political Science. If not lynched, I shall take refuge with the Lamonts for a while before escaping back to the ship to sleep. At noon next day I sail for Cherbourg and Southampton. In the meantime about a thousand people will try to see me on particular business—perhaps you among them to relieve the horror of it. And that's all. Absolutely all.

Now it is obvious that any attempt to exploit this sensation must be made *after* my departure, when people are talking about me. A performance in competition with me on the 11th would be the last word in managerial ineptitude. A previous production would involve not only this, but the possibility of a failure, or at least a deluge of hostile criticism, which would discount me heavily. Therefore on your life, nothing until I am gone.

What could you do anyhow? Give a single performance of *Methuselah* or *Man and Superman* in "the entirety" and lose a lot of money! Far better leave the performance to me and let the Academy of Political Science fill its pockets and leave mine emptied; for I shall not take a cent out of America on this visit, though the agents are ruining themselves with wireless offers of "the first five thousand dollars."

I don't quite see the lady you mention getting over the obsolescence of Brassbound. Of course up to a point she, or any attractive and sympathetic actress, can get away with it to the extent of two or three thousand dollars a week. But for an Ellen Terry success with it somebody very English, very uncommon, and with some reserve in her attitude towards the sentimental public, is needed. Mary Grey would be an experiment in that direction. The lady you prefer would be sure fire, not in the least experimental; but the play would date damnably.

But I can do nothing in the fashionable theatre at present prices. I shall leave it quite out of account henceforth. The play I am now engaged on is only for *publication* with *Too Good.* The one I finished in the first weeks of the tour, when I was too dog tired for anything but child's play, is only a comedietta for two people in three scenes, which will fill out the volume between the other two. It is time for the Guild to drop me, and for me to cease costing the Guild more than I am now worth to it.

I shall send this by air mail from San Francisco so that it can fly straight to you whilst I loaf round through the Canal. I doubt whether there is a service from Honolulu.

When GBS arrived in California, he spent a few days there, but he annoyed some of his liberal friends on this side of the water by putting himself under the sponsorship of William Randolph Hearst, the newspaper publisher, and having himself extensively photographed with him for the Hearst papers. When I mentioned this to Shaw on his arrival in New York, GBS tossed it off and showed me some of the photographs. "You'll notice," he said, "that my white beard catches all the light and no one even notices that Mr. Hearst is in the picture!"

On the day of Shaw's arrival in New York, none of the Guild Board members was at the Guild Theatre, and in the early morning GBS dropped by and had a talk with our business manager, Warren Munsell, inspected the theatre and the bust of himself in the lobby and returned to the ship. Had we been informed of the possibility of this visit, we would have had the red carpet out, but perhaps this is just what he wished to avoid.

The organization which sponsored Shaw's visit to New York was quite unknown to us and we were equally unknown to it, so that the Guild Board was not invited to the gathering given in Shaw's honor at the Metropolitan Opera House, nor were we able to purchase seats. I was able, however, to hear the speech over the radio, and although GBS was not in his best form, I doubt whether many who heard his clear, crisp, hard-hitting Irish-English diction over the air will ever forget the quality of his voice. Though he was but four years short of eighty, it was as clear, as young and unquavering as that of a man half his age. Unfortunately, at a certain part in his address, he became slightly confused for a few moments, and this was seized on by his detractors. But it made no difference to his admirers.

The following morning, Armina and I visited Shaw on the beautiful *S.S. Empress of Britain* and breakfasted with him. His other guests were Robert Lorraine, veteran of a dozen Shaw

comedies and one of his oldest friends in the theatre, Princess
Kropotkin, and Agnes de Mille's mother, Mrs. William de Mille,
who was the daughter of Henry George, the Single Taxer, whom
GBS had greatly admired. Despite his speech of the previous
day delivered before an audience of many thousands at the
Metropolitan Opera House and his tiring trip up the harbor and
through the streets of New York, the veteran playwright was
up early and in top form. Breakfast was scheduled for eight
o'clock, and with the usual promptness which prevails in the
Langner family, we arrived breathless at eight-fifteen, having
stumbled over casks, packing cases and other obstacles which
were dotted all over the pier as though the Fates were determined that we should be even later than usual.

When we arrived in the ship's dining salon, GBS was already there. Mrs. Shaw begged to be excused as she had had
but one meal in New York and it had given her ptomaine poi-
soning! We sat at the table and GBS talked—the rest of us listened.

"I witnessed a performance of a play in a Chinese theatre,"
he remarked. "While the show on the stage was interesting,
the show put on by the audience was even more enjoyable.
Throughout the performance the various members of the audience would raise their hands, and a skillful attendant sta-
tioned at the back of the theatre would throw a hot, wet towel
to them, with which they washed their faces and the backs of
their necks and, thus refreshed, settled down to enjoy the performance again." GBS suggested that a somewhat similar idea
might well be introduced in the European and American theatres, as undoubtedly nothing would be more calculated to wake
up an audience during a play than the application of hot towels
as a stimulant. I reminded GBS that during *Back to Methuselah*
we were in the habit of serving black coffee to the audience
during the intermissions, which was probably just as stimulating and undoubtedly more sanitary.

As we proceeded with breakfast, straggling figures began to
appear among the tables. When we had risen, several newspaper
reporters stepped forward. "Mr. Shaw," said one, "I am the man
who got into your cabin yesterday. Do you mind my having my
photograph taken with you?" "Not at all," replied GBS. "I am
ready for anything."

Then GBS rose and went on deck to meet the reporters, who

seemed like old-fashioned gentlemen compared with the gang of hoodlums who now began to take movies and photographs of him. Evidently under instructions to "get Shaw's goat," they did everything possible to irritate and disconcert him. In one instance, a lout set off a flashlight bulb almost in his face, amid loud guffaws, and took advantage of Shaw's shocked surprise to snap an absurd picture of him which was later published in a New York journal. Not one of these hoodlums showed the slightest respect for the man who was perhaps the most brilliant thinker and dramatist of our day. Although a number of intelligent questions was asked by the reporters of the New York daily press, those put to GBS by some would have been a discredit to the lowest grade of an elementary school. Here is a sample: "Would you like to go to the Zoo?"

Someone brought up the old joke about Shaw and Shakespeare. "What did you mean when you said that you were better than Shakespeare?" he was asked. GBS replied, "He and I were drawn to write a play on the same subject—Cleopatra. When I wrote my play I put the words 'Better than Shakespeare?' with a note of interrogation. This started the entire controversy which raged for many years. Of course I did not mean that I am a better dramatist than Shakespeare. I merely raised the question. Nobody could possibly beat Shakespeare in his own line. For example, I think that no one but Shakespeare could have written as great a play as *King Lear*. However, Shakespeare's ideas are of no use to young persons nowadays. They must read Shaw in order to get a liberal education. If they read Shakespeare for social ideas, they will get nothing which will help them today. Each nation must produce its own literature for its own time."

Then someone asked, "Do you think there should be a sort of over-dictator for the whole world?" Shaw replied, "I haven't contemplated that."

"And if there were such a dictator of the world, do you think you would be competent to fill the job?" asked the same great mind. To which GBS replied, rising, "Gentlemen, the time is up." We left the boat sadly, wishing that GBS might have taken away with him a better impression of our national manners.

The end of Shaw's American trip was explained in my letter to him and Mrs. Shaw dated April 25, 1933:

I do hope you had a nice trip back, and that you are now comfortably settled in England. I suppose you really feel the need of a long rest after all your irritating experiences here.

I wish I had been able to do something to avoid the final inconveniences of GBS's departure. I went up to one of the stewards and asked whether it wouldn't be possible to make some sort of a gangway for you to pass through. The steward leaned over, and with clenched teeth muttered, "You'd need fixed bayonets, sir."

The newspapers printed the answers to the questions quite accurately on the whole. In the condensed versions, however, they misrepresented quite a little, though not on any serious point. I think the enclosed clipping from the New York Sun, which I am attaching hereto, explains the reaction of the general public. The majority of people enjoyed the speech a great deal, and agreed with most of it. The newspapers, irritated with some of the remarks which had been made on the subject of the press, and also irritated with some of the arrangements which had been made at the lecture hall to take care of the reporters, tried to belittle the affair on the basis that it was "not funny enough." In other words, they expected a piece of entertainment instead of a serious talk. The Shavians were all delighted with the speech, and the others were irritated that you did not talk a lot of nonsense.

One of the effects of your trip has evidently been to throw the state of the world into utter confusion in your absence. You should have stayed in England, because now nobody seems to know where they are or where they are going.

I would like to close this episode on a note of sharp irritation at our manners in treating visitors to this country, distinguished or otherwise. While the news photographers are the worst offenders (there has been little improvement in their behavior in the last twenty-five years) this rudeness is characteristic of many of the news reporters as well as of the lesser officials in the passport offices, customs offices, etc. This attitude toward visitors, and especially toward colored visitors, is now being used as a reason for removing the United Nations from New York to a country where the delegates will not be subject to so many public insults. And all this *public* American rudeness takes place in a country where *private* courtesy and hospitality is at a higher level than almost anywhere else in the world.

In the case of GBS, his plays had endeared him to America long before he was recognized in England, and his visit here would have been a splendid opportunity for our newspapers to express their admiration and appreciation.

If we can ever learn to treat all our visitors, distinguished or otherwise, with courtesy and good breeding on the part of our officials, reporters and camera artists, we may make amends for our past mistake of attempting to goad a distinguished old man into making silly statements for silly newspapers.

CHAPTER EIGHT

The Apple Cart and Too True to Be Good

ALTHOUGH President Kennedy and Prime Minister Macmillan sometimes actually commit themselves on international affairs without first consulting with each other, we realize that Shaw was not entirely insane in suggesting, in *The Apple Cart,* that the United States form part of the British Commonwealth, preferably under the guidance of the British monarchy. However, he does seem entirely insane in suggesting that the British Commonwealth would turn down such a proposal with horror, since we are thoroughly accustomed, throughout the governments of Winston Churchill and Harold Macmillan, to cooperating with British premiers having American mothers and British fathers. As the Americans and the British move closer together under threats from Soviet Russia, we realize that Shaw was not so wrong in suggesting the possibility of far closer relationships between the two countries than now exist, though for reasons I doubt he would have approved. I also doubt whether he realized that his arguments about overproduction and underproduction are still going on in both countries, as well as arguments regarding the free licensing of patents and the wastefulness of breakages. All of these topical subjects, dealt with entertainingly in *The Apple*

Cart, are an accompaniment to some of Shaw's most brilliant and hilarious scenes on the subject of wives and mistresses—also still topical.

The Apple Cart was first produced in Poland and later in England by Sir Barry Jackson in the year 1929 as part of the Malvern Festival which was devoted to Shaw. Sir Barry coaxed GBS into writing plays which, but for this Festival, might not have been written.

Our first intimations that GBS was writing *The Apple Cart* came in a letter to Terry dated 8 February, 1929:

> By this time reports of my new play should have appeared in the American press, as it is some weeks since I wrote a letter about it to a lady in Detroit to whom I wanted to do a good turn, authorizing her to communicate the relevant parts of it to the papers and telling her how to set about it.
>
> It is a play in three acts: the first long, the second only a twenty minutes interlude, and the third nearly but not quite as long as the first. The period is towards the end of the present century. With the exception of the interlude, which is a duet for the leading man and his lady (who, by the way, does not otherwise appear), the action consists of a Cabinet meeting at which the King of England is present. The King is the principal man and has the sort of part that George Arliss shines in. Beside him there are two of his private secretaries, both of whom must be pretty good walking gentlemen. Two of the Cabinet ministers are women. The Prime Minister has a strong part; and there are five other ministers with character parts which you will have no difficulty in casting. There is also a young princess with one short scene. In all, nine men and four women, of whom one is a brilliant Millamant, one serious, one musical comedy, and the princess, as aforesaid.
>
> These are, of course, business details, not for publication. The book is at the printers. I expect proofs daily, and can let you have one ready for production as soon as your arrangements permit.
>
> The name of the play is *The Apple Cart;* and it is as unlike *St. Joan* as it possibly can be.
>
> P.S. The play will be produced in England next August

at a provincial Bühnenfestspiel, with *Methuselah, Heart-break House,* and possibly *St. Joan,* the particular Bay-reuth in question being Malvern in Worcestershire, near the Welsh border. Reinhardt may produce it first in Ber-lin; but I am rather dissuading him, as the politics in the play are very English.

If L.L. is about, tell him all this.

The Apple Cart was a prodigious success in England, largely because it was misinterpreted as a play in favor of the British royalty. Indeed in Dresden, according to Shaw, the perform-ance was actually prohibited as a blasphemy against democ-racy. What Shaw was really up to in his creation of King Magnus was to demonstrate that Supermen can exist even among royalty, and that such a Superman could easily get him-self elected Prime Minister even in a democracy. In Shaw's own words, *"The Apple Cart* exposes the unreality of both democ-racy and royalty as our idealists conceive them." But in writing one of his best plays at the age of seventy-two, he made the same mistake that he made with Andrew Undershaft in *Major Barbara,* who came out so splendidly in the play that audiences often felt that Shaw was writing in favor of millionaire muni-tions makers. The British King Magnus is portrayed as so great a leader in this play that the American Ambassador Mr. Van-hattan is sent to inform the King that the United States has de-cided to rejoin the British Empire, under his magnificent rule. That King Magnus refuses to permit this disaster to happen to England is only another indication of his genius as a Shavian Superman.

When a play is telling the audience one thing and a charac-ter in the play is telling them something else, the meaning of the play is bound to be obscured. Thus *The Apple Cart* in its original American production and its subsequent brilliant American revival by Maurice Evans never quite made the impression in this country which it might have done, for the audiences were never quite sure whether Shaw was writing in favor of monarchy or democracy. Actually, he was merely dem-onstrating the impossibility of preventing a brilliant man from rising to the top, even if he happened to be a king.

Today *The Apple Cart* is often remembered because of the magnificent comedy scene between King Magnus and his mis-tress Orinthia in whose boudoir he makes the famous dissertation on love and marriage. (Some writers have assumed that Shaw was writing a scene which had actually taken place between himself and Mrs. Patrick Campbell.) The audiences both in London and New York were immensely amused at the spectacle of the King and Orinthia rolling on the floor in a scene of physical violence which ends with an announcement from the Queen to remind him that "tea is waiting." Mrs. Pat Campbell is alleged to have stated apropos of this scene, "If Shaw ever ate a beef-steak, God help us women."

King Magnus was brilliantly acted in England by Sir Cedric Hardwicke at the peak of his career, and Edith Evans played Orinthia. We were urged to await the end of the British production and bring them over, but we were impatient to proceed on our own. In the summer of 1929 we lunched with the Shaws, and among the topics of conversation was the production of *The Apple Cart,* in which there were a number of Cabinet Ministers. Shaw asked me why we were producing it so late in the season, to which I replied that we had a large number of actors who were playing Cabinet Ministers in our play *Wings over Europe* on tour, and since it was hard to secure men whose appearance suggested Cabinet Ministers, we intended to wait for the tour to come to an end before producing *The Apple Cart.* "But that is all nonsense," said GBS. "Where did you get the idea that Cabinet Ministers look intelligent?"

On October 18, 1929, GBS was writing Terry:

The Apple Cart has been so far an enormous success; but it is still possible that the bottom may fall out of it suddenly when we exhaust the top stratum of the populace. However, many people who do not know the difference between a Cabinet and a camp meeting seem to find it amusing; so let us hope for the best.

When the play was placed in rehearsal in New York, I wrote GBS on January 21, 1930:

The Apple Cart goes into rehearsal today, and we are all very excited about it. It will open in about four weeks from the present time. We think the cast is A-1, and that it has a real chance. While some people say the question of a constitutional monarchy is something which has not troubled this country for the last hundred and fifty years, the fact that the American Ambassador goes over to England to re-consolidate the British Empire will, I think, give the play a great interest to American audiences.

On February 24, 1930, *The Apple Cart* opened in New York and the critical notices were mixed. The part of King Magnus was played by Tom Powers and his mistress by Violet Kemble Cooper, and along with the play the production was not too enthusiastically received.

On March 4, 1930, I pumped up as much enthusiasm as I could muster and wrote GBS as follows:

> Just a line to tell you that *The Apple Cart* is going very nicely in New York. It got over to pretty good notices, with one or two captious critics, as is usually the case. So far as the public is concerned, however, it is a "hit," unless I am very much mistaken. The first week's business was over eighteen thousand dollars, which compares very favorably with anything we have ever done.
>
> I think the cast is extremely able, and as good all around as we could give it. I do not know of anybody who could have played the King better than Tom Powers, with the possible exception of Alfred Lunt, who, however, has been very sick this season and is just leaving to get away on a long vacation. We had heard so much about the man who played the King in England [Cedric Hardwicke], that we thought at one time it might be a good thing to bring him over here, but we learned from our London representative that he was tied up for life!
>
> Cecil Lewis [a friend of Shaw's] complained of not hearing some of the actors very well on the opening night. This, I think, was due largely to his seat being very much to one side of the theatre, as well as the usual opening night nervousness of some of the actors, but we have been extremely careful on the subject of diction, as of course this play depends on every word being heard.
>
> The reception of the play in Baltimore was marvelous. It almost broke the record of the theatre for a dramatic play. I believe the total business was twenty-three thousand.
>
> The play has a very definite message for the United States, where we miss the presence of royalty more than you imagine.
>
> Armina has just opened in New York with the leading

part in a new play [*Those We Love*] and has been a great success. She is now a leading woman, and I am sitting home evenings leading a lonely bachelor existence. Lewis has been keeping me company by staying here for a couple of weeks. I have tried to help him in a number of ways, but I am sorry that I have not been able to bring these to a final issue.

The Apple Cart did not last longer than ten weeks in New York, while Armina's play ran for six months, so that my bachelorhood referred to in the letter lasted longer than the play.

The next new play we received from GBS was *Too True to Be Good*. Our first intimation that this play was completed and would be sent to us came in a cable dated December 4, 1931, reading as follows:

PLAY NOW IN PRINTERS HANDS COPY WILL PROBABLY REACH YOU BEFORE END OF MONTH THREE ACTS THREE SCENE SETS THREE HOURS SEVEN MEN FOUR WOMEN FIRST LEADING WOMAN SAVAGELY STRONG SECOND VULGAR CHAMBERMAID DIALOGUE MAINLY TEN MINUTE SERMONS EXPECT THE WORST KEEP THIS PRIVATE.

We expected the worst and we got it, and we kept it private. However, the sermons were not ten-minute sermons, they simply stopped the play from time to time. But we were happy to receive it and to have the fun of producing it. Those were the halcyon days of the Theatre Guild, when we were able to afford to use our profits from one play to produce another, which was easy for us at a time when we could produce six plays for the cost of one play at present (1962).

On receipt of the manuscript of *Too True to Be Good* I remembered what Shaw had once said on the subject of plots. "In my opinion," he stated, "it's quite unnecessary for a playwright to bother himself about a plot. I believe it would be quite possible for a writer to start two people off with a conversation and fill the entire evening." "Yes," I replied, "provided the conversation is good enough. But of course you're the only one able enough to write such a conversation." "Naturally," he replied, "I don't recommend this for anybody except myself." When I read *Too True to Be Good* I thought,

"At last! Here is the play without a plot which Shaw has been talking about, and the dialogue is certainly delightful." At the end of the first act, one of the characters (The Microbe) turns to the audience and says, "The play is now virtually over; but the characters will discuss it at great length for two acts more. The exit doors are all in order. Goodnight."

Shaw's comedy, which was intended to ridicule the sufferings of the footloose idle rich, fell on indifferent ears in the depths of the depression period of 1932. The audience was disconcerted by the loose form of the play, even though the comedy scenes delighted them. Moreover, they felt that Shaw's lecturing had spilled over into the theatre and counteracted the play's entertainment values, which in themselves were hilarious. Indeed, this play contains some of the funniest lines and situations Shaw ever wrote.

Theresa Helburn had the brilliant idea of casting Beatrice Lillie, the Canadian-British comedienne, in the part of the sex obsessed Nurse-Housemaid Sweetie. Her appearance, her walk, her intonations, and even the raising of her eyebrows, all produced hilarious laughter for which GBS was in no way responsible. The part of the athletic daughter, who foreshadowed Epifania in *The Millionairess,* was played by the athletic comedienne Hope Williams, who wrestled nightly with decided comedic effect with Beatrice Lillie until the play closed, and thereafter betook herself to a ranch in Montana where she disappeared from the theatrical scene. The part of the young burglar Aubrey, played by the attractive English actor Hugh Sinclair, ended in a long speech lasting over five minutes, which simultaneously terminated the action of the play and the patience of the audience.

Though *Too True to Be Good* is being produced on Broadway in 1963, I have always thought of it as highly suitable for revival by the *avant-garde* or off-Broadway theatre, where its formlessness will in no way mitigate against its success.

The play is especially interesting for the light it throws on Shaw himself at this period of his life. It opens with a large-sized Shavian microbe who sits groaning in a chair, complaining that his misery was due to measles, which he had caught from the Patient, "a poor little rich girl" who had become a hypochondriac as an escape from an overprotective mother. "These humans are full of horrid diseases," complained the Microbe: "they infect us poor microbes with them; and you doctors pretend that it is we that infect them. You ought all to be struck off the register." Then after polishing off the doctor in hilarious Shavian style, we are introduced to two delightfully lighthearted characters as a pair of burglars, Sweetie masquerading as a hospital nurse and her boy friend Aubrey, who has the brilliant idea that instead of stealing the rich girl's £20,000 necklace, he will persuade her to steal it herself, then all three of them go off together and spend the proceeds of the theft on an extended jamboree. At the end of the play Aubrey, the erstwhile burglar, returns to his early vocation, that of a preacher, and preaches to the audience in a speech which purports to tell both what the play and life is all about and leaves the audience gasping with admiration at the magnificent language, without being made particularly aware of what Shaw is trying to say. But perhaps it can best be understood if we realize that the preacher is Shaw himself, and that he is revealing his state of mind in the year 1932, when he says, ". . . all I know is that I must find the way of life, for myself and all of us, or we shall surely perish. And meanwhile my gift has possession of me: I must preach and preach and preach no matter how late the hour and how short the day. . . ."

But a long speech dropped in at the end of a play does not become integrated into the play unless its roots are firmly planted in the story and characters. Shaw's final speech in this play may be regarded as belonging to the Preface, which was written later, and, as was becoming more and more the case with GBS, had little to do with the play.

Too True to Be Good was as indifferently received by the critics as by the audience, and it closed after a run of fifty-seven performances at the Guild Theatre in New York. Shaw himself was affected by the bad notices he received, for he wrote later on in the opening words of his Preface that "Somehow my play, Too True To Be Good, has in performance excited an animosity and an enthusiasm which will hardly be accounted for by the printed text . . . over and above the resultant querulousness to which I have long been accustomed I thought I detected an unusual intensity of resentment, as if I had hit them in some new and unbearably sore spot."

Another play in our Shaw cycle was *Getting Married,* which was produced on March 30, 1931, at the Guild Theatre. This magnificent outpouring of Shaw's views on every aspect of the subject of marriage was, because of its lack of play structure, impossible to treat in any other way than as a conversation piece. Called a "disquisitory" play when it was written in 1908, it had become a discursive play when we produced it in 1931, even though it contains an ebullient flow of some of Shaw's most brilliant lines on such subjects as free love, family life, adultery, divorce and children; and indeed he ran the gamut from lechery to platonic love. For those who seek an explanation for Shaw's famous correspondence with various women, the situation of the Bishop who, in the play, has been receiving anonymous love letters from a woman named Incognita Appassionata, may be illuminating. "She says she is happily married," says Mrs. Bridgenorth, "and that love is a necessary of life to her, but that she must have, high above all her lovers . . . some great man who will never know her, never touch her, as she is on earth, but whom she can meet in heaven when she has risen above all the everyday vulgarities of earthly love." And the Bishop adds, "Very good for her; and no trouble to me. Everybody ought to have one of these idealizations, like Dante's Beatrice." GBS had several!

We gave the play an excellent production, our cast including Romney Brent, Peg Entwistle, Margaret Wycherly, Henry Travers and Dorothy Gish; but much of the conversation fell flat, partly because many of the grounds for divorce, such as adultery which must be combined with physical cruelty, did not exist under American law, nor do they exist *in toto* in England today. The play ran for only six weeks and closed somewhat ignominiously in mid-April.

Having myself written a number of one-act comedies on the subject of marriage and divorce, one of the favorite subjects for playwrights during the teen-age period of our century, I sent a printed copy of my *Five One Act Comedies* to GBS with a letter telling him of the difficulties writers on the subject of marriage suffer (and still do) from the American dramatic critics' conventional attitudes. This is Shaw's reply:

> The plays are very good: I read them all through with undiminished appetite; and so did my wife. But you will find the same difficulty with them as I did with my *Philanderer*. The circle of freethinkers to whom your outlook on family life is commonplace is astonishingly small. It is hard to imagine that men with the morals of tom-cats

and the conversation of camp followers are so convinced of the sacredness of indissoluble monogamy that they are unable to understand a play in which legal ties do not settle everything; but they are mostly like that; and even critics who have picked up what I may call problem play jargon are as scandalized as Victorian governesses when their own cackle is brought home to them on the stage. Now that you have tried how cold the water is I think you may venture a little deeper than one-act into modern life.

Getting Married contains some of the most witty and eloquent lines ever written on the subject of women and their place in the world. Indeed, for this reason alone the play will bear revival, especially if those lines which relate to obsolete matter are removed. In fact, the play is greatly overwritten (the sign of a great writer) and is in the form of a continuous act without intermissions. However, we had mercy on our audiences and provided two. Even the stage directions in this luminous comedy are delightful and contain one of Shaw's best witticisms: "To know nothing, is to forgive everything."

Unfortunately the breed of actors capable of putting across this kind of play is rapidly dying out in this country due to the importance which has been given to the training of performers in "realistic" methods of acting. Hundreds have been trained by a system of phony Stanislavsky and pseudo-psychoanalysis into a highly vocal group of neurotics who scarcely dare move without help from their analysts who must now be supported by them along with their agents. However, many excellent and talented actors have survived this training and, in a few cases, have benefited from it. They are now numbered among our best. Unfortunately, those who train these actors have thus far been unable to teach them the sprightly speech and bravura bearing of "high comedy" needed for Shaw's plays. It was difficult to cast *Getting Married* in the year 1931 with American actors; it is well nigh impossible to do so in the year 1962.

Styles of acting move in cycles, and one of these is now on the move, led by the very people who formerly swept us into the jungle of realism associated with the expression "method acting." Elia Kazan, Lee Strasberg, *et al.*, who have contributed so greatly to the theatre of realism, are now separately leading a new movement of "style" which may result in a coming generation of actors in the theatre who are taught to speak the sprightly dialogue of Shaw and the poetic language of Shake- speare in good understandable English. If and when this hap- pens, it will be possible to produce Shaw well again in this coun- try without having to import most of the actors from England and Canada.

CHAPTER NINE

Shaw and the Supermen

T H E nineteen thirties was the period marked for history by the great world depression and the rise of Hitler to power, following in the footsteps of Mussolini in Italy and Franco in Spain. These Fascist dictators, alike only in their contempt for democracy and parliamentary government, filled the lime-light on the stage of European politics, and most of the serious playwrights of the day, both in this country and in England, were deeply concerned about the direction in which Europe was drifting. Shaw's own concern resulted in his writing, be-tween the age of seventy-seven and eighty-two, three full-length plays, *The Simpleton of the Unexpected Isles* (1934), *The Millionairess* (1935-36) and *Geneva* (1938), as well as some lesser works, such as *On the Rocks* (1933). It is a re-markable tribute to his extraordinary mental vitality that the first two of these plays were both entertaining and actable, *The Millionairess* having achieved popularity on the stage in Eng-land, the United States and elsewhere. Some of these plays seem to have owed part of their inspiration to what was going on in Russia under the dictatorship of "Superman" Stalin.

I was once of the opinion that GBS's socialism, like beauty, was only skin-deep. However, I am convinced that the burning convictions of his younger days, though somewhat dampened by his enjoyment of the affluent life of an English country gentleman, remained with him to his death and were the source of many of his trenchant criticisms of the society of his day. On one occasion, when he was praising the progress of the Soviet government, he remarked to me, "I gave them many of their best ideas!" "Including the idea that writers are not permitted to express themselves freely?" I asked. "No," he replied with a grin. "They did not follow *all* my ideas."

In 1931, he visited Moscow with a party that included Lady Nancy Astor and was reported to have behaved like an enthusiastic schoolboy, praising almost everything he was permitted to see. While the Communists received him officially "with immense fervor" according to St. John Ervine, the limelight was stolen by his companion, the outspoken Lady Nancy Astor, who shocked Stalin by asking him to his face why he had killed so many Russians.

Shaw's plays were not well-known nor was his social philosophy accepted in Russia, since his Fabian or evolutionary Socialism placed him among the Socialist reactionaries. Shaw, however, was so pleased by his reception there that soon after he wrote his American lady correspondent, Molly Tompkins, on 13th August, 1931, "My visit now seems like an extraordinarily jolly dream: never in my life have I enjoyed a journey so much. You would have been disgusted at my reception as a Grand Old Man of Socialism, my smilings and wavings and posings and speechmakings."

GBS did not visit any concentration camps, so far as the records show, nor did he publicly attack the tight censorship of writing or the arts of which he disapproved, and which still prevails there; had he done so there might have been less "smilings and wavings."

The relative unpopularity of Shaw's plays during the Czarist regime was commented upon by Stanislavsky when he visited this country with the Moscow Art Theatre, in the year 1923. We were presenting *Androcles and the Lion* and *The Man of Destiny* at the Garrick Theatre at the time, and since I had spent several evenings with him visiting Theatre Guild and other productions (we conversed in broken French), I took Stanislavsky to the Garrick to see these two Shaw plays. Afterwards I conducted him back stage and introduced him to some of the actors, including Claire Eames, Edward G. Robinson, Romney Brent (who made a delightful Christian lion) and Tom Powers. The little group gathered on the stage and heard with delight Stanislavsky's praise (in French) of their acting. Then he remarked that "Shaw has never been popular in the Russian Theatre, and this was especially true during the Czarist regime, for they recognized in him the handwriting on the wall" (*l'écriture sur le mur*). These are the very words he used, for they made a vivid impression on Romney Brent, who reminded me of this fact many years later. How curious, I thought, no matter how detested by the Czarists, Shaw's plays, as well as the novels of Dostoevsky, Tolstoy, Gorki and other critics of the old regime were nevertheless permitted by the Czars to be read and seen by the Russian people despite their obvious attacks on the social conditions of the time. Yet the Communists go much farther than the Czars in suppressing the works of their own great writers, such as Pasternak, whose *Doctor Zhivago* is still under censorship in Russia. Shaw however turned a blind eye to all this while in Russia, although had he been alive when the Pasternak incident occurred, I am sure he would have raised his voice vociferously for the freedom of the writer.

According to statistics collected by Lucille Kelling, Dean of the School of Library Science, University of North Carolina, only seven of Shaw's plays were presented in Russia from 1904 to 1932, and between 1932 to 1951 only eight were produced in Moscow. However, the printed plays and essays have enjoyed a far greater vogue.

As GBS and the Sidney Webbs, the high priests of Fabian Socialism, grew into old age, the Soviet murderings and purges began to die down, and their faith that Socialism could be achieved by peaceful Fabian methods changed into endorsement of the Communist dictatorship. By the time Shaw was in what he himself called "his dotage," he began to think he had invented Soviet Communism, at least most of its beneficial aspects. Indeed, in his message on the founding of The American Shaw Society, July 1, 1950, he stated the following inaccurate and contradictory facts:

> I was one of the inventors of Fabian Socialism now established as the policy of the U.S.S.R. I helped to set the religion of Creative Evolution with its feet on the ground

because I saw that an established religion in the world is wholly credible, and that without religion men are political timeservers and cowards.

That the Soviets had neither adopted Fabian Socialism nor religion escaped GBS at the age of ninety-four.

(It is difficult to realize that many of my younger readers in the USA do not know the meaning of the expression "Fabian Socialism." During the eighties and nineties Shaw, Beatrice and Sidney Webb, Graham Wallas, Annie Besant, E. R. Pease and many other liberals and socialists formed a group of social reformers in London under the name of the Fabian Society. In general they believed that Socialism could be attained gradually under parliamentary democracy. They are thus distinguished from the Communists who mainly believe that their ends can be achieved only by plundering those who now own property and the means of production, and usually murdering the owners. The name "Fabian" was derived by them from the Roman General Fabius Cunctator because they believed that "long taking of counsel" was necessary before they could attain their objective. The Fabian Society was ultimately absorbed by the Independent Labour Party, which it helped to create.)

Shaw's best plays are those which do not contain preachments, and these were written in his earlier years. As a Fabian Socialist, believing that Socialism could arrive by peaceful means, Shaw spent the greater part of his political life and writings to show that this was possible. He and his colleagues in the Fabian Society were the opponents of revolutionary Socialism as advocated by others under the name of Communism, based on establishing a Socialist dictatorship by the killing and plundering of those who possessed property or the means of production. It was no accident that he kept his Socialism out of *Heartbreak House* for example, and did not attempt, in the play itself, to ascribe all the reasons for World War I to the old shibboleths of the Fabian Socialists of his day. However, he used almost all of these arguments in the Preface, in which he blamed the war on the indolence of the British upper classes, their lack of interest in politics or science, their inherited wealth, their preoccupations in an amateur way with art or literature, and finally their capitalism; and on the other hand, he blamed equally the inhabitants of Horseback Hall "consisting of a prison for horses with an annex for the ladies and gentlemen who rode them, hunted them, talked about them, bought them and sold them, and gave nine-tenths of their lives to them. . . ." Years later he put the blame where it largely belonged, on the Germans under the leadership of the Kaiser, Ludendorff *et al.* This naturally did not endear him to the Hitlerites.

Shaw, in *Heartbreak House* itself, shows a Chekhovian British society which still exists, in part, despite the great changes in social responsibilities which are continuing to evolve. The Heartbreak Houses are still there in England, even though often supported by the coins of tourists who come to inspect their bygone glories. The British working man still dearly loves his Lords. And the Horseback Halls and their horse owners continue to thrive as the social goals of the mercantile classes who have now bought up many of the homes of the aristocracy on profits derived from nontaxable "capital gains." And the House of Lords, the peerage and the royal family may well continue to exist in a welfare state along parliamentary socialistic lines long after their left-wing detractors have been lost in oblivion.

Shaw, in his Preface to *Heartbreak House,* paints a magnificent word picture of what happens in a democracy at war. One thing he learns—he must keep his mouth discreetly shut. "As for myself," he wrote in the year 1919, "why, it may be asked, did I not write two plays about the war . . . ? The answer is significant. You cannot make war on war and on your neighbor at the same time." And he goes on to add that "When men are heroically dying for their country, it is not the time to shew their lovers and wives and fathers and mothers how they are being sacrificed to the blunders of boobies, the cupidity of capitalists, the ambition of conquerors, the electioneering of demagogues, the Pharisaism of patriots, the lusts and lies and rancors and bloodthirsts that love war because it opens their prison doors, and sets them in the thrones of power and popularity. For unless these things are mercilessly exposed they will hide under the mantle of the ideals on the stage just as they do in real life."

Shaw, throughout most of his life, was utterly opposed to the slaughtering of his fellow men for any reason whatsoever, and he carried this to the point where he even strongly opposed the killing of animals for food. It was, in my opinion, only when his mind began to be confused in his late seventies and eighties between his admiration for the Superman which he saw embodied

in such men as Lenin, Stalin, Mussolini and Hitler, and his dis-
trust of the voters, that he began to turn a blind eye to the
slaughtering of his fellow human beings which was the horrible accompaniment to all these dictatorships. Then, when his
disillusion with Fascism set in, he disclaimed his former advocacy of Mussolini and partial advocacy of Hitler, and gave
his allegiance to Stalin. Thus, only the few plays and prefaces
which were written toward the end of his life were tainted with
this thinking, and these mercifully were among his least good
theatre pieces.

It would be interesting to be able to leap forward into the
future for fifty years and to look back and appraise which of the
two economic systems, the modified capitalism of the Western
countries or Communism, has captured the destiny of mankind. If, as Premier Khrushchev recently stated with the arro-
gance by which a man often covers his own doubts, our grand-
children will all be Communists, then Shaw may have backed
the winning horse when he abandoned his evolutionary Socialism during his eighties and nineties. But if the Western system turns out to be the winning horse, it will be partly because of what Shaw contributed to liberal thought and action
throughout the world during the major part of his life. So, in
either event, Shaw will be on the winning side.

Shaw's next full-length play after *Too True to Be Good*
was *On the Rocks,* written in 1933 while the great depression
of the thirties was at its height. In it, GBS, at the age of seventy-
seven, broke his usual rule of reserving the Preface for his political views, and filled the play with them instead. It begins
with a parade of mobs of the unemployed marching in Trafal-
gar Square, and ends with a parade of mobs marching in
Downing Street, singing "England, arise"; with interminable
speeches from Cabinet Ministers in the acts between. In the
play, the Prime Minister (said to have been suggested by the attractive but inefficient J. Ramsay MacDonald of the Labour
Party) is at sixes and sevens as to how to deal with the depression, until a vibrant lady with all the ideas of Bernard Shaw
takes him to a retreat in Wales and brainwashes him so that on
his return he has all the Shavian remedies for all of England's
ills. The title of the play might easily have been changed to
How I Would Govern England by Bernard Shaw. The chain
of economic depressions can be broken only by Socialism, abolition of the Houses of Parliament and the upper classes, establish-

ment of a dictator type of leader and a dozen other items in the Shaw larder for improving the world. Nothing is said, however, about the economics which brought the United States out of the depression and consisted mainly in increasing the earning and consuming power of the working classes, along with a certain amount of price fixing and subsidy which remain with us to this day.

GBS did not send the play to me but gave a copy to Lee Simonson, who brought it to New York where it was read without enthusiasm by the Guild Board. On December 23, 1933, GBS wrote Terry on the subject as follows:

My dear Terry

I gave Lee Simonson an early proof of *On the Rocks;* but it is now obsolete, as I have since produced the play here, and made many changes, especially in the stage business, as I found when the scene was set up that there was a third door on which I had not counted. The enclosed revised copy is correct. But probably the play will be published by Dodd, Mead & Co. before there is any question of a New York production.

I should like to know at the Guild's convenience whether it proposes to do this play or not. It is in a way very local, although the political situations are now so alike in all countries that the points will carry everywhere. Here the audiences laugh from beginning to end; but they are not as yet excessively numerous, and I suspect they are mostly the same people every night. A very strong and agreeable personality, very English, and with a pleasant voice is indispensable for the leading part. Lorraine could do it better than anyone else known to me. I mentioned this to Lee. Hipney is the next most important part. It made a very marked impression here.

I am presuming that the blessed old Guild is still in existence: at all events *you* are, as your welcome Christmas greeting testifies.

The Guild having taken a negative position, GBS again wrote Terry from R.M. *Rangitane,* at Wellington, New Zealand, on 24th April, 1934, as follows:

My dear Tessie

Your letter of the 6th Feb. did not reach London until

after my departure for New Zealand; and its pursuit of me was long and tortuous.

I take it that I may now deal with *On the Rocks* as discarded by the Guild and free to find shelter wherever it can. In London it flopped in the most annoying manner: huge first night success, unanimously good press (for once) presaging an unlimited run, audiences apparently delighted by every line, AND receipts £400 a week! I had insisted on an experiment at half the regular theatre prices; but this involved a slightly out-of-the-way new theatre, and the general playgoer would not come, though the fans came over and over again. In short, it was a magnificent success with the people—say 5000 or so—who are interested in politics. To the others it meant absolutely nothing. After the first few weeks it settled down to £40; and the shutters had to go up before the management was quite cleared out.

During this voyage I have written one full length play and begun another; but the finished one is so fantastic, and in great part so hieratical, that it is useless except perhaps for a Festival performance at Malvern (two or three shows only). I am writing myself off the theatrical map, partly through senile decay, partly because I am no longer interested in the sort of thing that has any commercial value in the theatre. Consequently unless I can find a fresh set of desperados, standing where the Guild did in the days of *Heartbreak House* and *Jane Clegg*, I am out of the running.

Is there such a thing? If so, dear Tessie, give it the address of your superannuated, G. Bernard Shaw.

Had there been an off-Broadway theatre in existence in New York at the time, this would have been the place for *On the Rocks*. But if its politics did not interest the British theatregoing public, still less would they have interested the American public. *On the Rocks* lived up to its title so far as this country is concerned.

The Preface to *On the Rocks* was devoted to a cold-blooded examination, "on its own merits," of the political necessity for killing people. In it GBS reached the conclusion that "the essential justification for extermination . . . is always incorrigible social incompatability and nothing else. . . . The only country which has yet awakened to this extension of social re-sponsibility is Russia." Thus in this Preface we find the seeds of an anti-Shavian idea, "the extermination of people," which was to find fuller expression in two later plays, *The Simpleton of the Unexpected Isles* and *Geneva*.

The Theatre Guild's hero-worshiping of Shaw was nowhere better demonstrated than in our production of *The Simpleton of the Unexpected Isles,* his allegorical play about the Judgment Day which we produced in New York at the Guild Theatre on February 18, 1935. Taken at its face value, the play seemed to say that on the Day of Judgment, Angels of Destruction will arrive on earth, and as a result, all the useless people on the earth will vanish into thin air, and the lives which have no use, no meaning, no purpose will fade out. We will have to justify our existence or perish. Only the elect will survive. Since we of the Theatre Guild regarded ourselves as of the elect, and cer-tainly did not regard ourselves as useless, it seemed a comfort-ing sort of idea, even if we surmised only dimly what Shaw meant by "the elect." However, in the play itself he charac-terized in hilarious headlines those useless people who van-ished on Judgment Day.

> Stock Exchange closes: only two members left. House of Commons decimated: only fourteen members to be found: none of Cabinet rank. House of Lords still musters fifty members; but not one of them has ever attended a meeting of the Chamber. Mayfair a desert: six hotels left without a single guest. Fresh disappearances. Crowded in-tercession service at Westminster Abbey brought to a close by disappearance of the congregation at such a rate that the rest fled leaving the dean preaching to the choir. At the Royal Institution Sir Ruthless Bonehead, Egregious Professor of Mechanistic Biology to the Rockefeller Foun-dation, drew a crowded audience to hear his address on "Whither have they gone?" He disappeared as he opened his mouth to speak. . . .

While Shaw propounded the general idea that "the Day of Judgment is not the end of the world, but the end of its child-hood and the beginning of its responsibility," this had very little to do with the action of the play, which was mostly concerned with the happy sexual life of six parents representing Eastern and Western civilizations who bring forth four beautiful Eurasian children, two boys and two girls, the latter two seducing an innocent young English curate in a scene which might well be regarded as questionable—even in these days of theatrical improprieties.

Somewhat bewildered by the formlessness of the play, we turned it over to Romney Brent, a young actor-director who was born in Mexico and thus qualified to deal with such exotic characters as the two young girls named Maya and Vashti, and we invited him to direct it. He read it and reread it, but since he could not understand it, and since we could not explain it, he declined the honor but offered to play the part of the simpleton-curate who was seduced by the two beautiful Eurasians. We therefore engaged an excellent director named Henry Wagstaff Gribble, noted for his gay comedy *March Hares,* who had a reputation for dealing successfully with improbable theatrical situations. The two leading roles, the Priest Pra and the Priestess Prola, were excellently played by McKay Morris and Alla Nazimova, both of whom gave convincing performances in parts in which sermonizing took precedence over emotion and action. The cast also included Lawrence Grossmith, Rex O'Malley and Viola Roache, all excellent performers.

Nazimova, not unexpectedly, had difficulty in mastering a role in which she fluctuated between a *religieuse,* a seductress, a sybil and a saint, and she finally settled for the seductress, which came more naturally. However, her interpretation sometimes became incongruous when she carried the seductress too far into the saintlier aspects of the role. One evening she would give a brilliant performance, the next evening a ghastly one. "I was bad tonight, wasn't I?" she once asked me in her dressing room after the play. "Yes, but you were wonderful yesterday evening," I replied, comforting her. "Tell me, Lawrence," she said, "what is the difference between my performance tonight and my performance yesterday?" This usually called for a lengthy interrogation. No actress of my acquaintance could play a part in so many different ways as Nazimova. Whatever kind of character she started with, on a particular night, she ended with. The playing of this role, which earned her no great credit, resulted in a pact between her and Romney Brent to play together in Ibsen's *Ghosts,* a project which they brought off later on with great acclaim. While the play was in preparation Theresa Helburn received the following comments from GBS:

I have no notion of what they are doing with *The Sim-pleton* in New York, except that they muffed their attempt to get Mrs. Patrick Campbell and got Nazimova instead. I have a horrible fear that they will use Honolulu costumes (or no costumes) instead of Indian ones, and present the four phantoms as brown savages with nothing on but garlands of flowers.

Will you tell them that if they want to abbreviate the title for an electric sign, they must call it *The Simpleton,* and not *The Unexpected Isles?*

The play was received in New York with the usual mixed notices from the critics. Its humor was delightful, its sex-ridden story was hilarious, but its last act with the dramatic arrival of the Angels and its philosophical conclusion was generally incomprehensible. On February 21, I wrote GBS as follows:

We did not cable to you about the *Simpleton* because it seemed as though we could not say anything which could not keep, after reading the perfectly absurd notices written by the dramatic critics. We enjoyed working on the play very much, and it certainly did not deserve the things which were said about it. A number of people who saw the play on the opening night have written to the critics protesting against the tone of the notices. My own feeling in the matter was that the greater part of the play was mostly enjoyable, but it seems to be the fashion nowadays to object to ideas being aired in the theatre—that is, more than one idea at a time.

I was looking over the list of plays which are now current in New York, and there are only three out of about thirty which really have an idea behind them of any kind whatsoever. One of the critics actually stated that he thought that the best way to write about an idea was to write a few columns in the newspapers.

On the part of the Guild, I feel that we did everything we possibly could to make a good production. We employed excellent actors throughout, and we paid particular attention to their diction. We had them speak distinctly so that they could be heard plainly, though you could certainly never tell this by the notices, as the majority of them are written as though the critics had not even bothered to listen. However, I could go on *ad infinitum.*

We are all naturally very disappointed, and we are especially disappointed that the play should have been received with so much ill nature.

With kindest personal regards to you and Mrs. Shaw,
and hoping that you will not be too disappointed.

Shaw wrote later on in the printed Preface, "The increasing
bewilderment of my journalist critics as to why I wrote such
plays as *The Simpleton* culminated in New York in February,
1935, when I was described as a dignified old monkey throwing coconuts at the public in pure senile devilment." Shaw
explained in the Preface to the printed play, which was published later, that he introduced the exotic group marriage situation which occupies three quarters of the play, "only to bring
into the story the four lovely phantasms who embody all the
artistic romantic and military ideals of our cultured suburbs."

When we turn to the Preface to find out what Shaw was really
driving at, we discover that the Angel of Judgment who caused
the useless "ladies and gentlemen" to vanish was an allegorical
representation by GBS of the Bolshevik Commissar Djerjinsky
who organized the dreaded Communist Tcheka (later called
the GPU and MVD), the Soviet Government apparatus of
death and destruction for all who opposed the Communist party
line. How Shaw justified this interpretation can be understood
only by reading the Preface (written later) from which I quote
the following:

> For the Tcheka was simply carrying out the executive
> work of a constitution which had abolished the lady and
> gentleman exactly as the Inquisition carried out the execu-
> tive work of a Catholic constitution which had abolished
> Jupiter and Diana and Venus and Apollo. Simple enough;
> and yet so hard to get into our genteel heads that in mak-
> ing a play about it, I have had to detach it altogether from
> the great Russian change, or any of the actual political
> changes which threaten to raise it in the National-Socialist
> and Fascist countries, and to go back to the old vision of a
> day of reckoning by divine justice for all mankind.

Since Shaw was carefully disguising in this play what he
really meant by the Day of Judgment, it was no wonder that we
of the Theatre Guild, the critics and the general public, were mis-

led into believing that we were concerned mainly with an innocent allegory which at its worst suggested that future races would intermarry and the useless people would disappear. Indeed, but for this explanation in the Preface, I defy any intelligent reader of the play itself to see any parallel between the painless disappearance of the so-called useless people in the allegory and the torture and bloody executions of the Spanish Inquisition and the Soviets in real life. Shaw fooled everybody to his complete satisfaction, but not to the satisfaction of those he fooled when they learned later on they had been fooled. And I was one of them.

The play, while charming as an allegory to me and to those who did not know Shaw's preposterous explanation, turned out to be neither good theatre nor good propaganda, and although well acted and simply staged, it did not run beyond the five weeks' subscription period. And the heavy financial loss which we incurred on the production of this play led us to look much more carefully into the question of whether we would produce Shaw's next play.

Shaw sent us a copy of his next newly written play, *The Millionairess,* in 1937 and we read it at once. The general consensus of Theatre Guild opinion was that the play was written in two theatrically incompatible moods. It was felt that the visit to the "sweat-shop" in Act III was written in the vein of complete realism, while the rest of the play was intellectual high comedy. It was also hard to become too sorry for the "sweat-shop" clothing workers, when as a result of the unionization of the garment workers in New York City, they were among the best-paid classes of labor in the world.

GBS had constantly told us that this was a role for which Katharine Hepburn's dominating character was especially suited, but Katharine Hepburn begged to differ. She turned down the part and the Guild (with some sense of relief) told GBS that they would not produce it. However, I informed my colleagues that if they did not produce the play, I would.

Out of these conflicting differences of opinion came the first production and public performance of the play in England or the United States, at the Westport Country Playhouse in the summer of 1938, with the title role excellently played by Jessie Royce Landis, but without much support from the rest of the cast. The play ran for the usual eight-performance week and was extremely well received by the audiences.

Despite the brilliant dialogue, the play actually suffered from being in two distinct moods, and the character of Epifania, the Millionairess, even in the capable hands of Miss Landis, seemed strained and unpersuasive. The play floated into what seemed to be oblivion as a somewhat disjointed conversation piece. I pocketed my losses and conjectured that my colleagues had been right.

Not so. Performed differently and in the manner GBS had insisted from the start—that is, with Katharine Hepburn in the title role—the play was revived after his death in 1952 and was received with approbation both in London and New York. Shaw stirred up our interest in *The Millionairess* when we suggested in 1940 that Katharine Hepburn play *Saint Joan,* by writing us on April 3 of that year as follows:

> My play *The Millionairess,* with Edith Evans in the title part, is next on the list at the Globe Theatre in London. In the original version I made the woman a boxer; but, on the stage, that was unconvincing and unladylike. So I have made her a Judo expert. Judo is what we vulgarly call jujitsu, which is magnificently spectacular. The part requires just such a personality as Miss Hepburn. Has she ever read the play?

On my very last visit to Shaw we brought up the matter again, and asked for his permission to produce *The Millionairess* with Kate Hepburn. He asked whether she was a good athlete and when I answered yes, he said, "Watch out for the scene where she applies jujitsu to her leading man, or she'll kill him if she isn't careful." Later on, when we produced the play with Hepburn, it was a miracle that she did not kill her leading man, Cyril Ritchard. Ritchard is a brilliant actor, a big man who stands six feet two in his stockinged feet and weighs about 192 pounds. One particularly exuberant performance by Katharine Hepburn resulted in her heaving him in the air, bringing him down on the floor like a sack of potatoes, and tearing a ligament in his right leg which caused him to limp for several months! After that she was more careful.

The British and American productions of *The Millionairess* which took place two years after Shaw's death were largely the result of the combined efforts of Katharine Hepburn, the Theatre Guild and Tennent Productions of London. Two Australian actors, the aforesaid Cyril Ritchard and Robert Helpmann, who played the Egyptian doctor who ultimately marries the Millionairess, buttressed the fine performance of Kate Hepburn. Hepburn's own story of how she came to play *The Millionairess* shows the vicissitudes of the theatre. When the Theatre Guild sent her the play in the year 1937, with the full intention of producing it in New York (notwithstanding its defects) if she would play the lead, she read the play with great interest. She read the first act and liked it; she read the second act and liked it less; she read the third act and liked it not at all; she read the fourth act and disliked it. She said, "No, thank you," despite GBS's constant reiteration that she was made for the part and the part was made for her. Ten years later, she had a "hunch" about the play and took it in book form out of her library. Much to her surprise, as she read it her reactions were reversed, and by the time she reached the end of the play, she was enchanted by it and wanted to play the role of Epifania.

She was in England at the time, having completed a tour in Australia for the Old Vic, under the direction of Michael Benthall. Whether playing the parts of Katharine in *The Taming of the Shrew* and Portia in *The Merchant of Venice* made her appreciate *The Millionairess* more, I do not know; but she talked with Michael Benthall about the possibility of playing Epifania and he was enthusiastic. She planned to appear in the play first in England, under the auspices of Tennent Productions, and then to open it in New York for the Theatre Guild the following season. She and Michael telephoned Hugh (Binkie) Beaumont, the resourceful head of Tennent's, and invited themselves to dinner at his home. They promised that after dinner they would offer him a surprise, and they did. They offered him *The Millionairess* on a silver platter while the coffee was being served on another silver platter. In turn, Binkie offered them a surprise. He had already produced *The Millionairess* with Edith Evans in the title role ten years before, and it was such a failure he decided not to bring the play into London. "But you didn't have me in it," said Kate, with appropriate lack of modesty. "Nor me directing it," said Benthall.

Fortunately for us all, Beaumont was unable to withstand their enthusiasm. The play went into rehearsal under an agreement between the Guild and Tennent. It opened at Liverpool at the same theatre where it had failed ten years earlier. "When did you realize *then* that it was a disaster?" Kate asked Binkie. "Ten minutes after the curtain went up." He looked very glum after her very incomplete dress rehearsal. "And when did you know it was a disaster *now?*" she asked. "Ten minutes after *you* came on," he replied. Since Kate had no costumes ready for the dress rehearsal, she draped herself in sheets, and for the tricky cellar scene, she borrowed a stagehand's hat and coat. She bought them from him later and wore them right through the London and New York runs—possibly the only instance on record of a stagehand dressing a star.

Armina and I visited the play in Newcastle-on-Tyne on our way to Scotland and were delighted with the performance and production. Just as Shaw had prophesied, Hepburn was superb in the part, her dominance and stridency being balanced by her essential sweetness and honesty of character. She resembled the winds, half typhoon and half zephyr. During the early performances, Kate was having difficulties with her entrance in Act I, being petrified by the applause which greeted her and which made it impossible for her to speak for almost half a minute. She had a brilliant idea for solving this problem. She came on stage, looked around the room, then went off again, slamming the door. The audience applauded wildly. After the applause died down, she re-entered and played the scene. Unlike the first production, the play was brought to London, and it and Hepburn received excellent notices. I quote the following from an almost unanimous press. "A human hurricane," *Daily Express.* "Makes every moment glitter," *Daily Mail.* "The rhythmic beauty of her sledge hammer playing," London *Times.* "Vitality comes bursting out of her," *Daily Telegraph.*

During the fall of 1952, Kate was ill and there was some question as to whether the play could be brought to this country, since she was not feeling able to play the heavy role in New York. But indiscretion triumphed over discretion, and Kate decided to play the ten weeks booked at the Shubert Theatre, which were almost completely sold out before we opened. Two days before the opening, I asked her to postpone it for a day or so to avoid forcing her voice. Her reply was, "If you postpone it, I'll be worse. I'll be much more nervous waiting." So we opened as advertised, and the reception of Kate and the company was similar to what it had been in London. Later on her performance became more and more dominating, and she insisted on straining her voice until it shook the rafters of the Shubert Theatre. "Where is the best place to hear *The Millionairess?*" someone asked me. "On the pavement outside the

theatre," was my almost truthful reply. Fortunately for all concerned, she soon lost her voice, and it was restored thanks to the
ministrations of Dr. Craig and the Dixon Voice Institute. This
play, which was our last Shaw production in New York, ran for
a limited engagement of ten weeks, and there was not a vacant
seat throughout the eighty boisterous performances. This was
one of the few plays of Shaw which yielded a profit for the
Guild. We shared it with Kate, who worked for Actor s Equity
minimum salary, plus half the profits, if there were any, and at
first it looked as if she would be working for next to nothing.
But for this unusual and generous arrangement on her part,
I doubt if we would have been able to produce the play at all
in New York for such a short engagement.

In Shaw's Preface to *The Millionairess* he writes on the subject of Bosses, their advantages and drawbacks. He wrote a special ending for the play for Russia and countries with Communist sympathies, in which the Millionairess makes the following speech in reply to a remark from Blanderband that she is a
bloated capitalist:

> I am a capitalist here; but in Russia I should be a
> worker. And what a worker! My brains are wasted here:
> the wealth they create is thrown away on idlers and their
> parasites, whilst poverty, dirt, disease, misery and slavery
> surround me like a black sea in which I may be engulfed
> at any moment by a turn of the money market. Russia
> needs managing women like me. In Moscow I shall not be
> a millionairess; but I shall be in the Sovnarkom within six
> months and in the Politbureau before the end of the year.
> Here I have no real power, no real freedom, and no secu-
> rity at all: we may all die in the workhouse. In Russia I
> shall have such authority! such scope for my natural pow-
> ers! as the Empress Catherine never enjoyed. I swear that
> before I have been twenty years in Russia every Russian
> baby shall weigh five pounds heavier and every Russian
> man and woman live ten years longer. I shall not be an
> empress; and I may work myself to death; but in a thou-
> sand years from now holy Russia shall again have a patron
> saint, and her name shall be Saint Epifania.

I have no information that *The Millionairess* has ever been
performed in the USSR with or without Shaw's special ending,
but with the official Soviet attitude toward religion, I doubt

whether Epifania will ever be dubbed a Soviet saint.

The next play we received from GBS was *Geneva.* It was the first full-length play of his which we refused to produce for what may be termed "ideological" reasons. This will be explained in the next chapter.

CHAPTER TEN

We Battle with
Shaw over Geneva

DURING all our years of correspondence, I had refrained
from ideological arguments of any kind with GBS. However,
we were to arrive at a strong clash of opinions when, in August
of 1938, I received a privately printed copy of his latest play
Geneva. By this time Europe was dominated by four dictatorships, those of Hitler, Mussolini, Stalin and Franco. The possibility of a war with Hitler's Germany was on everyone's
mind, and the Theatre Guild, wherever possible, had been producing plays which would arouse the nation to the dangers to
democracy everywhere should Hitler's dream of world dom-
ination by the German "Superman" come to be generally accepted. On reading the copy of *Geneva,* I was furious with the
way Shaw in this play had given lip-service to the dictators and
had dismissed Hitler's treatment of the Jews—a treatment
which was later to culminate in the killing of over six million
of them in the concentration camps of Buchenwald and Oswie-
cim. I delivered a frontal assault on GBS by letter on August
26, 1938, which, believe it or not, caused him actually to revise
the third act of the play and to change the character of the
Jew. "To please you, Lawrence," he replied, "I have written up

the part a bit." Shaw also wrote me, "You may now put the copy I sent you in the fire as useless, or, better still, sell it as a curiosity!" Here is what I wrote GBS after reading the play:

Dear GBS

Thank you very much indeed for sending me the privately-printed copy of *Geneva*. I read the play immediately, and while I enjoyed it very much in the main, I was so deeply hurt by certain parts of it that I feel I should write you immediately about same.

I refer especially to the part "the Jew" plays in this play, and which seems to me to contradict the attitude you have taken for over seventy years of your life. I do not believe that you will want future generations of Jew-baiters to quote you as part authority for a program of torturing, starving and driving to suicide of Jews all over the world. Yet, on page 65, you give Battler (obviously Hitler) a speech in which he justifies everything that has been done recently in Germany and Austria, on the ground that in every country "the foreigner is the trespasser." As the thought is presented so convincingly by him, it seems that you do not take into account that Jews have lived in Germany for over 1700 years; that they have contributed largely to the cultural and scientific life of Germany; that during the last war alone over thirty thousand Jews died in the German armies, and that but for a Jewish scientist, Haber, who invented the method of abstracting nitrogen from the air (which scientist later committed suicide) the Germans would have been defeated in 1916 instead of 1919. You give the Jew merely the weak answer: "For my race, there are no frontiers," as though the German Jew of today had anything to do with the historic reasons, beginning with the Roman armies and ending with Torquemada and others, as a result of which some of the Jews found themselves in Germany.

Furthermore, you justify Hitler as though he had merely opened his doors and allowed the Jews to depart, taking with them enough to start them off in other countries. However, in order to tend towards the extermination of the race and to enrich his own Nazi followers, every schoolboy knows that, as a result of Hitler's actions, the German Jew who wishes to leave Germany finds every pos-

sible obstacle to departing with any means of subsistence
which will enable him to gain admittance or continuance
of livelihood in another country, while those who remain
there are subjected to increasing torture. You justify this
torture on page 66 by stating that Hitler is not responsible
for what is done by his underlings. ("I cannot be everywhere, and my agents are not angels.") But, in a dictatorship, who is responsible? On page 82, you have Battler
state on this point: "I do not condescend to defend myself.
I have already remarked that the Jews are an obnoxious
species, which we refuse to tolerate just as we refuse to
tolerate venomous snakes." Instead of giving the Jew an
historic answer backed up by facts, you merely have him
present the weaker side of his case; to wit, "We Jews have
been driven by persecution into trade and finance until
we have become more skillful at them than our lazy per-
secutors. This has made us their bankers and employers,
and to that extent their masters. The remedy is very simple. They have only to cultivate their brains as energet-
ically as they cultivate their muscles. Then they will no
longer be our slaves . . ." etc., etc. The idea implied by
this weak answer, that all that the Jews have contributed
to German civilization can be expressed as "trade and finance," is an absurd libel on a people which have en-
riched German culture in every field which is higher than
trade and finance.

Is not the Jew entitled to answer to the German accusation that the Jews are an obnoxious species, that nevertheless Germany and the rest of the world have numbered
among the brightest lights of German culture such men as
Albert Einstein, Hertz, Mendel and Franck, in science;
Mendelssohn, Rubinstein, Gustav Mahler and Bruno Walter, in music; Wassermann, Ehrlich, Freud and Adler,
in medicine and psychiatry; Henrich Heine, Feuchtwanger
and Zweig, in literature, and Franz Werfel, Schnitzler and
Reinhardt in the theatre? Yet you give the Jew only the
pitiful answer of a reference to his accomplishments in
German "trade and finance." And can anybody properly
call the German iron-masters and bankers "lazy perse-
cutors"? The Germans as a race are probably the most in-
dustrious on earth.

Then again you follow the teachings of Julius Streicher

in making much of the point that over 1900 years ago the ancestors of the present-day Jews killed Christ. I believe that if He lived today in England the English would kill Him; that if He lived in Ireland the Irish would kill Him; and that the same is even more true in Germany. Is it fair to leave unanswered this accusation against people living today, whose misguided ancestors committed this crime? Yet you give the Jew no answer, though you are not sparing with your words on the other side of the equation. In case you doubt the truth of the stories of the injustices which you defend in this portion of the play, I am enclosing herewith an article written by Mr. Dodd, the late ambassador to Germany, who is not a Jew, but was present in Berlin as a disinterested witness to what has been taking place in Germany in the last few years. Read this and see whether, if the same thing were done to Irishmen in England, you would not burn with the injustice. And, incidentally, how would you like it if all Irish books, and especially, your books, were burned by the English because the Irish were writers of radical literature of the kind calculated to damage the fighting instincts of the British race? Also incidentally, if you happened to be living in Germany instead of Great Britain, you would find yourself in a concentration camp, and the penalty for having written *Geneva* would undoubtedly have been a bullet through your head, for dictators have very little sense of humor.

The final insult to the Jewish race which is contained in your play is when the Jew, hearing of the end of the world, decides to try to buy up the securities at a depleted value. Surely, no one would be so stupid, especially the Jew, to whom, at least, you are willing only to ascribe superior intellect in trade and finance! The Jew in your play is permitted to say nothing regarding the more spiritual aspects of his racial heritage; nor to act on that heritage; nor show his contribution of such thinkers as Moses, Christ, Marx, Spinoza, etc., all (like yourself) opposed to established tyrannies of power and thought. He is the creation of Streicher, not of Shaw.

In the unpublished version of *Geneva* which you have sent me, you have crossed out some of the passages on pages 82, 83 and 84, which contain some of the above. I do not know whether it is your intention that these passages should appear in the printed version, but I know that it is your habit to revise your plays before they are actually printed. In *St. Joan,* you actually deleted nearly thirty pages. As one who has venerated you for practically all his life, and has especially admired your fairness and, above all, your humanity and kindness, I do most sincerely ask you to reconsider the position you have given the character of the Jew in this play. Shakespeare, by the character of Shylock, and Dickens, by the character of Fagin, have added greatly to the cross of hatred which future generations of Jews must bear. You, who have always been so understanding through your entire life, will surely not want to add another figure to a collection which breeds intolerance and racial hatred.

I am fully aware that whenever a comic Irishman is put upon the stage, all the Irishmen rise in their wrath and write letters to the newspapers. When anyone puts a comic Jew on the stage, the same things happen. You and I both come of races that are inordinately sensitive to this sort of thing, but do not overlook the reason: Both races have had hundreds of years of living as minorities in which they have constantly had to fight an assumption of superiority by the majority. This is a sufficient explanation for this hypersensitivity. But my criticism of your character of the Jew does not spring from the fact that you have made him a comic figure. You have not done this. You have made him a pitifully inferior mouthpiece to express his case, thus playing into the hands of the breeders of racial hatred by ranging yourself unconsciously on their side.

In a broader sense, judged by the standards of the latter speeches of your own play *The Simpleton,* I think you have missed even a more important point in the present play. I refer to the fact that, while the judge, at the end of the play, excoriates both dictatorships and democrats in equal terms, nevertheless, the impression is left strongly that you range yourself on the side of the dictators. This is done especially in the character of Bombardone and his magnificent speech on page 72, which ends with the words: "Out of the liberal democratic chaos comes form, purpose, order and rapid execution." But if you will send your mind back over the political history of mankind, you will realize that, out of dictatorships too comes ultimately the same kind of chaos. It is merely postponed. Democracies breed liberalism and chaos, and dictatorships breed tyranny ultimately leading to chaos and oppression. People will not tolerate tyranny and oppression more than a generation or so. Then they come back to democracy, and later on to liberalism and chaos all over again. Strong leaders like Mussolini and Hitler arise, and for a brief moment in the history of the world, their regimes seem admirable from the standpoint of efficiency and "getting things done." But does it last? You give the historic answer in *The Simpleton*. Looking out over the future, you saw that man could never submit indefinitely to tyranny; that he would never be willing to be a well-fed, well-housed political slave. The cry for liberty will always ring out in the world, as long as the world exists. This is the ultimate truth, the truth by which man has progressed upward and onward towards his ultimate destiny. The present dictatorships are mere ephemeral halting places on the way.

I wonder whether you have ever stopped to contemplate the part you have contributed to this democratic chaos, with which you are now so impatient. St. John Ervine once remarked to me that you have more profoundly influenced your generation than any other man living. The effect of your influence has been exactly the opposite of that of the dictators. You have preached tolerance, justice, love of the common man, freedom, economic fairness, elevation of women; and, in England and America, at any rate, your disciples are numbered by the millions. Yet you seem to justify Fascism with its intolerance, racial hatred, economic slavery, degradation of women, fanning of the war spirit, etc., mainly on the ground that its dictators are "Supermen" and the Supermen "get things done." Believe me, GBS, before you successfully attacked Victorian morality and economics, the plutocratic rulers of England were strong and "got things done."

Why not have yourself brought before the bar at the World Court on the ground that you have preached liberalism, tolerance, justice and the other qualities which have permeated all your writings and made the liberal nations so largely what they are today? And make your accusers the very dictators whom you now seem to admire, and then justify yourself for what your teachings have accomplished. I believe that, if you do this, you would add a spice to the play, which to my mind it lacks at the moment. Now that you are restored to health again, I hope you will consider what I have said with your characteristic good humor. I especially hope you will forgive the length of this letter and will understand its spirit, which I am sure only echoes the thoughts of millions of others who love you as I do, and have had their lives and thoughts influenced so strongly by you.

P.S. I have not shown *Geneva* to the Theatre Guild yet, and you will appreciate that this is purely a personal reaction.

20th September, 1938

Dear Lawrence Langner

Can you wonder at Hitler (and now Mussolini) driving out the Jews? Here am I who have written a play in which I make ruthless fun of British Cabinet Ministers, of German and Italian Dictators, and Cockney young women, of the Buchmanite Oxford movement, of Church of England bishops, and of the League of Nations. Everyone laughs. Not a voice is raised in their defense.

But I have dared to introduce a Jew without holding him up to the admiring worship of the audience as the inheritor of all the virtues and none of the vices of Abraham and Moses, David and Isaiah. And instantly you, Lawrence, raise a wail of lamentation and complaint and accuse me of being a modern Torquemada.

You ask me how I would feel if the British Government burnt my books because I am an Irishman, and then put Irish characters on the stage and made fun of them. Lawrence: the Irish have banned my books; and in *John Bull's Other Island* I myself have been far less kind to the Irish characters than I have been to the Jew in *Geneva,* who is introduced solely to convict the Nazis of persecution. But you will not allow him to do exactly what an able Jew of his type would do when Gentiles were swallowing a terrifying Press canard: that is, go into the money market as a bear speculator and make his fortune.

You really are the most thoughtless of Sheenies. However, to please you, I have written up the part a bit. Musso let me down completely by going anti-Semite on me; and I have had to revise the third act to such an extent that you may now put the copy I sent you in the fire as useless, or, better still, sell it as a curiosity. Only 40 copies of it ever existed; and most of them were worn to tatters at rehearsal in Malvern. So go in as a bull speculator.

Meanwhile wait until I send you a revised copy. You may show it to the Guild; but they had better leave it to the Federal Theatre and the 50 cent public, who are a much steadier source of income to me.

Why doesn't the Guild come to terms for a revival of *The Apple Cart* with Cedric Hardwicke, who made a tremendous success with it in London whilst it went for nothing in New York?

Have you ever considered what would have happened to the United States if the Ku-Klux-Klan had found as competent a leader as Hitler? There is a play for you in that.

Yours as always
G. Bernard Shaw

October 7, 1938

Dear GBS:

Thank you for your letter of the 20th September. If I am really one of the most thoughtless of "Sheenies," then you are one of the most inconsistent of "Micks."

Since you are rewriting the part of Mussolini, I hope that you will make it quite clear that his anti-Semitism does not spring from any nobler source than the fact that he believes it is a good way to stir up the Arabs against the British. This shows the tremendous value to the world of having supermen dictators, who at the stroke of a pen, can sacrifice the future of thousands of individuals on the altar of racial superiority. It is to laugh.

Practically all the great nations of the world have been racial mixtures. The mixture of the Nordic blood with the Latin blood produced the English and French races; the German blood, without Latin inter-mixture, producing the Junker.

The Irish as a race were greatly improved by the fact that many of the ships of the Spanish Armada foundered on the coast of Ireland, thus producing that group of the

Irish people known as the "black Irish," a mixture of Celt and Spaniard, from which most of the men of genius of Ireland have been produced. A number of the Spaniards were Maranos—or converted Jews, which resulted in a certain admixture of Jewish and Irish people. Undoubtedly, you are one of the striking examples of this mixture, since you possess all the virtues of Moses, Spinoza, Heine and all the other Jewish prophets. Then, take your money-making ability. Nine-tenths of the radical playwrights starve to death; you make a fortune at it. Then look at your Socialism. Don't you know that, according to Hitler, all Socialists are Jewish? Yes, GBS, the truth will out. You, too are a Sheenie; and as to that red beard of yours, did you not know that the medieval Jew always had a red beard? A friend of mine recently visited what remains of the Pharisees. He found that they had red beards and blue eyes. You are undoubtedly a Pharisee throw-back.

And as I look back on twenty years of my life wasted in the American theatre, I realize how un-Jewish I have been. The only thing I have left for my support in my old age is the sale of various letters and privately printed copies which you have sent me from time to time. I have treasured them for sentimental reasons, but now you, with your characteristic money-making instinct, suggest that I sell them on the bull market. Thanks for the tip.

All joking aside, I shall be tremendously eager to read *Geneva* when it comes.

I imagine that the amazing proceeding of the last three weeks must have confirmed your views about the stupidity of democracies. There seems no doubt about the fact that you can only destroy Fascism with Fascism. Too bad, because I suppose, once they begin imprisoning the radicals in England, you will be led to the slaughter. However, there will always be a home for you over here with us, in "the land of the free."

As a result of this correspondence, GBS revised his play. Those who read the play in the revised versions (it was revised more than once) may wonder what all this pother is about. I advise them to look at the original printed proof sheets now in the Theatre Guild collection at the Yale Sterling Library in order to realize why I was so upset and angry.

We did not produce *Geneva,* even with the anti-Semitic speeches mostly omitted, for it seemed to us a dull conversation piece, despite the importance of the issues which it discussed but did not dramatize. Moreover, we did not wish to risk the financial sacrifices involved, especially after our losses on *The Simpleton.* Later on, Terry and I went to Canada to see it produced by Maurice Colbourne and Barry Jones. They wanted us to bring it to New York under our banner, but it did not impress us sufficiently to cause us to change our minds. However, Colbourne, Jones and Gilbert Miller took the chance. The play opened in New York on January 30, 1940, and met with the complete failure which we had anticipated, although it ran for several months in London.

Geneva in all its versions is an interminable debate full of unrelated diatribes against the state of the world, with the scale tipped toward the dictators, "the men who got things done," and against the democracies with their lack of social progress, their disorganization, their parliaments, and their poverty. It was silent on the subject of the poverty which existed (and still exists) in the dictatorships whose causes Shaw expounded so favorably.

The preface to *The Millionairess,* entitled Preface on Bosses and signed August 28, 1935, shows GBS's state of mind at the time *Geneva* was incubating more clearly than the actual preface to *Geneva* written in 1945, seven years after he sent the play to me. By this time both Hitler and Mussolini were dead. (*Geneva* was actually written in 1938, less than two years before the outbreak of World War II.)

It is interesting to note how GBS, misled by his worship of the Superman and disgusted with the fumblings of democracy, regarded Mussolini as an inspired hero in the year 1935. After explaining in the Preface to *The Millionairess* how Mussolini led the March on Rome with demobilized soldiers who "fell on the Syndicalists with sticks and stones. Some, more merciful, only dosed them with castor oil," Shaw goes on to say with admiration:

They carried Mussolini to Rome with a rush. . . . It seemed just the occasion for a grand appeal for liberty, for democracy, for a parliament in which the people were supreme: in short, for nineteenth century resurrection pie. Mussolini did not make that mistake. With inspired precision he denounced Liberty as a putrefying corpse. He declared that what people needed was not liberty but discipline, the sterner the better. He said that he would not tolerate Oppositions: he called for action and silence. The people, instead of being shocked like good Liberals, rose to him. He was able to organize a special constabulary who wore black shirts and applied the necessary coercion. . . .

Mussolini proved that parliaments have not the slightest notion of how the people are feeling, and that he, being a good psychologist and a man of the people himself to boot, was a true organ of democracy.

In the same Preface, Shaw expressed his admiration for Hitler, but he qualified it by taking a furious whack at his anti-Semitism:

Hitler was able to go further than Mussolini because he had a defeated, plundered, humiliated nation to rescue and restore, whereas Mussolini had only an irritated but victorious one. He carried out a persecution of the Jews which went to the scandalous length of outlawing, plundering, and exiling Albert Einstein, a much greater man than any politician, but greater in such a manner that he was quite above the heads of the masses and therefore so utterly powerless economically and militarily that he depended for his very existence on the culture and conscience of the rulers of the earth. Hitler's throwing Einstein to the Antisemite wolves was an appalling breach of cultural faith. . . . Now no doubt Jews are most obnoxious creatures. Any competent historian or psycho-analyst can bring a mass of incontrovertible evidence to prove that it would have been better for the world if the Jews had never existed. But I, as an Irishman, can, with patriotic relish, demonstrate the same of the English. Also of the Irish. If Herr Hitler would only consult the French and British newspapers and magazines of the latter half of 1914, he would learn that the Germans are a race of savage idolaters, murderers, liars, and fiends whose assumption of the human form is thinner than that of the wolf in Little Red Riding Hood.

We all live in glass houses. Is it wise to throw stones at the Jews? Is it wise to throw stones at all?

No one reading these lines will imagine that GBS had any sympathy for anti-Semitism. Had he known of the impending systematic slaughter of six million Jews from all over Europe at the behest of this mad fanatical dictator Hitler, he would have recoiled in horror from any admiration for him. As it was, after the defeat and deaths of Mussolini and Hitler, he wrote in 1945: "Contemplating the careers of these two poor devils one cannot help asking was their momentary grandeur worth while? . . . They were finally scrapped as failures and nuisances, though they all began by effecting some obvious reforms over which party parliaments had been boggling for centuries. Such successes as they had were reactions from the failures of the futile parliamentary talking shops." Poor devils, indeed! Worthwhile, indeed!

Here we see Shaw's dilemma as an old man clearly defined. To him parliaments were failures. He had invented the political Superman, with acknowledgments to Nietzsche and other German philosophers. But the brave new world of dictatorships under the "Supermen" Hitler and Mussolini were much more ghastly failures than the democracies, costing the world untold millions of its youth at a price we are still paying. Again Shaw was too decent, too kindly a man to approve the dictatorships of Moscow with their cruel Tcheka, MVD, etc., with their brainwashings, torture, slave camps in Siberia, firing squads and the rest of the apparatus for liquidating those who opposed the party line. So he invented in *The Simpleton* an Angel of Judgment to "liquidate" the useless people (the ladies and gentlemen, the nonworkers) by having them painlessly disappear, "fade out." But he continued to hero-worship Stalin. On his eighty-fifth birthday he stated, "When I met Stalin in 1931 I knew I was face to face with the greatest statesman in Europe. And the personal impression he made on me did not change my opinion." Had he lived long enough, could Shaw have been de-Stalinized by Khrushchev? I wonder.

GBS at the age of ninety, when he wrote the Preface to *Geneva*, was writing in a state of considerable confusion. Speaking of people's political ignorance and delusion which he felt was curable by simple instruction as to the facts without any increase in their political capacity, he went on to state, "I am ending as a sage with a very scrappy and partial knowledge of the world. I do not see why I should not have begun with it if I had been told it all to begin with: I was more capable of it then than I am now in my dotage."

But in spite of his "dotage," now and again the old old man speaks in a voice of inspired prophetic clarity. What greater indictment of the present-day "cold war" could be written than the words of the Judge of the World Court in *Geneva* (rewritten after the deaths of Hitler and Mussolini) as he castigates the two dictators Battler and Bombardone as scoundrels.

> Your objective is domination: your weapons fire and poison, starvation and ruin, extermination by every means known to science. You have reduced one another to such a condition of terror that no atrocity makes you recoil and say that you will die rather than commit it. You call this patriotism, courage, glory. There are a thousand good things to be done in your countries. They remain undone for hundreds of years; but the fire and the poison are always up to date. If this be not scoundrelism what is scoundrelism? I give you up as hopeless. Man is a failure as a political animal. The creative forces which produce him must produce something better.

Everything said above by Shaw now applies to Stalin according to Nikita Khrushchev. In hero-worshiping Stalin Shaw himself failed "as a political animal." It is only fair to realize that this was a repudiation, due to senility, of the social and political beliefs held for most of his life, which endeared him to so large a following throughout the civilized world. However, by this time his life-work, of such great value for the historical period in which he lived, as well as for future generations, was already completed—and completed magnificently.

CHAPTER ELEVEN

The Latter Days

I N 1938, Armina and I wrote a play which was partly suggested by Shaw's reference to the Oneida Community of Oneida, New York, in his Preface to *Man and Superman*.

We dedicated it to Mr. and Mrs. Shaw and were deeply touched by a sentence written by GBS at the end of a postcard acknowledging our dedication.

> We are dreadfully old, and forget everything; but we have not forgotten you.

Mrs. Shaw's health began to fail in the latter part of the thirties. The last time Armina and I saw her was on our visit to England for the London production of our play of the American Revolution *The Pursuit of Happiness*. We tried to take GBS with us to see a matinee, but he pleaded that he had read the play, which he found rather shocking; and that he now avoided the theatre as the plague. We learned through the newspapers of Mrs. Shaw's death at the end of the summer of 1943. Armina and I wrote GBS letters of sympathy, which he did not answer. Instead he sent us a beautiful photograph of Mrs. Shaw, as though words were meaningless on such an occasion.

Over a year after Mrs. Shaw's death, GBS wrote the story of her illness to his friend Molly Tompkins in the following touching words:

> I am a vecchio, nearly eighty eight and a half. I am also a widower. Charlotte died on the 12th September 1943. I was not in the least grieved; for she was only a year younger than I; and it was time for her to go; but I was deeply moved. Her four years illness threatened to have a dreadful end; but a miracle intervened: she suddenly became younger than I had ever seen her, and incredibly beautiful, she had thirty hours of ecstatic happiness before she ceased to breathe.

Few women attain their heart's desire to the extent that Charlotte Shaw did. Her chief ambition in life was to use her fortune to help a man of genius, and by her marriage to Shaw her income was the least contribution she made. Of far greater importance was her ability to make and maintain a home where GBS could work peacefully; her constant companionship and willingness to travel with him on all occasions, and especially during his declining years, on long voyages which gave him the privacy to write his later plays; and above all her sound common sense which was a counterbalance to his tendency to theorize on every and all subjects, and the inspiration which guided him to write two of his greatest plays, *The Doctor's Dilemma* and *Saint Joan.* I shall forever be grateful to her personally for helping me from time to time when I was having arguments with her illustrious husband, and also for encouraging me in my own work when moments of doubt were defeating me.

The story of Mrs. Shaw's funeral service was later recounted to Armina and me by someone who attended. Accompanied by Lady Astor and his faithful secretary, Miss Patch, Shaw drove to the service. He was silent and preoccupied. Then some of Mrs. Shaw's favorite music was played on the organ. After the resounding tones of Handel's *Largo* rang out, Shaw began to sing as though inspired, and his eyes shone and his voice sounded young and clear, his spirit soared as though he were singing to his beloved Charlotte, as though he felt that her presence was near him and she did not wish him to grieve for her. After this, purged of his grief, Shaw became himself again, and when he made some passing quip on his way home, Lady Astor remarked, "You really *are* a wicked old man!" When this story was told me, I remembered again Shaw's telling me that Saint Joan herself had guided his hand as he wrote his play about her. Behind the philosopher and the poet stood the mystic. Perhaps he felt that Charlotte Shaw was not really dead—but had merely passed over into another dimension of space in which they would meet again.

The February after her death, *The New York Times* published the following story about Mrs. Shaw's Will.

MRS. SHAW LEFT FUND TO TRAIN IRISH IN SOCIAL GRACES TO END "SHYNESS"

LONDON, Feb. 16—After forty-six years of married life with one of this generation's most famous Irishmen, the late Mrs. George Bernard Shaw, in a Will probated to-day, left $400,000 to teach the Irish the rudiments of so-cial conduct and to abolish from their lives the social de-fects of shyness and inarticulate conversation.

The first Irishman interviewed after the explosive pro-visions of the Will became known—her famous writer playwright husband himself—hastily denied he was a true Irishman, but the rest of Eire is yet to be heard from and London is awaiting the expected articulate reaction with heads bowed against the storm.

Mr. Shaw approved his wife's plans for the Irish in his characteristic forthright manner.

"You see, they need it," he said. "They get no training. They have no manners. They are ignorant."

When it was pointed out that Mr. Shaw himself was an Irishman, his quick Irish wit found an answer.

"I'm only an Irishman by birth," he protested. "Really, I'm a Londoner."

Mr. Shaw, who will be 88 next July, revealed that the will not begin until after his death.

campaign to teach the Irish confidence and self-expression

"That part of the Will doesn't come into operation un-til I am dead," he said. "Already a considerable number of people have written me from Ireland to get hold of it. They aren't going to get it."

One of the first organizations to make a public comment on the Will was the Workers' Educational Association, whose spokesman declared the real remedy would have been to offer workers a broader education instead of try-

ing to produce "courtiers who would mince before aristocracy."

Mr. Shaw had an Irish answer for the association.

"They want money like every other organization in the
country," he said. "Mr. Churchill's attitude is my attitude
—what I have I hold."

On February 18, after reading the above, I wrote GBS on
the subject, and I also reprimanded him (to no avail) for his
attitude about the production of his plays during the war.

> Thank you or Miss Patch, or both, for sending me the
> picture of Mrs. Shaw, which I will certainly treasure. It
> brought back some old memories and especially of the
> week we spent at Stresa. Going through some old papers
> I ran across some snapshots of you and her which I am en-
> closing.
>
> I see from the paper today that she has left a fund to
> train the Irish in some social graces. Most of the Irish I
> know have too many social graces, but there are certainly
> plenty that I do not know.
>
> Morris Ernst, the lawyer of the Dramatists Guild, is try-
> ing to work out something about your taxes. He may get
> in touch with you when he returns to London. We would
> certainly like to do some Shaw plays. The theatre needs
> them badly, and it is too bad that your congregation—
> after supporting you for many years—and now that we
> need your works in the theatre, we cannot produce them
> because of this curious position you have taken. I find my-
> self in just the same boat that you are in—practically ev-
> erything I earn is taken by the Government, but do I
> stop working? Not a bit of it! The people need the thea-
> tre in wartime and whether you or I made the war has
> nothing to do with the question. These audiences sup-
> ported us when we needed them. We should support them
> now they need us.

I received no reply to the above, and some years were to
elapse before I actually *saw* GBS again, although we continued
to correspond.

During the latter part of the thirties, Armina and I completed our play entitled *Suzanna and the Elders* on the subject
of Communism and the Oneida Community, to which our at-

tention had been drawn by Shaw's reference to the socialist experiment in his Preface to *Man and Superman*. As Father
Noyes, the founder of the community, had many theories in
common with GBS, I suggested that GBS was a reincarnation
of Noyes, and we asked him if he would like to read the play.
I received a reply postcard in GBS's handwriting:

> I am interested in Oneida and have talked to and cor-
> responded with some of the survivors and with that hard-
> bitten capitalist-employer who was the result of the at-
> tempt to produce another Noyes.
>
> But the incarnation theory seems to us quite the mad-
> dest of even your notions.
>
> However, send the play along: we are always delighted
> to hear from you on any excuse.

After the play opened and closed in New York, we sent a
printed copy of it, published by Random House, with the dedication to Mr. and Mrs. Shaw. And I hope one day to see it revived. It is an actual fact that after the lashing we took from
the New York critics, and the failure of this play, our second
in succession, we gave up writing plays for New York City, a
decision which I now regret, and which goes absolutely counter
to the advice I have given so often to other writers from time
to time. Thereafter my plays were given in Westport only,
without any attempt to bring them to New York.

After Mrs. Shaw's death, GBS spent considerably more time
at Ayot St. Lawrence, near his bibliographer, F. E. Loewenstein. Miss Patch, at a visit we had with her in London, was
somewhat caustic about the goings on at Ayot St. Lawrence,
"Mrs. Shaw wouldn't have given half these hangers-on house
room," she once remarked. Shaw was busily engaged in putting
his papers together in preparation for his death and worked
just as hard on his writing as he did while she was alive. In
the seven years which elapsed after her death, on all occasions
when we saw him, he never once referred to her, and we did
not discuss her.

On July 26, 1946, Shaw was ninety years old and in full
possession of his faculties. What a magnificent old man! We cabled him our birthday greetings as follows:

> Your statue is in our lobby and your memory is in our
> hearts. Love and happy birthday. Terry, Lawrence and
> Armina.

When my autobiography *The Magic Curtain* began to reach completion, I asked GBS if I might have permission to publish some stories about him and I sent him some chapters for him to read over. In replying, he stated:

> I can neither permit nor prevent the publication of books about myself. You must act of your own responsibility without asking my leave or anyone else's. Why should I grudge you that freedom?
>
> But I implore you not to describe me as a "lovable human being." It will bring a million begging letters on me by the next post. Rather present me as detestable, avaricious, merciless, contemptuous, and everything else odious enough to discourage people from writing to me. Otherwise you may hasten my already imminent death.

GBS was also good enough to say that he would pose for some pictures for the book, and his friend Mr. Loewenstein took these on some film I sent him. I particularly like one in which Shaw posed, pen in hand, with furrowed brow, to show what the Genius looked like when he was working. These pictures were taken when he was in his ninety-second year.

During January, 1947, when Theresa Helburn and I were in London, we decided to call on GBS. I saw Miss Patch who made the appointment with him and gave us printed instructions on a card as to how to reach Ayot St. Lawrence.

The following day Terry and I hired a limousine and as we settled down in our car, we studied the printed directions which Shaw himself had written, showing us how to reach his country home. Only a playwright could have written such directions, and only a stage manager could have followed them.

Driving through the snow we read, "The lane twists about and rises and dips and rises again. At the top of the second rise, at a signpost marked 'to Welwyn,' bear left into village of Ayot St. Lawrence. Drive through it past the ruined church; and at the end, where the road divides, Bernard Shaw's gate is facing you in the angle." Our chauffeur was no stage manager, and it is not surprising that we got lost several times in the snow. We finally arrived at the ruins of the church and descended from our car at Bernard Shaw's gate, fully expecting to meet the ruins not only of a church but also of a playwright. As we drove toward the Elizabethan village of Ayot St. Lawrence, my memory strayed back to the first time I had seen

GBS when I was a boy of fifteen, lecturing at the Fabian Society on "The Position of the Artist under Socialism." Here I was in England in 1947, and if England was not exactly under Socialism, at least Socialism was under way, and here was GBS enjoying the income of a capitalistic millionaire. It would be interesting to see what had happened to him.

We walked through the snow to the porch of Shaw's red brick house, and the door was opened by a bored-looking housekeeper who had doubtless let in many boring callers during the past twenty years. She showed us into a comfortable little sitting room with four large chairs drawn up in front of a glowing coal fire. Around the room there was a good deal of bric-a-brac, a model of a small break-front desk, and a Chinese scroll on the wall. Theresa and I sat in front of the fire and thawed out until GBS appeared and greeted us. He was no longer the tall, handsome white-bearded figure I had once known, but resembled a Chinese philosopher or sage carved out of yellowing ivory, for his hair was streaked with yellow and his beard was shorter and irregular, as though he had bitten it off around the edges. I thought of Jacques' speech on the Seven Ages of Man in Shakespeare's *As You Like It*. At sixty-five Shaw had resembled "The justice . . . with eyes severe and beard of formal cut, full of wise saws and modern instances." As a vegetarian, however, he was lacking "the fat round belly with good capon lined." A lining of good vegetables, no matter how filling, can never produce the effect of a lining of good capon.

Shaw at the age of ninety-one was still in the sixth age of man, wearing gray plus-fours in which he looked indeed "the lean and slipper'd pantaloon," and he walked, acted and thought like a man in his early seventies. "How are you feeling?" I asked. "My legs are letting me down," he said, "but otherwise I am perfectly well." He motioned us to be seated and sat in the large armchair at the side of the comforting fire. Then he put us at ease by discussing the English winter weather. Terry mentioned that she was going to Edinburgh with S. N. Behrman's play *Jane* and that she dreaded the cold. "You should go a lot further north to the Orkneys," said GBS, allowing his imagination to run riot. "You will find a subtropical climate there due to the Gulf Stream which will astonish you," and he described a kind of island paradise where the winter warmth is so great that large fuchsia trees grow and bloom outdoors. "Why don't they make the Orkneys into a winter resort?"

Shaw before his fireplace

Shaw at the door of his cabin workshop at Ayot St. Lawrence

Three views of Shaw in his workshop

George Bernard and Charlotte Shaw
Shaw greets Lawrence Langner in June, 1950, a few months before GBS's death

The Westport Country Playhouse, where numerous Shaw plays were produced (*above*)
The recently refurbished Playhouse, ready for the projected Shaw Festival

Jessie Royce Landis as she appeared in *The Millionairess* at Westport, the first production of the play in the United States or England

Dolores Grey in the Westport production of Pygmalion *(above)*

Vanessa Brown and Tom Helmore in *The Philanderer* at the Westport Playhouse

Celeste Holm and James Daly as Adam and Eve in the abridged version of *Back to Methuselah,* presented at Westport

Terry asked me on the way home. "GBS was probably romancing," I replied. "He still loves to discover something different from everybody else."

"What are you doing these days?" asked Terry. "I am being quite busy," said GBS. "First of all I am writing a new play for the Malvern Festival. There will be some plot and a good deal of conversation. I don't get so many new ideas now. After I had finished writing the play, I found that several of the things I had written had already appeared in some of my other plays. You know," he said, as though he was quite surprised at the fact, "it's rather hard to get new ideas at ninety. I rewrote the play and took out everything I had said before and now it's in fine shape." I asked if we might do it in New York after the Malvern production. "Certainly," he replied, "if you want to! It's called *The Unfinished Comedy.*" (Later the play was retitled *Buoyant Billions.*)

Talking of world issues, Shaw didn't think it mattered very much whether every nation shared the secret of the atomic bomb. "One thing ought to be self-evident to everybody," he said. "None of the peoples throughout the world want to destroy themselves. Indeed," he said, "from one point of view it's too bad the Japanese didn't appeal to the conscience of the world after the atom bomb was used at Hiroshima. I think the conscience of the world would have stopped the United States from using any more of these bombs, just as the conscience of the world stopped the use of poison gas." I told GBS I knew the use of poison gas had been stopped, not because of the conscience of the world, but because everybody had plenty of it. However, he stood his ground as usual.

At about this time the housekeeper, no longer bored, entertained us with a tea tray and an appetizing assortment of cakes. Terry presided over the pouring and offered GBS a cup of tea. "No tea for Mr. Shaw," said the housekeeper sharply. "Mr. Shaw drinks this." And she handed him a glass of greenish-looking fluid which smelled like stewed acorn juice and which may have been the elixir of life for all I know.

Glass in hand, Shaw smiled benignly at us, and sipped his vegetable juice from time to time. "How is the theatre in America?" he asked. We told him our problems and how mounting costs were making it increasingly difficult to take chances on experimental or noncommercial plays. "I see," he said with a smile. "You are caught between the cruel landlord and the *re-*

lentless playwright." As we had hoped to persuade GBS that his royalties, the highest in the world, ought to be reduced somewhat, I winced at the way he pronounced the word "relentless." "The theatre is not merely up against the landlord and the relentless author, but rising salaries as well," said Terry. "I agree with you," said GBS, and for a moment I thought, "Aha! Being a capitalist millionaire has taught him something." "The actors are overpaid," he said, "and it's entirely unnecessary. They would all be willing to work for less." And he instanced how Miss Gertrude Kingston told him that she had to ask a West End Manager forty pounds a week in order that she might get a good dressing room, for they had a habit of putting the inexpensive actors on the upper floors. However, she was willing to work for a third of that amount with Vendrenne and Barker because she was on a yearly (repertory) contract and could count on work all the year round. "Until you get the theatre on that basis, you'll have to overpay," he added. "As to myself, I am now a classic. Of course I have to have my royalties, but if the royalty is only nine pence, why, I touch my hat and say 'thank you.'" "How can anyone put on one of your plays and pay only nine pence royalty?" I asked. "Oh, some village amateur dramatic group," he replied. "They do the classics."

We expounded the theory that since it costs at least fifteen thousand dollars a week to operate one of Shaw's plays, his royalty of 15 per cent was too high. "I'll make you a proposition," said GBS; "I'll give you my plays royalty free up to fifteen thousand dollars." Our faces lit up happily, but only momentarily. "Any receipts over that I'll take half—and of course," he added, "you'll have to play in a very large theatre." A rough calculation showed that GBS would gain considerably more on this basis than before, so we said, "No, thank you. We'd rather pay the fifteen per cent." As a capitalist millionaire, GBS hadn't changed so very much, I thought.

We talked happily of many more things until it was time to leave. "We'll be back here soon with *Oklahoma!,*" said Terry cheerfully, as we put on our coats in the hall, "and you'll have to come to see it." "No," said GBS rather sadly, "I'm afraid I won't. I've lost all interest in the theatre, and I'm not much interested in anything else either."

He insisted on coming out of the front door to see us off. The snow was all around us as he stood outside the door, the light falling on his bare head and hair and giving him a translucent quality, almost saintly, like a halo. "I'm afraid you'll take cold," I called. "Nonsense," he said as he stood there, a friendly smile on his face. "Thanks for coming," and he waved good-bye, smiling his charming old smile.

On our way back Theresa said that she thought he must lead a lonely life so far out in the country. I said I didn't think so —that I felt the key to his character was to be found in the Preface to *Man and Superman,* in which he wrote that there are no passions like the passions of the mind. I thought that GBS had indulged this passion all his life, and that as he grew older he had more chance to indulge it, and that with it he would never be lonely. He showed no symptoms of tiring, although our visit lasted nearly two hours.

In May of 1947, Armina and I visited Ayot St. Lawrence with Gabriel Pascal. We did not have much time alone with GBS, but we discussed the possibility of presenting *The Devil's Disciple* and *Heartbreak House,* which he gave us permission to produce. He asked us to continue looking after the amateur and stock rights of his plays, which at his request we had handled for him in the United States for over twenty-five years. "From a business standpoint you must now consider me as dead," he remarked with great vitality.

GBS then took us for a walk through his grounds and showed us the little cabin where he wrote his plays. Although he complained about his legs giving way under him, he opened the French windows, and without an overcoat, despite the coldness of the weather, walked us down a little hill, on one side of which stood a statue of St. Joan which he had recently purchased from a lady sculptor living in the village. The walk to his cabin took several minutes, and when we arrived there, we looked through the windows into the interior. The small, low shed in which he had written so many of his plays was entirely plain and without character, furnished with a couch-bed, a table and papers untidily scattered around. GBS assured me that although over ninety-one, he continued to work in this cabin each day, writing articles or working on contracts for motion pictures and other rights, which he worked out in his meticulous Pitman's shorthand and sent to London for his secretary Miss Patch to type. He very seldom visited London, however, where Miss Patch conducted her office in his apartment in Whitehall Court.

During the summer of 1950, my wife Armina and I were in London for the opening of our English production of Rodgers and Hammerstein's *Carousel* and we asked GBS if we might visit him. The answer came back on the usual postcard, telling us to come but that he had been ill with lumbago. This was destined to be our last visit.

We arrived in Ayot St. Lawrence in the late afternoon, and soon after, GBS came into the room, looking frail and bent over, and walking with the aid of a stick. "Don't talk such nonsense," he replied to my remark that I thought he looked well. "I am decaying and disintegrating. I am not the man who wrote those plays." We sat and talked to him for a while, and he seemed gentler and more contemplative than ever before. In the course of our conversation he remarked, "Lawrence, I have told you several times now, you must regard me as being officially dead. I have made all arrangements so that my business affairs will proceed just as though I *were* dead." "But, GBS," I replied, "whenever we want to do a play of yours, we still ask your permission, even though the Guild and the Westport Country Playhouse have produced over twenty of your plays." He answered in tones which sounded rather virile for one officially dead. "What, *only* twenty?" "Yes," I replied, "that's more than any other management has ever produced." By this time GBS was coming to life rapidly. "I've written fifty," he said with a smile. "Why don't you do the other thirty?"

As previously related, we then asked GBS's permission to produce *The Millionairess* with Katharine Hepburn, in accordance with his suggestion made some years earlier.

He explained that he would never permit his plays to be done on television or in cut versions on the radio, and when Armina remarked that cut versions of Shakespeare had been done successfully on radio, his eyes twinkled as he remarked, "My dear girl, it's bad enough to do that to Shakespeare, but it's sacrilege to cut Shaw!" I told him that I had brought a movie camera along to take a picture in place of the one which Pascal had muffed. "Come outside," he said. "If it's a movie camera, it calls for a director. Now you, Armina, will take a picture of the door to stimulate the interest of the audience. Then, after a moment of suspense, the door will open and I will come out. Then I will sit in my chair, Lawrence will come around the corner and I will rise and greet him cordially." GBS acted out the picture as planned, but when it came time for him to rise from his chair and greet me, the ninety-four-year-old actor was somewhat less than sprightly. I shall always cherish this picture, and the one that follows it. "I think I'd better not see you off," he remarked, and I remembered his old custom of walking down the driveway to wave us good-bye. My last picture of him standing by the roadside endeavoring to draw his bentover body into the erect position in which he had always held himself, while he smiled and waved to us, brought tears to my eyes. Two months later he was dead. There will never be another of his ilk in our time.

During the past forty years, the Theatre Guild presented more of Shaw's plays than any other management (seventeen), while the Westport Country Playhouse has presented eight. On balance, our relationship earned as much for GBS as it had cost the Theatre Guild. But our presentation of his plays to American audiences gained us a following which benefited all the other writers whose plays we produced during this period. But more than that, we counted his plays among the most precious contributions to the modern theatre, and in presenting them, we fulfilled one of our best reasons for existing.

I felt singularly ungrieved at GBS's passing, when I learned the news of his death, because I knew how much he had wanted to die. I knew he felt that he had outlived his own brain and body when he remarked to me, "Lawrence, I am not the man who wrote those plays," and he did not want to outlive that man. That man was a leader of our generation all over the world—in the theatre and out of it—and that man knew his days were over. The theatre has been very fortunate in the fact that some of the great geniuses of the world have written for it. One of these was Shakespeare, another was Shaw. The fact that Shaw was a great reformer, philosopher, thinker, and humorist —that fact that he used the theatre as his medium of expression, has made the theatre a greater place for his being in it, and it is a lesser place for his passing.

After we learned of Shaw's death, I suggested that the Theatre Guild sponsor a Memorial Service dedicated to his memory. This took place on November 19, 1950, at the old Guild Theatre (now ANTA Playhouse). Before the ceremony I received a telegram from Maurice Evans who had revived several of Shaw's plays, reading as follows:

IF IT HAD BEEN POSSIBLE FOR ME TO BE IN THE
AUDIENCE OR ON YOUR STAGE TODAY THERE WOULD
BE ONLY ONE THOUGHT IN MY MIND, THE HOPE THAT
LAUGHTER WOULD BE THE KEYNOTE OF THIS MEMO-
RIAL PERFORMANCE STOP SHAW WAS A MERRY MAN
AND THE TRIBUTE WHICH WOULD PLEASE HIM MOST
WOULD BE YOUR MERRIMENT RATHER THAN YOUR
TEARS.

The ceremony took place under the joint auspices of the Theatre Guild and the American National Theatre and Academy.
Warren Caro, our Executive Secretary, was in charge of the affair for the Theatre Guild and acted as master of ceremonies.
The speakers made the occasion one of high celebration that
the theatre had been blessed with so distinguished a genius, in-
termingled with grief at his passing.

The New York Times reported the proceedings in the following words by J. P. Shanley:

> With little solemnity, but much warm feeling, the the-
> atre paid tribute here yesterday to the late George Ber-
> nard Shaw.
>
> The scene of the memorial service for the author and
> playwright who died on Nov. 2 at his home in Ayot St.
> Lawrence, England, at the age of 94, was the ANTA
> (American National Theatre and Academy) Playhouse,
> 245 West Fifty-second Street.
>
> It was an appropriate setting. As the Guild Theatre, a
> title it retained until it was taken over this year by ANTA,
> the playhouse opened a quarter of a century ago, on April
> 13, 1925, with the presentation of Shaw's "Caesar and
> Cleopatra." Lionel Atwill and Helen Hayes were in the ti-
> tle roles.
>
> Burgess Meredith, who played a scene from "Candida"
> at yesterday's observance, with Peggy Wood and Walter
> Abel, delivered a brief preface to the presentation which
> was in keeping with the spirit of most of the one-and-three-
> quarter hours tribute.
>
> "We're doing two things contrary to the master's
> wishes," he declared. "First, we're doing this for nothing;
> the other thing we're doing is cutting it."
>
> John Chapman, drama critic of The Daily News and
> President of the New York Drama Critics Circle, said that

yesterday's observance was "not a memorial to Mr. Shaw's body but a celebration of his spirit."

Other participants in the program were Clarence Derwent, president of Actors Equity Association; Arthur Schwartz, President of the League of New York Theatres; Sir Cedric Hardwicke; Theresa Helburn, co-director of the Theatre Guild; Melville Cooper and Warren Caro, executive secretary of the Theatre Guild, who presided.

In my opinion, the best parts of the service were Shaw's own words, for at the conclusion Peggy Wood, Burgess Meredith and Walter Abel played the last scene from *Candida;* John Gielgud read the "Statement of Faith" of Dubedat from *The Doctor's Dilemma,* and Katharine Cornell, with a sweep of emotion which carried the audience along with her, read the great speech of Saint Joan and ended the Memorial with the ringing words, so applicable to Shaw himself, "O God that madest this beautiful earth, when will it be ready to receive Thy saints? How long, O Lord, how long?"

Unfortunately, in writing an account of Shaw's Memorial Service for *The Magic Curtain,* I forgot to mention the fine tribute paid to him by the late Esmé Percy who had played in many of Shaw's plays in London and directed even more. I hope I can undo an injustice to his memory by printing part of his letter to me of June 21, 1952.

There was just one thorn in my flesh and that is that my name should have been omitted from the list of actors who took part in the Theatre Guild Memorial celebration to GBS. If I am to judge by the tremendous reception which my rendering of the *Diet* speech from Shaw's latest play received, and the personal congratulations I received (yours among them) I conclude that my contribution was worthy of the occasion and of my reputation as a Shavian actor—indeed, as an actor it was my proudest moment in my last visit to U.S.A. Oh drat! All this must read as intolerably vain, but to be mentioned in such books as yours, is the only means of an actor to be remembered by posterity—*Vanitas Vanitatum* it may be, but there you are! . . . Forgive this tedious rigmarole of a letter, but I feel you will understand and therefore forgive or at least excuse, though GBS in a more impish mood declared that to understand everything was to forgive nothing!

Nearly fifteen years have elapsed since Shaw died, but his voice has not been silenced. He has more to say about the world of the future than most of the *avant-garde* writers of today who are muddying the theatre of England and America with their peculiar obsessions.

I end this chapter on two of Shaw's aphorisms from his Preface on Doctors (*The Doctor's Dilemma*), which apply particularly to himself:

Use your health, even to the point of wearing it out. That is what it is for. Spend all you have before you die; and do not outlive yourself.

Do not try to live for ever. You will not succeed.

Part Two

CHAPTER TWELVE

Shaw as a Businessman

SHAW died leaving one of the largest fortunes ever amassed by a writer. This amounted to the sum of £367,233 (about $1,222,000) before taxes. This was due to his ability not only as a writer but also as a businessman. He employed no play agents and printed his own books, his publishers working for him instead of *vice versa*. Every time he had a difference of opinion with us on a business matter, he almost invariably turned out to be right.

GBS had no false modesty about himself. He regarded himself as an excellent businessman, and in this respect he was entirely correct. Despite his socialistic convictions, and perhaps because of them, he loved the possession of money, not for hoarding purposes as a miser does, but because he placed a high value on himself and expected everyone else to do the same. He was paid the highest royalties of any author in England and the United States during his latter years, and he was generally adamant in refusing to reduce them, even if this meant closing a play. According to his biographer, Archibald Henderson, his friend Lady Astor once wittily observed, "More than any Socialist I have ever known, Shaw is obsessed with concern for private property—particularly his own."

The late Maurice Wertheim, one of the Guild's directors and its financial genius, once prepared a detailed balance sheet showing how the high Shaw royalties made it impossible for the Guild to make any profit out of his plays. When I showed Shaw Wertheim's figures, he barely glanced at them. "I remember seeing a balance sheet like this," said Shaw, "prepared by the Shuberts in connection with Forbes-Robertson's production of *Caesar and Cleopatra*. It came to me along with a letter saying they couldn't possibly keep the play running in New York at the Shubert Theatre unless I reduced my royalties. I refused, and the play ran for several months longer!" I admitted we would continue to present his plays, even though we lost on them, and the matter was dropped. We did this, not because we liked losing on his plays, but because of our admiration for him. Besides, our subscription audiences constituted a Shaw congregation, and in the halcyon days of the theatre in the twenties we were usually able to make up our losses on Shaw from the profits of other plays.

Shaw's customary royalty was a sliding scale which usually amounted to 15 per cent of the box office receipts; however, he charged amateur theatrical societies, repertory companies and other less commercial forms of theatre at the rate of so much per performance. Indeed, he was so proud of his royalty scale that he was blind to the fact that throughout his lifetime, institutions such as the Theatre Guild were seldom able to pay their way by producing his plays. While GBS had earned about $350,000 in royalties from the Guild, the Guild in turn had lost about the same amount in the production of his plays. On one occasion GBS remarked to me that the Guild had kept him out of bankruptcy and this was probably true of the period when we were producing *Heartbreak House, Back to Methuselah* and *Saint Joan*.

Lest there be any doubt of Shaw's keen interest in money, and the basis for this on a dignified level, GBS expressed himself strongly on the subject in the Preface to *Major Barbara* in the following words: "The universal regard for money is the one hopeful fact in our civilization, the one sound spot in our social conscience. Money is the most important thing in the world. It represents health, strength, honor, generosity and beauty as conspicuously and undeniably as the want of it represents illness, weakness, disgrace, meanness and ugliness. Not the least of its virtues is that it destroys base people as certainly as it fortifies and dignifies noble people."

"Money is the most important thing in the world," he wrote with conviction, and this did not prevent him from advocating that everyone should receive the same income in *The Intelligent Woman's Guide to Socialism and Capitalism.* I have always found it difficult to reconcile Shaw's love of money and his driving an excessively hard bargain with those who produced his plays with his professed Fabian Socialism and his outspoken admiration for Soviet Russia in his later years. However, consistency is the mark of little men, and GBS was on the side of the angels in wishing to see all men become equally well off, something which appears to be impossible under either Communism or capitalism.

On one occasion during the early days of the British Labour government and the welfare state, while I was visiting him at Ayot St. Lawrence, I asked him, "How does it feel to live under Socialism?" "Good heavens," he replied, "we are not living under Socialism here, but under Trade Unionism." What an apt name for our present society, I thought, remembering the trade unionism in the American theatre, which is rapidly driving good plays and good management out of business. Later on an old friend of mine, who had given up producing plays in this country in disgust, remarked to me, "Don't irritate me by referring to the economic system under which we live in the United States as 'free enterprise' when the theatre is dominated by no less than fourteen labor unions, each of which becomes more unreasonable and dictatorial as the years roll on."

Shaw's business ability is well illustrated by the following letter dated 26th April 1923 in the early days of the Guild's activities:

> Your telegram announcing the apparent success of the D's D. has just arrived. But I believe nothing but box office returns. Caesar is quite another pair of shoes. It needs a classic actor: you can find ten Dicks and fifty Bluntschlis more easily than one Caesar. However, I am all for it if the man can be found.
>
> Have you ever thought of the Don Juan in Hell scene from *Man & Superman* as a separate show? At the Court Theatre here years ago, with wonderful dresses by Ricketts against a dead black stage, it was unexpectedly successful in holding the audience.

The above paragraphs show GBS in the guise of a theatrical manager and salesman for two of his plays. Shaw wrote, "I believe nothing but box office returns" in evaluating the success of a play. This is a cold-blooded, hard-boiled businessman speaking. Our failure to find "a classic star actor" for our revival of *Caesar and Cleopatra* was a large contributing factor toward its early demise. To Shaw was also due Paul Gregory's all-star production of the long *Don Juan in Hell* scene from *Man and Superman,* with the famous actors Charles Laughton, Agnes Moorehead, Charles Boyer and Cedric Hardwicke which toured the entire United States, north, south, east and west, with probably less than 25 per cent of the audiences understanding what Shaw was driving at. The public paid to see this well-known group of actors and to hear them enunciate Shaw's beautiful rhythmic prose. For a man who believed in "nothing but box office returns" it must be counted a great success, and others are recommended to produce it again from time to time in the future, remembering that when it was performed originally in the Court Theatre in London it was *"unexpectedly* successful in holding the audience."

Shaw properly complained about his heavy taxes and for several years refused to have his plays presented because of them. Indeed, our American actors and writers are taxed so heavily that many of them are forced to leave the USA and work abroad in order to be in a position to save enough to live in comfort in their old age. As I write these lines, the Hollywood technical unions are flocking to Washington to impress upon Congress that these writers and actors should be hauled back to the United States in order that our overpaid stagehands and technicians can batten off their talents while they are being strangled by income tax laws which make it impossible for them to put away in their prosperous years sufficient funds to support them in their lean years. And the Congress of the United States has consistently ignored encouraging the writers, actors and artists of America, as it has the inventors of America. In this connection the National Inventors' Council, of which I was the founder and Executive Secretary for over twenty years, has never been able to promote passage through Congress of a simple bill by which the government will be required to pay for the inventions it appropriates. No wonder the Russians are overcoming our inventive lead, and even gaining on us!

GBS was understandably concerned about the income taxes which operated so unfairly when they took most of his earnings in his good years and gave him nothing back in his bad years. When I wrote GBS on October 24, 1941, suggesting revivals of some of his plays, I received the following answer:

> William Brady also wants to revive *You Never Can Tell* with a magnificent cast; but I am sufficiently ruined already by Katharine Cornell's revival of *The Doctor's Dilemma* and the *Pygmalion* film with royalties taxed 27% in the States and 95% here. I shall have to let Gabriel Pascal film *Arms and the Man* to keep him alive; but that is all for the duration (of the war) : I may die at any moment now; and what is to become of all the people provided for in my will if my property is swallowed up by this infernal way? Don't mention another production to me unless you can guarantee a flop worse than *The Apple Cart* or *The Unexpected Isles*. However, I rejoice in the recovery of the Guild from its phase of apparent slow extinction. It sounds more like its old self now.

Writing again later on for permission to revive one of his plays, I received the following postcard dated February 3, 1942:

> The war taxation forces me to ration revivals of my plays very drastically. But to throw away a good revival is as bad for the Guild as for me, or nearly so; as I presume the profits are taxed pretty heavily. Anyhow I am out of business until I can *reduce* my income to a point at which it becomes possible to live on it.

In my reply I stated:

> . . . Thanks for the information about the taxes. The reason why the Theatre Guild wants to put on your plays is not to make profits—we cannot do that, nor have we been very successful as profit makers—it is because of the lack of plays and the great need of the public for comedies. You force us back to Shakespeare and Molière. It is so long since the Guild made profits that we are not worrying about the taxes on them.
>
> Nobody can tell me that you are out of business—especially yourself!

It is interesting to note that my letter was written while we were in rehearsal with *Oklahoma!* and my reference to profits shows clearly my state of mind at the time. This musical play ultimately earned over $3,600,000, probably a record for any musical play, except *My Fair Lady,* although most of it, thanks to the supertax, went to the United States government.

Unlike most other authors, GBS refused to sell his motion-picture rights along with the first production of his plays. It was lucky for him and his estate that this was so. By holding on to all his subsidiary rights, he had a large income in his old age which enabled him to live in his accustomed style, in spite of the fact that most of his new plays, written and produced in his lifetime after *The Apple Cart,* were neither artistically nor financially successful in this country, with the exception of *The Millionairess.* Indeed, most of these later plays (again excepting *The Millionairess*) were produced for prestige rather than for their intrinsic merit. But an author who can keep up his best work until over the age of eighty is a rarity; indeed, almost unheard of.

When we were visiting the Shaws at Stresa, GBS one day gave me his opinion on what should be considered the correct attitude for a writer on selling plays. "Never wait to sell a play," he said. "As soon as possible after the first play is written, begin the next." This attitude was successful in his own case, for by the time he sold his first play he had several more ready for production. He also remarked, "Every young playwright should remember that one out of every three plays written by Shakespeare was a failure." How often I have cited these two remarks to talented writers who had stopped writing because they had not sold their last play. Under present-day theatrical economics, Shaw's advice is increasingly apt, as production becomes increasingly difficult to achieve.

"Build up your copyrights," was Shaw's invariable advice to young writers. They sustained him in his old age and proved that writers as a rule do far better by retaining their copyrights than by working on a motion-picture salary, no matter how large.

I once asked GBS for his opinion of play agents. He never used them himself and was negative as to their value. He stated, "I remember watching an auctioneer selling watches at a country fair. He never took long in making a sale, even if he sold some at a loss. It did not pay him to spend more than a certain time on each watch, as he could do better by selling in quantity. The play agents use the same technique. They cannot afford to spend more than a certain time on selling each play. If it is hard to sell, they prefer to work on the ones which are easy to sell." Of course this was before the days when agents acted as business managers, tax advisors, psychiatrists and investment counsel to their stables of authors and actors.

Shaw's almost savage retaliation against unauthorized productions of his copyrighted plays is illustrated in the following correspondence. One such production, by a manager who shall be nameless, was about to be made of *Arms and the Man.* When Shaw heard of it, he wrote me as follows on December 2, 1947:

> I never sell nor assign my copyrights. I deal solely in licenses. I am bound by written contracts only, not by alleged promises and so-called gentleman's agreements.
>
> Reputable travelling repertory companies can obtain licenses to play in repertory my pieces on the road as they can play Shakespeare's, on condition however, that they publish no claim to hold any rights or an exclusive license, *and specially that their license does not empower them to revive the play in New York or elsewhere for a run.*
>
> I hereby authorize the Theatre Guild, acting as my agent as it has done for years past, to require Mr.———— to produce and exhibit the contract under which he claims (if he has claimed) to have any authority to revive *Arms and the Man* on Broadway or elsewhere.
>
> This had better be done through a lawyer. Mine is Benjamin H. Stern, of Stern and Reubens, 7 East 45th Street.
>
> If Mr. ———— should prove obdurate we must proceed for an injunction.

I called up the manager who had announced the play and read him the letter over the telephone. Needless to say, the production was called off.

When Shaw was in his eighties, he turned over the administration of his plays to the British Society of Authors and the British Public Trustee. In 1946, he issued a set of iron-clad business rules in which he set forth his demands with all the finality of a dictator. "No rights may be assigned," he thundered, "nor sold nor alienated from the estate under any circumstances." And he added, "Procedure must be by license only; and no licenses should be granted for longer than five years." Shaw's love of business detail and his attitude toward what he called "parasitic intervention" is shown in the following paragraph taken from his instructions:

> Licenses should be non-negotiable and non-transferable, and agencies should be withdrawn if sublet. Every possible step should be taken to prevent parasitic intervention between those who actually perform the services delegated and the Author.

His hand reached out after death and pointed out the hard path the motion-picture companies would have to travel in order to produce pictures made from his plays:

> Film agreements should be between the responsible financing company and the Author, with, if necessary, clauses making employment in the production of named individuals of the essence of the contract, but in no case making these individuals parties to the agreement. With such clauses to protect them they can make their own contracts.

He was not too happy about the foreign translations of his plays in the latter part of his life, so he decided:

> In the case of foreign licenses the Author's license must not undersell the earnings of the most highly paid native authors, and should exceed them where the latter is a sweated profession according to English standards.
>
> Foreign agents should not be authorized to operate beyond the political frontiers of the State in which they are resident except in cases where the language is the same as in Brazil and Portugal, European Spain and the Argentine. The rule should be for one language one agent and one translation only; and in choosing between States regard should be had to the severity or liberality of their censorship.

Despite Shaw's arrangements with the British Society of Authors, and the excellent work done by Elizabeth Barber and her staff, Shaw could never quite give up the supervision of his business affairs, even in his nineties. Possibly this gave him some occupation which was welcome, despite his frequent grumbling about being overwhelmed with work. Even after his creative writing was ended, his creative business sense continued as exemplified by his will, which he constantly changed as one legatee after another died before him. The final outcome of this kept hordes of lawyers active for years, and some of the results are as ironic as the third act of a Shaw comedy.

In looking over my files, I find the following cable from Shaw, dated April 12, 1949, in reply to a suggestion which I cannot trace to publish an extract of dialogue from one of his plays:

MOST CERTAINLY NOT, IT WOULD KILL THE PLAY DEAD. NOT A LINE OF IT MUST BE ACCESSIBLE EXCEPT BY A VISIT TO THE THEATRE.

Brother playwrights, please note!

CHAPTER THIRTEEN

Shaw's Personal and Business Relations with the Theatre Guild

IN ALL our dealings with Bernard Shaw after our first legally executed contract on *Heartbreak House,* we had no contract with him other than an understanding in the form of a letter. It was a one-sided arrangement, for he promised us the first refusal of his plays, while we on our part did not guarantee to produce them. That it resulted in the production of more than twenty-five of Shaw's plays by The Theatre Guild and the Westport Country Playhouse shows that this relationship of mutual trust certainly did not hurt the author.

During my annual trips to Europe to visit my London office, I always called on the Shaws. It was my desire that the Guild should cement our relationship with him, and I tried in vain to have this set forth in writing. Notwithstanding the fact that The Theatre Guild had produced so many plays by Shaw, the only agreement we had with GBS, other than the original *Heartbreak House* document, was the following, written on a half sheet of notepaper dated June 14, 1922, in reply to a letter of mine asking for a contract to produce his other plays on the same terms as *Heartbreak House.*

Yes: your letter of the 12th correctly summarized our understanding except that though I have stood out for a minimum payment of $2500 win, lose or draw I have never asked for an advance, or been in a hurry for a contract. Of course I have no objection to either; but I wish to affirm that it is the Guild and not the Author that gets these attacks of nerves. . . .

Meanwhile I am not to deal with the plays in New York without giving the Guild a look in unless I yield to an overwhelming impulse to treat them shabbily and lose my reputation for being the most reasonable man now living.

To this should be added the following legend on the back of a picture postcard from Madeira in 1923:

Now the Actors Theatre, which has done pretty well with *Candida,* wants to reap the harvest you have sown; but I am telling them and all other applicants that you have an option on all my plays, and that they can have only your leavings, if any.

Everybody wants to start a theatre on Shaw. I tell them that they who sow the seed must reap the harvest and that you have an option on all my plays. Lorraine wants *Man and Superman!* But you had better reserve that.

After Katharine Cornell had appeared in *Candida* for the Actors Theatre (sponsored by Actors Equity Association), he established a warm personal relationship with her, and gave her the right to produce and play in a revival of *Saint Joan.* From time to time others tried to produce Shaw's plays in New York but were invariably turned down by him until after World War II.

When the supply of new Shaw plays dwindled, we tried to project plans for the production of his earlier plays. One of the most ambitious of these was for a Bernard Shaw cycle which I explained in the following letter of January 22, 1925.

This is to confirm my cable to you telling you of the plans of the Guild to do substantially a complete revival of your plays, as a "Bernard Shaw Cycle." We plan to start next October, using the Garrick as the production centre, and placing the plays in other Theatres in which it will be possible to play from $12,000 to $15,000 per week.

By this system, the plays which succeed can play to capacity business, while those which do not do so well, will not cause us to lose so much as to put a crimp in the cycle.

The plays which we expect to produce during the two or three year period are as follows:

Arms and the Man	*Fanny's First Play*
You Never Can Tell	*Captain Brassbound's*
Major Barbara	*Conversion*
The Doctor's Dilemma	*Mrs. Warren's Profession*
Man and Superman	*Pygmalion*
Getting Married	*Androcles*

I returned here to find the Guild enjoying great prosperity. Our first play, *The Guardsman* was an enormous success and has moved to the Booth Theatre where it will run until the Summer. Our next play *They Knew What They Wanted* written by a young American, Sidney Howard, has been phenomenal. It looks as though it will run for almost two years. We have leased the Klaw Theatre for this play. We expect *Caesar and Cleopatra* to do splendidly in our new Theatre.

I gather from the papers that you have gone to Madeira. I thought at first that you had taken this trip instead of coming to America, but on second thought I decided it was a mere preliminary, as you probably want to be fit as a fiddle on arrival here. I see that Robert Lorraine, after announcing *Arms and the Man* and *Man and Superman,* and throwing the Guild into hysterics, calmly departed for England and will probably not be heard from again.

Did GBS hail this ambitious project with joy? Not a bit of it. He merely asked if, in effect, we were releasing certain other plays "for other adventurers to mangle," and he pointed out a danger in the cycle which we ourselves would have heartily welcomed. Here is his reply on a postcard—a postcard which seemed to indicate that our proposal to produce eleven of his plays was hardly worth the postage stamps on a letter:

What about *The Philanderer, Misalliance, Methuselah* and *Heartbreak House?* Am I to take it that you are through with the two last and off the two first, and that I can let other adventurers mangle them?

The cycle scheme is all very well, if you can put it

through; but don't forget that the more successful the plays may be the more you may overwork the concern.

The Guild eventually produced eight of the plays of the cycle, and the rest of them were produced in Westport. The idea of a Shaw repertory company was also considered from time to time by the Theatre Guild. The last occasion was in connection with our summer theatre at Westport, where it may again take shape as a Theatre Guild Shaw Repertory Company.

From time to time we had correspondence with GBS regarding a revival of *Captain Brassbound's Conversion*. The transaction regarding Mrs. Fiske is not clear to me, but the following letter of June 31, 1931, addressed to "Dear-whoever it is" is revealing:

Dear-whoever it is

I have had misgivings occasionally about *Captain Brassbound's Conversion* ever since you compelled me to turn down Mrs. Fiske's offer. The play requires special treatment, as it has only one woman in it, and it is quite useless unless that one woman is a big gun, very English, very attractive, and *not young*. I dread your shoving it on with one of your pretty young American ladies in it.

Now it happens that Mr. James Fagan is going to New York at the end of August to produce his play *The Improper Duchess,* which has been successful here. His wife Mary Grey, though she is not in the cast, will cross with him. Why not engage her to play Lady Cicely and get Fagan to produce it? She has played the part, and has all the qualifications, including that of being no use for small parts: She is a big gun or nothing. Managers are afraid of her because she is not like everyone else, which is exactly what is wanted for *Brassbound.* The New York press was, I understand, very polite to her when she played in Fagan's *And So to Bed.*

My new play will not, I am afraid, please everybody. It is not meant to. So do not expect another *Apple Cart* or *St. Joan.*

The new play was *Too True to Be Good* and it pleased quite a few people. We did not accept the suggestion to use Mary Grey in *Captain Brassbound.* Later this play was produced by John Haggott and John Cornell at our Westport theatre with Jane

Cowl and Arthur Margetson. It was one of the most satisfying Shaw productions ever to be made at our Westport Playhouse.

Before and during World War II, our relations with Shaw were affected by a number of circumstances. Our failure with his later plays *Too True to Be Good, The Simpleton of the Unexpected Isles* and *The Apple Cart* had been discouraging. The revival of his older plays required "star" actors, who took a large percentage of the profits; Shaw's own royalties, amounting to fifteen per cent of the gross with no picture rights included, made the revivals an expensive luxury. But these were not the only reasons why we no longer followed our earlier adage, "When in doubt, play Shaw." As explained already, he had acquired a very real fear about income taxes and forbade the production of his plays on the ground that his taxes would ruin him.

I wrote GBS on August 30, 1940, at the time when the air raids over London were beginning to grow heavy, about the formation of the National Inventors' Council, in Washington, D.C., the purpose of which was to mobilize the inventors of the country for the war effort. To this he replied:

> Your National Inventors' Council is all to the good. Our own people have been hard at work and expect to have something that will surprise Jerry after Christmas.
>
> I gather that the Guild after a narrow escape from extinction, has now regained some of its old success and prestige. The New York public can now subscribe to it without fear of suffering from my plays. The Federal Theatre experiment (I regret its untimely murder) seems to have proved that I am not a highbrow author and that my true sphere is where no seat costs more than fifty cents.

On October 15, 1945, after a long hiatus in producing GBS's plays, Terry and I sent him a cablegram reading as follows:

> RUMORS OF REVIVALS OF YOUR PLAYS BEING CIRCULATED AROUND BROADWAY. WE ASSUME WE ARE STILL ACTING AS YOUR AGENTS. ALSO IF YOU ARE RELEASING NOW FOR NEW YORK WOULD LIKE TO CONTINUE OUR CONTROL OF PLAYS WE HAVE PRODUCED ESPECIALLY PYGMALION, ARMS AND THE MAN, DEVIL'S DISCIPLE, ANDROCLES AND THE LION, SINCE WE MADE THE LAST SUCCESSFUL PRODUCTIONS OF THESE. WOULD FEEL

VERY BADLY IF THEY WERE RELEASED TO OTHER MAN-
AGEMENTS WITHOUT OUR HAVING FIRST CHANCE AT
PRODUCTION OURSELVES.

To this we received a cabled reply dated October 22nd:

GO ON AS BEFORE SUBJECT TO MY RIGHT TO AU-
THORIZE DIRECTLY WHEN ADVISABLE, BERNARD SHAW.

Later on, other New York managers were in touch with GBS,
and he gave them the right to perform individual plays. One of
these was Maurice Evans, who discussed the possibility of a
production of *Man and Superman*. We received a postcard
from GBS on the subject dated 7th of July, 1946, reading as
follows:

Maurice Evans has a personal non-exclusive license to
play *Man and Superman* in repertory on his tour. It is an
express condition that the license will be withdrawn if he
claims any further privilege or interferes with any new
production. He has been reminded of this.

Obviously, however, it would be very good business
for the Guild to cast him for the lead in its production.

My plays are now classics open to all managements like
Shakespeare's, except for the royalties. First come, first
served!

The "first come, first served" seemed like a repudiation of
our earlier business arrangements, and on April 24, 1946, we
asked for a resumption of the policy under which we produced
one play a year.

As you know, half a dozen times during the war we
tried to do one of your plays, only to be turned down by
you on account of the income tax situation. This inter-
rupted our relationship, and other people have been quick
to pick it up again before we realized that you were again
willing to release your plays. As a result, numbers of your
plays are being announced for next year, and the Theatre
Guild, which used to be your home, seems to have been
abandoned by you.

As the years go by, you are still our favorite author. I
well remember after the first world war, the excitement
there was in doing *Heartbreak House, Back to Methuselah,*

St. Joan, and all the others. I think we did fourteen plays in all.

In those days, when anyone else wanted to do your plays, you used to refer them to us, and you wrote me, "Where you sowed, others may not reap." At the present time, the actors do not bother to come to us to do the plays, but make arrangements with you directly, so we are left out in the cold. We would very much like to have done *Man and Superman.* Now Maurice Evans tells me that he got the rights directly from you and is considering whether he will allow us to be the managers. This, of course, puts us in an inferior position. We would like a resumption of the old situation where we would definitely agree to do one play a year, and when other parties wrote you (other than Katharine Cornell, in view of her old relationship with you), you would refer them to us so that the Guild could continue to function as the manager. Actually, it has been very difficult for us to make any plans for a Shaw revival because there can be four or five of them all running in competition with one another and thus hurt each other's business.

In case you have forgotten it, and there is no reason why you should not have forgotten it, you wrote us a letter setting forth your gentleman's agreement with us, and I am attaching a copy of this letter hereto. Since we diligently tried to do your plays throughout the war, the agreement was certainly not broken on our part.

On June 27, 1946, I wrote again, reiterating our position:

Morris Ernst tells me that you told him you did not want to see him as you were writing directly to me.

I want to congratulate you on the occasion of your ninetieth birthday and wish you everything you wish for yourself. The Theatre Guild is now twenty-seven years old and going stronger than ever. Terry and I run the Guild, and Armina is our first assistant.

We want to return to our practice of doing a Shaw play every year. We wanted to do this during the war, but your income tax wouldn't let us. Now that the war is over, everyone else wants to come in. At the end of the last war, when no one was doing your plays over here, the Theatre Guild made a great success of *Heartbreak House, St. Joan, Pyg-*

malion, Arms and the Man, The Doctor's Dilemma, The Devil's Disciple, etc., etc. All in all, we did fourteen plays, of which four were world premières. . . .

We would like to make the following arrangements with you: that except in the cases where you have already made direct arrangements, e.g., Katharine Cornell and Gertrude Lawrence, before leasing a play to someone else in this country, you will first consult with us and see whether we are willing to do it the following season, in which case you will hold it for us. If, however, we are not willing to commit ourselves to doing the play the following season, then the play can be released to whomever else you may select.

We were particularly disappointed to read an announcement that Maurice Evans was going to do *Man and Superman.* This is a play both Terry and I have always wanted to do for you, and we can certainly cast it very much better and do much more for it with our subscription list, which now amounts to over 150,000. We have since learned that Maurice Evans has postponed *Man and Superman,* and this will be the first play we would like to produce.

The Theatre Guild has always been known as the home of Bernard Shaw in this country, and we hope to continue the policy of at least one Shaw play a year. Years ago I coined the phrase, "When in doubt, play Shaw," which is really one of the three basic mottoes of the Guild.

We have just had three new plays by Eugene O'Neill delivered to us, and we are going to do two of them this season.

With kind remembrances in which Terry and Armina join me.

At the same time we continued to present GBS's plays on Broadway, we also represented him in connection with his amateur rights in the United States and Canada. This has continued since our first Shaw productions, under the management of Miss Sara Greenspan of the Theatre Guild, who has acted as personal watchdog on Shaw's behalf over all these years.

During a visit to GBS in 1947, he raised the question of why we were taking care of his amateur rights for the USA and Canada. He had forgotten that twenty-five years earlier he had asked us to do so. On May 2 I made the following proposal to govern our future relations, since many other American producers were announcing unauthorized productions of his plays:

On looking into the matter, I find that the sum which we sent you last year for amateur rights was £2,000., (about $5,600) and not $2,000., as you mentioned. Also, that we have been collecting these amounts for you for the last twenty-five years at *your own request.* We have a special department of the Guild that takes care of this kind of business for other authors as well as yourself and it is no trouble to handle it.

Now, since you are "getting ready to die," as usual, I suggest that we make the following arrangements:-

1.) The Theatre Guild to have the first call to do at least one Shaw play a year in the U.S.A., and, so long as we present a Shaw play each year, we are your American representatives.

2.) During your life, all offers for first class revivals of your plays are to be forwarded to you, together with the names of the actors for your approval. Plays are to be licensed on the principle of "first come, first served." In forwarding offers to you, the Guild will furnish information regarding the financial standing and position in the theatre of any producer who wishes to produce a first class revival of a Shaw play.

3.) Stock and repertory rights will not be referred to you, but handled by us as heretofore. We pay the money into the Irving Bank, which transfers it to your Bank. This money *does not* go to the British Society of Authors and we shall not send any statements to them.

4.) Upon your death, all royalties to be paid over to the Public Trustee.

5.) In the event of the liquidation or dissolution of The Theatre Guild, Inc., or its successors, this arrangement to be transferred to the Authors' League (Dramatists Guild Branch) of the U.S.A.

If you will agree to the above, you can die in peace knowing that your plays are in good hands in America and, if we do anything we should not (which, of course, you believe we will!), then you are free to haunt us for the rest of our lives. However, as I fully expect you will send a wreath for my funeral, all this part about dying seems quite academic.

If my letter seems to treat of Shaw's "getting ready to die" too lightly, the reader should note that at this time it was a constant subject of conversation with him. But old as he was, his mind was young, and he was as much at home with business details as many a younger man. Here is what he replied to my proposal on 6th May, 1947 (aged ninety):

> You don't understand my difficulty about managerial control of my plays. You think I am complaining of the sums paid to me by the Guild. I am not. Put that out of your head.
>
> Your letter says not a word about the main point, which is, what you are to get for your trouble?
>
> My experience is that when a management gets control of a play it takes a rake-off for its licenses. Sometimes the licensee sublets for another rake-off, the net result being that the production is sweated the last penny it will bear, and even beyond it, instead of benefiting from the moderation of my sliding scale. I am determined to put a stop to this by every means in my power.
>
> Now the accounts of the Guild have never included any charge for collecting. This is what has never satisfied me. You cannot have been doing it for nothing. If we are to go on as before—it must be on the understanding that no performing licensee is to be charged more than my standard sliding scale, and consequently that The Guild's charges for collecting must be definitely settled as a percentage of the fees due to me.
>
> Is that clear?
>
> The rest of your letter calls for no comment, except that you have nothing to do with the Public Trustee or the London Society of Authors. The law will take its course when I die.

GBS had forgotten that we deducted the usual 10 per cent commission for collecting his royalties, which deductions appeared on his statements. In addition to collecting his royalties, Miss Greenspan had to answer thousands of letters from professionals, amateurs, summer theatres, little theatres, schools and colleges, most of which were requests for permission to present the plays. Until the Society of British Authors came into the picture in the year 1947, all correspondence on this subject passed between Miss Greenspan and Shaw's secretary, Miss Blanche Patch, who had a dry sense of humor of her own. Here are extracts from some of her letters to Sara Greenspan:

19th April 1948

Dear Miss Greenspan,

I hasten to thank you most warmly for the nylon stockings. It is indeed kind of you to send me such a handsome present by Miss Helburn. I had tea with her at the Savoy Hotel, and we had a good chat together. I very much doubt her being able to see GBS as he is, at the moment, firmly opposed to having *any* visitors. The older he gets—and he is nearly 92—the more he retires into his shell. However, we can but be thankful that his sight and hearing are really not too bad, so that he is able to amuse himself, and is not dependent on a "companion," which he would loathe.

You asked me if I had seen *Oklahoma.* Yes, I was at the first night at Drury Lane when the Langners were here. As a matter of fact they told me to let Tennents know if I wanted to go again, but there was a bit of a muddle with the Drury Lane people when I tried it for some friends, and anyhow GBS thoroughly disapproves of "free seats," and would probably say "Serve you right" if he knew I'd tried to get in without paying.

5th November 1948

. . . Considering his age GBS keeps very well and is pouring out a lot of his shorthand material for me to transcribe. Not always too easy, as he is now apt to leave out necessary symbols. However, rather remarkable for a man of his age to be able to do it at all.

7th December 1948

. . . now that they have been enabled to deduct this percentage from the sums Maurice Evans pays to the Irving Trust (as you must know they are pretty considerable), I have given up bothering about it, and after all it means that GBS gets rather less. And this should please him, as he is always saying he can't afford to earn more money owing to heavy taxation.

14 January 1949

. . . GBS keeps much the same and for his age is extraordinarily mentally active. I have occasional week-ends with him, but at this time of the year find the house much too cold for me, and there is nothing particularly attractive in the village. He likes being alone and says that cold suits him so there is nothing to worry about as far as I am concerned.

Terry called on GBS early in 1947, and she told him of the difficulties in financing his old plays without the picture and subsidiary rights, and an over-all fifteen per cent royalty. In a letter dated 14 February 1947 in which he addressed her as "My dear Tess" he expressed his opinion on the royalty situation in characteristically Shavian manner:

It is out of the question for me to change my standard terms. If I did it for the Guild I should have to do it for everybody; for I must not have two prices. If the Guild cannot afford my plays it can simply not perform them.

But why can it not afford them? My 15% does not come in until you have given 8 performances to capacity; and below that figure you pay only 10%, 7-1/2%, and 5%, which suits the smallest set of village amateurs and the biggest New York success. I ask for no advances nor guarantees nor star salaries. If I raise your 15% figure from $14,000 to $15,000 you will think me a cheap skate and undercut my plays as you did *The Apple Cart* and *The Unexpected Isles.*

So let us say no more about terms, which I have not raised for more than fifty years, though the cost of living has rocketed since then. I listened to you without the smallest intention of changing: the charm was yours.

The new play—if such a senile effort can be called a play—is finished, printed, and ready for the next Malvern Festival (this year or next is not yet fixed) at which it will see the light for the first time. It is not yet named: you may call it TRIPE provisionally.

I enjoyed your visit very much.

The "catch" in the above letter is that although the cost of living had gone up, so had the price of theatre tickets, so that GBS's royalties compensated him for his rising costs, while making it financially far more difficult for us. His remarks about *The Apple Cart* and *The Unexpected Isles* are incorrect, as he never reduced his royalties to us under any conditions.

On March 24, 1948, at the time we were producing Shaw's *You Never Can Tell*, he was writing me complaining that "it is most desirable that something should be done to make the commercial managements conscious that I have written other plays besides 'Pygmalion.' " He further went on to say:

> . . . I am finding that we must make an end of the utterly anomalous arrangement whereby you have to act as both agent and theatre lessee with the strongest interest in pre-venting my plays being produced anywhere except in your theatre or on your tours.
>
> Paul Reynolds acted as my agent (for books) 60 years ago; and I see that his son is still carrying on. Chambrun has acted for me, also a scion of the Brentanos. Fanny Holtzman is very friendly. But I don't know whether they are good and disinterested for play business. Is there any agent whom you would prefer to anyone except yourself? Let me have a line on this. I shall die presently, and must leave my affairs in businesslike order.

The above statement was nonsense, for we were not "thea-tre lessees." We had been acting for him mainly for his ama-teur rights; had we really acted as his agents for professional New York Broadway productions, we would have had every financial inducement to license his plays to any and every commercial management. But very few could pay his price.

One of the main reasons why it became difficult for the Guild or any other management to produce Shaw's plays after the war, when taxation problems seemed to be lifting somewhat with the abolition of the supertax, was because of the rising costs of producing plays. In our young days, we financed our own plays, and whenever we made a profit from a play, we used it to produce other plays. After the successful production of Philip Barry's *The Philadelphia Story*, starring Katharine Hepburn, we realigned our business policy to follow the trend which now exists in the commercial theatre, which is to form syndicates financed by so-called backers, who were called "angels" when they lost their money in a play and were called "financiers" when they made a great profit.

The revival of Shaw's plays without any participation in picture rights, as well as the high royalty, made it difficult to finance his plays in the regular Broadway theatre. Quite apart from this, some of his later plays were very talkative. Perhaps one of the most remarkable, *In Good King Charles's Golden Days,* while it contained sparkling dialogue, had no plot. Thanks to the interest of Day Tuttle, formerly of Smith College in Northampton, Mass., we arranged for his production of the play in an off-Broadway theatre, the Downtown Theatre on East 4th Street, New York City. The rent was low, the seating capacity small, the actors' salaries infinitesimal and Shaw's royalties minimal. As a result, when *Good King Charles* received excellent notices, it was able to run for nearly two years in the depths of Greenwich Village, and this is said to be one of the longest runs of any Shaw play in the USA.

For the benefit of those interested in the economics of the theatre during Shaw's lifetime, I quote the royalty clause which was contained in Shaw's contract, and from which he did not deviate. Reduced to theatre language it means that he charged a royalty for each performance of 5 per cent on the first $250; 7-1/2 per cent on the next $250; 10 per cent from $500 to $1,500; and 15 per cent over $1,500. We found ourselves nearly always paying Shaw in the 15 per cent bracket, or 5 per cent more than any other author.

Here is Shaw's exact terminology:

> The Manager shall pay to the Author Fifteen Per Cent (15%) of the gross receipts at every performance given under this Agreement when such receipts exceed fifteen hundred dollars ($1500.); Ten Per Cent (10%) when they exceed five hundred dollars ($500.) and do not exceed fifteen hundred dollars; Seven and a Half Per Cent (7-1/2%) when they exceed two hundred and fifty dollars ($250.) and do not exceed five hundred dollars; and Five Per Cent (5%) when they do not exceed two hundred and fifty dollars ($250.), it being understood that when the specified sums are exceeded the corresponding higher percentages are to be paid on the entire gross receipts and not according to the American custom of different percentages on the successive increments; and it is

further understood that the Manager may calculate the percentage on the average of the gross receipts during the week instead of on the actual receipts at each particular performance. Provided always that if the said play be omitted from any performances given by the company within the week, the gross receipts shall not be averaged in calculating the percentages for that week.

Our last project for producing a group of Shaw's plays was presented to him on July 18, 1947, as follows:

Following are some of our plans for your plays for next season.

1. *You Never Can Tell:* I had a series of conversations in Hollywood with Edmund Gwenn and Cedric Hardwicke. Gwenn is too busy to play the part of the waiter now, but might do so later. Hardwicke is tied up until January. He says he would fancy playing the part of the waiter himself. What do you think? When we do this play, we will take in Mr. Fischer as a partner to give him an opportunity of making some money out of it. We may bring this off fairly early in the season.

2. *The Devil's Disciple:* We are looking for a good cast for this play. What do you think of using John Gielgud? He is a splendid actor and has a lot of dash. Possible American candidates are Spencer Tracy and Katharine Hepburn.

3. *Arms and the Man:* We would like to produce this play during the forthcoming season and are trying to line up a cast.

We are still awaiting a copy of your new play as soon as you get it from the printers. I am also awaiting with great interest some copies of the photographs that you took of us all.

You Never Can Tell was the last play we produced of Shaw's during his lifetime, and the story and correspondence which follows shows how keen was his mind and his business acumen at the age of ninety-one. GBS replied to my letter on a postcard:

Judith in *The D's D* is weakly sentimental; Katharine Hepburn is too strong for her. Dick is not a raffish profligate: he is a tragic figure in black, like *Hamlet,* or Buckingham in *Henry VIII.* I must let Alfred Fischer go where he chooses, as he did very well for me in Germany; but you should be able to give him as good terms as any other management, or better; and I should prefer yours. Hardwicke would of course be perfect as the waiter. It would be wise to wait for him.

We informed GBS that if and when we produced *You Never Can Tell,* which was to be successfully revived in a London production directed by Peter Ashmore, we would take in Mr. Fischer (Shaw's former German manager) as an associate producer, and such an arrangement was made with Mr. Fischer. We finally decided not to wait for Sir Cedric Hardwicke, but to produce the play with another well-known English actor Leo G. Carroll, and we notified GBS of our intention to proceed.

The entire project was under way when we received a cablegram from GBS on October 14, 1948:

> PRODUCE NOTHING OF MINE UNTIL PRESIDENTIAL ELECTION IS OVER. SHAW.

In view of the above cable, we deferred our production of *You Never Can Tell* until after the end of the year. We brought over some players from England, as well as the bearded English director, Peter Ashmore, who looked for all the world like Shakespeare's younger brother (if one ever existed). He came to New York before the others, and a theatre was engaged. However, on January 10, 1949, when we were just about to go into rehearsal, we received a new cablegram reading as follows:

> TAXATION OBLIGES ME TO DEFER FURTHER REVIVALS. GBS.

I cabled in protest and on January 17, 1949, our Miss Greenspan received a letter from Miss Patch, Shaw's secretary, from which I quote the following:

> You might tell Mr. Langner that I passed on his cable about *You Never Can Tell* to GBS, but have not much hope that the latter will relent and allow a production. At the moment he is obsessed by the idea that he can't afford to earn any more royalties owing to the tax he has to pay on them; but as the tax cannot be more than he would receive, I cannot follow his reasoning. However, there it is.

Hindsight compels me to admit that it was too bad we did not cancel all the contracts and follow GBS's instructions. It would have saved us a great deal of money and trouble. However, since we had already entered into the production contracts on *You Never Can Tell* with his blessing, we cabled him that his request had come too late for us to stop the production. Moreover, Peter Ashmore, who had directed the same play in London, was already at work.

Unfortunately, while *You Never Can Tell,* a charming comedy, written with Shaw's youthful verve, was liked in Boston and Philadelphia by our audiences and by the out-of-town critics, the drama critics in New York took it to pieces, notwithstanding the fact that it was, in my opinion, given an excellent production and was very much liked by our public; in fact, to test this out, we took a vote of the fifteen-thousand-odd subscribing New York members of the Theatre Guild at the time, and well over two thirds were delighted with the play. However, running expenses were very high, and we felt it expedient to close after a few weeks.

GBS was furious with the Guild when our revival received bad notices from the New York press. Here is what he wrote to "My dear Tessie" on 27 March, 1948, after the New York opening:

> An absolutely damning press. You see now what comes of producing my play when I forbad you to do so. You have thrown it away from sheer incompetence. There was in it a first-rate revival but not up against *Man & Superman,* compared to which it is the most threadbare old hat.
>
> Serve you right, but where do I come in? Decidedly I must get an agent at once. We shall meet in April if you dare look me in the face and I am still alive.

Due to an engagement GBS had with Pandit Nehru, Terry missed seeing him when she was in England that spring. To make sure that she understood his attitude about the Guild, he wrote her a postcard on June 6, 1949:

> Note, dear Tess, that I have promised the Guild nothing, and that after the production of Y.N.C.T. in defiance of my explicit instruction to the contrary, with the result that a valuable revival has been thrown away on a foredoomed and forewarned failure the T.G. is now at the top

of my black list.

Tell it to stick to its film business and write me off. GBS

Anyone reading these remarks might well imagine that they represented the end of our friendship. Not at all. GBS had an affection toward us which outbursts of this kind did not destroy —once he gave vent to his anger, there was an end to it. On several later occasions, Terry, Armina and I called on him at Ayot St. Lawrence and had the most friendly reception.

With *You Never Can Tell,* this brought our total of Shaw productions in New York City including revivals, to twenty-two of his long plays, or about three quarters of his major output.

It would be fun for the Guild, as GBS suggested before his death, to produce all his other plays, but to do this would call for a substantial government or foundation subsidy and the discovery of the Fountain of Youth for the Langners, neither of which seems an immediate prospect. However with the development of a Westport Theatre Arts Center devoted to the playing of comedy, and the possible home of a Bernard Shaw Repertory Company, who knows what the future may bring forth? GBS's name is particularly associated with the Westport theatre because a considerable number of his important plays have been produced on the stage of the Country Playhouse, including the première of *The Millionairess* with Jessie Royce Landis.

Other notable Shaw plays presented at Westport were *Fanny's First Play* with Claudia Morgan and McKay Morris; *The Showing Up of Blanco Posnet,* with Zachary Scott; and one of the best productions I have ever seen of *Arms and the Man* with José Ferrer, Kent Smith and Uta Hagen. There was also a brilliant performance at Westport of *Captain Brassbound's Conversion* with Jane Cowl and Arthur Margetson, in an excellent production by John Cornell and John Haggart. Jane Cowl as Lady Cecily Waynflete in *Captain Brassbound's Conversion* was outstanding, and she achieved one of her best performances and looked her most beautiful in the part. The miracle of her appearance was obtained under considerable difficulties, caused by her invariable practice of bringing her own electrician to the theatre with a long mirror, which he held before her while she examined her lighting at every important position. In doing this she was proven entirely right, because in a famous earlier production of *Romeo and Juliet* she achieved an excellent performance and made one of the youngest-appearing and most beautiful Juliets I have ever seen in the theatre, at an age well past forty.

Other Shaw plays presented at Westport by other producers were *The Devil's Disciple,* with Maurice Evans and Dennis King; *Man and Superman,* also with Maurice Evans; and also a very striking production of *Heartbreak House,* with Beatrice Straight and Peter Cookson in the leading roles. We also presented a brilliant production of *The Philanderer,* directed by Romney Brent, with the leading roles all excellently played by Tom Helmore, Claudia Morgan, Vanessa Brown and Rex O'Malley.

Finally, it was at the Westport theatre that *Pygmalion* with Dolores Grey and Tom Helmore was presented for the inspection of Lerner and Loewe as a step in the ultimate production of *My Fair Lady,* as explained in Chapter 15. It is for these reasons that the Westport Country Playhouse has been selected as a suitable home for a permanent Bernard Shaw Repertory Company next season or the season thereafter.

CHAPTER FOURTEEN

Shaw in Motion Pictures, Radio and Television

WE HAD many interesting and sometimes amusing encounters with GBS on the subjects of motion pictures, radio and television. In the conflict between his integrity as an artist and his instincts as a businessman, he never wavered in his determination that his works should not be cheapened in their transfer to these mass media, and he refused many lucrative offers which did not include his personal supervision.

Many attempts were made on both sides during our relationship for the Guild to assist GBS in producing his plays in motion pictures, radio and television; but in general there were other individuals more competent and more interested. Among these were a young Englishman named Cecil Lewis and the fantastic Hungarian-American impresario, Gabriel Pascal, who, by his brilliant motion picture *Pygmalion,* earned a niche in the motion-picture Hall of Fame for producing one of the best motion pictures ever made. We were more successful in introducing Shaw into the field of radio, as explained hereafter.

As far as I know, Shaw showed his first interest in talking pictures after he appeared in Fox Movietone (a combination of a silent picture and a sound track) and delivered a lecture on a variety of subjects. I was present at the New York opening, and on June 29, 1928, I described it in a letter to GBS in the following terms:

This is written just after seeing you in the Fox Movietone, which not only reminded me that I had not heard from you for some time, but also made me regret that I hadn't.

I am sorry that you were not present at your American première. You would have enjoyed it immensely. You were given the place of honor in the program. The first picture showed the changing of the guard at Whitehall, giving a rather British atmosphere to the proceedings. The band played very realistically and one could even hear the gravel crunching as the soldiers marched. This was followed by sham warfare, with bombs dropping in every direction, shrapnel shrieking through the air, the rattle of machine guns, tanks vaulting over the ground, infantry firing in all directions and rockets screaming through the sky. One felt the great moment was at hand. The Movietone orchestra struck up that ancient but honorable melody, the words of which begin "There was an old Scotsman at the Battle of Waterloo," and the name of George Bernard Shaw flashed across the screen. What there is of Scotch in your ancestry, and whatever you may have been doing at the Battle of Waterloo, has evidently been kept a dark and hidden secret from the world. A moment after, you appeared on the screen, your very charming and very clearly enunciating self. Indeed, your voice contrasted very favorably with the brass bands and the sounds of warfare which had immediately preceded it.

I rather think your imitation of Mussolini did not do justice to yourself. Had Mussolini given an imitation of you, one could have understood him and forgiven him, but not even "The Intelligent Woman's Guide to Socialism and Capitalism" will put you right with the radicals in this country. The final irony of the evening, however, undoubtedly goes to the picture which followed your appearance. It was called "The Red Laugh" and portrayed scenes during the Russian Revolution in which all the villains were bolshevists and anarchist agitators, while all the heroes were Grand Dukes. You must place in all your contracts hereafter a clause that you must not be used for propaganda purposes.

I received no reply, perhaps because I also suggested that he use this medium for lecturing to women's clubs on the subject of his forthcoming book, *The Intelligent Woman's Guide to Socialism and Capitalism.*

GBS first mentioned the subject of motion-picture performances of his plays in a letter dated January 2, 1930, which introduced the attractive young Englishman named Cecil Lewis whom he liked and had befriended.

> Meet my friend, Cecil Lewis. He has gone over on a broadcasting job; and when he has finished it he will be available for anything in our line that may turn up. I wish you would talk to him and put him up to what he may need putting up to. He will tell you all that is necessary about himself. He is a playwright and a producer and quite good company.
>
> As his appearance is attractive you had better warn Terry that it is no use: he is married and has two children.
>
> P.S. I have just been offered $75,000. for a musical film of *The Devil's Disciple.* I am replying that one *Chocolate Soldier* is enough for me: consequently, Nothing Doing.

GBS hated what was done to his play *Arms and the Man* when it was used as the basis of the libretto for *The Chocolate Soldier,* with excellent music by Oskar Straus. Indeed, according to Dr. Henderson, Shaw insisted that the program of the operetta contain an apology for the "unauthorized parody of one of Mr. Bernard Shaw's comedies."

After meeting Cecil Lewis, I wrote to GBS:

> Mr. Cecil Lewis called with your letter of introduction, and I have done everything I could to help him while he has been here. I have placed the Guild's acting resources at his disposal, in case he is at a loss to secure the necessary talent for producing plays over the radio. I have also introduced him to a number of personal friends, and they all like him very much.

On February 15, 1930, we received the following letter from GBS. Alas, we did not realize the important opportunity this presented to the Theatre Guild, for it might have led to our producing all of Shaw's plays in talking pictures had we so desired. However, our heads were in the clouds and we were wrapped up in our Repertory Acting Company which at that time seemed far more important to us.

Here is GBS's proposal:

Do you think there is any serious chance of The Guild doing anything with *Arms and the Man* as a talkie? Goldwyn is pressing me about it; and Stern cables to ask whether he may name $150,000 as my price in a deal which is proposed. There is no immediate prospect of my entertaining these proposals; for Goldwyn wants to cut the play down to forty minutes; and I suspect some of the other applicants of wanting to film, not *Arms and the Man,* but *The Chocolate Soldier.* Also Mary Pickford is very keen to do *Caesar and Cleopatra;* and, generally speaking, my film market is getting excited. Meanwhile my hands are tied by our understanding about the Guild having a shot at talkie producing; but it is obvious that on coming to close quarters with such a very laborious and expensive new departure, you may find it quite impractical —if, indeed, you have not already done so. How does the matter stand? I am in no hurry; but I cannot wait unless I see a reasonable chance of something happening.

I have to thank you very cordially for your reception of Cecil Lewis on my introduction. He was greatly gratified by the way you treated him, especially as his head is full of schemes of film work on my plays.

I answered on March 7th:

I received your letter regarding *Arms and the Man,* and the Guild's situation as regards talking pictures. I have also talked this matter over with Cecil Lewis, and Mr. Stern. There is no doubt about the fact that several of the talking picture companies would be willing to finance us in the production of some of your plays. However, when it gets down to talking finances, and the question of royalties arises, as well as the idea of doing your plays without changes, we seem to make no headway. It is therefore our opinion that we would only be hindering you if it is your desire to sell outright to the "talkies" with no restrictions.

The thought occurred to us that we might act as your

agents, somewhat along the lines that we have acted in connection with your amateur rights, attending to the business matters for you, and especially representing you on the artistic side, but we do not want to push this idea in any way unless it is one which appeals to you. We know that in any event you would not release plays that we were either doing or contemplating doing, and we know that when it comes to handling the business end, you are very much better at it than we are.

I feel that either the "talkies" will have to modify their program practice and do your plays *in toto,* or you will have to modify your plays and allow them to be cut down by the "talkies." Cecil Lewis and I thought that it might be a good idea for him to try to get scenarios in shape so that they would be satisfactory to you and would constitute a compromise between what you wanted and what the "talkie" people want. I doubt whether the plays could be done in their full length on the screen, not because the plays are not sufficiently interesting, but because one cannot spend two hours listening to shadows. The real flesh and blood interest is missing, and the general experience seems to be that a "talkie" will talk you to death in about a quarter of the time it takes a stage production to do the same thing. [How wrong I was!]

We are much too alive to the future of the "talkies," however, to utter any dictum on the subject. It may very well be that within the next year or so we may ask you to let us do one of your plays as a Theatre Guild "talkie." It was for this reason that my cable expressed the hope that our relinquishing *Arms and the Man* would not mean that we were no longer interested in the situation.

Nothing came of Cecil Lewis's excursion over here in New York, so he went to Hollywood in an endeavor to sell some of Shaw's picture rights. There were some attempts on his part to stir up picture interest in *Arms and the Man;* one of these emanated from Twentieth Century Fox, but it transpired that they were attempting to make a picture of *The Chocolate Soldier* to which Shaw would not consent. I telegraphed a friend at this company as follows:

GUILD HAS RELEASED ARMS AND MAN BUT RECENT
LETTER FROM SHAW SEEMS TO SUGGEST THAT HE WILL

NOT CONSENT TO ARMS AND MAN BEING BOUGHT FOR
CHOCOLATE SOLDIER. HAVE TRANSMITTED YOUR SUG-
GESTION TO HIM.

The suggestion was of course turned down. Cecil Lewis was
not successful in promoting a talking picture for GBS and returned to England.

When Terry Helburn took a leave of absence from the Theatre Guild and spent a year or more in Hollywood at Columbia
Studios in 1935, GBS wrote her expressing his opinion on the
motion-picture industry as it then existed. While conditions
have changed greatly, his basic criticisms of why an important
author should avoid Hollwood are still vastly pertinent and
probably will continue to be so for generations to come.

15th February 1935

I am glad that I have at last a correspondent at Hollywood who has some sense. There is no question of my attitude changing: all my plays are in the market for filming,
and have been ever since Hollywood began to realise, however feebly, that a talkie is something more than a movie
with spoken sub-titles.

But there is a good deal more for it to realise besides.
For instance, that the talkie has killed the old system of
buying the world rights from the author. I have just concluded an agreement for a German film of *Pygmalion.*
But under the existing law the film must be made and distributed by Aryan German firms. Else the necessary German permission for the export of my royalties would be
refused by the Government. Fox Films might have had
this job, including the English language rights, if they had
consented to guarantee my German royalties; but they
threw the whole affair back on my hands with the remark
that they are only interested in the English language
rights of *Pygmalion.*

Another example, R.K.O. makes proposals for the filming of *The Devil's Disciple* with John Barrymore as the
star. But when they submitted a scenario I had to cry off:
it was quite impossible; and I then saw that I must make
my own scenarios, as Hollywood is not within half a century of knowing how to handle my stuff. I accordingly
made a scenario of *Pygmalion.* The German studio (Kla-
gemann) jumped at it, and, when Fox backed out, agreed

with me for the German language.

Then came the great question of the *St. Joan* film with Elisabeth Bergner. I had to make the scenario for that; for nobody could cut the dialogue and write the new scenes except myself. A Hollywood studio would have given the job to the bellboy and been firmly persuaded that his hokum was really good screen stuff which would carry my literary touch to victory.

R.K.O. did not get as far as the bellboy. Their notion of a scenario was a man lecturing on a series of pictures, like the old dioramas of my youth.

I contemplate the popular Hollywood productions in despair. The photography is good, the acting is good, the expenditure is extravagant; but the attempt to tell a story is pitiable: the people expend tons of energy jumping in and out of automobiles, knocking at doors, running up and downstairs, opening and shutting bedroom doors, drawing automatics, being arrested and tried for inexplicable crimes, with intervals of passionate kissing; and all this is amusing in a way; but of what it is all about neither I nor anyone else in the audience has the faintest idea. Scenically, histrionically, photographically, and wastefully, Hollywood is the wonder of the world; but it has no dramatic technique and no literary taste: it will stick a patch of slovenly speakeasy California dialect upon a fine passage of English prose without seeing any difference, like a color-blind man sticking a patch of Highland tartan on his dress trousers. When it gets a good bit of stuff it takes infinite pains to drag it down to its own level, firmly believing, of course, that it is improving it all the time. So you see it is not very easy for me to deal with Hollywood; and it will probably end (or begin) with European productions of my plays, adapted to the screen by myself.

Many thanks for your letter. I presume you are doing business for Columbia and not wasting your young life in the studio. You must be quite priceless; for I have yet to find anyone connected with films who has the faintest notion of what the word "business" means.

It was not until Gabriel Pascal appeared on the scene some years later that Shaw's motion-picture career really began. From time to time Pascal visited us and discussed various projects for simultaneous play and motion-picture production of Shaw. We found ourselves being drawn into what appeared to be a series of fascinating ventures. Pascal—nicknamed "Gaby"—was a smallish man with a roly-poly body and a vivid imagination. In some other incarnation he must undoubtedly have been a religious leader, so intense was the fanaticism he put into his film making. With the eyes of an eagle, the rotundity of a Buddhasatva, the contemplative brow of a prophet and the relentless jaw of a Napoleon, Pascal combined all the astounding qualities of the oriental, the occidental and the accidental. His mental life was a series of grandiose acrobatics; and GBS loved to hear Gaby talk. In fact, his conversation was one of his most charming qualities. Within a few moments, he put you at your ease and made you accept him as one of the outstanding geniuses of our time, something which you continued to accept under the hypnosis of his charm.

Gaby's naïve belief in his love affair with destiny was one of his most endearing qualities. Another quality was his power to project, from his vivid imagination, word pictures of what he would like to transform into motion pictures. Thus, in describing the story *The Snow Goose* by Paul Gallico, Gaby informed me that he had made a trip to northern Canada and there had been introduced to a very beautiful snow goose. "Lawrence," he said, "I want to tell you this snow goose had the most beautiful face I have ever seen. In a close-up she will look even more beautiful than Garbo."

The years before World War II were enlivened by the fact that Pascal was now working with Shaw on various talking-pictures projects and was also trying to set up joint Theatre-Guild-Pascal stage-and-picture ventures with such actresses as Katharine Hepburn.

Gabriel Pascal played an increasing part in the story of the Theatre Guild and Shaw, with his constant urging on us to form a joint theatre and film company. It therefore seems appropriate to repeat Gaby's appraisal of himself in his own words in relation to Shaw, which appeared in *GBS '90*, published for Shaw's ninetieth birthday by Dodd Mead & Company, Inc., 1946.

After long years of erring and searching, as it was predicted to me by a Hindu "Perfect Master," I arrived one day in the spirit of playing my life's part at GBS's flat on

Whitehall Court. I told him that I was Richard Dudgeon
and I believe that he himself was convinced that I was the
materialization of his *Devil's Disciple*.

When finally, after that certain Friday, the 13th of December, 1935, which he called, "Auspicious day in the history of Art," we became friends and partners in the great
venture to conquer the millions of the world with the
screen versions of his plays which during the last fifty years
have been reserved for a few ten thousand of the so-called
intelligentsia, I realized that I must stop playing the role;
that I must do the job and henceforth let others play. . . .
GBS would have been the greatest scenario writer for the
screen if I had met him twenty-five years earlier, but even
at this late stage he started his new career as scenario
writer with terrific fervour, enthusiasm and unbelievable
visual knowledge.

Gaby had nothing in his pocket but an invitation to make
pictures in China. He therefore said to Shaw on the 8th of December, 1935:

"Look here, GBS, I am leaving the 15th of this month
for China, but I am ready to wait until Friday, 13th, four
o'clock—which would be an admirable day to sign a contract."

Nothing happened and Gaby waited until the fateful Friday.

It was a quarter past three . . . it was half-past three
. . . it was a quarter to four . . . still no telephone, no
contract. At a quarter to four I started to pack my tooth-
brush, and some imaginary luggage; imaginary because I
had nothing. My Hindustani friend was delighted that I
was going to the East and declared triumphantly a few
minutes before four o'clock: "You see, he has not understood you, he has not believed in you." Suddenly, Big Ben
struck, and the door bell rang. A messenger boy entered:
"Are you Mr. Gabriel Pascal?"

"I am." And just as Big Ben was sounding the fourth
stroke he handed me a big envelope. I opened it. It was
the contract of *Pygmalion* and the photo of GBS signed
and inscribed: "Auspicious day, Friday, 13th December."
Shaw proved that he is not only a great scenario writer but
a great *metteur en scène* of Life. . . .

The talking picture of *Pygmalion,* with Pascal as producer and Shaw as story and dialogue writer, was magnificent. Wendy Hiller as Liza won the hearts of audiences and the plaudits of critics all over the world.

During World War II, we kept up an intermittent correspondence with GBS which reflected the wartime moods on both sides of the ocean. GBS continued to write in his usual sprightly manner, and dealt with the dropping of bombs as casually as though they were tennis balls.

In the year 1940, when Shaw was busily engaged in making the film of *Major Barbara,* I wrote him the following letter to indicate that we and Pascal were anxious to make a motion picture of *Saint Joan* with Katharine Hepburn.

> Thanks for your letter about Katharine Hepburn. I can assure you that she would make a most wonderful St. Joan, and certainly from the standpoint of popularity I very much feel that she would make a great success in it in both stage and screen.
>
> I am hoping to see Kate here in a few days and to talk to her some more about the situation. Perhaps I will be able to hand Mr. Pascal, Katharine Hepburn in one hand, and $500,000 in the other—as a result of which all my dreams will come true.
>
> Meanwhile, if the idea interests you, please do not hesitate to talk to Pascal about it. I believe it will be very easy for me to raise the money if Kate is to play the part.
>
> All my best wishes to you and Mrs. Shaw. When may we expect a new play?

To this Shaw replied as follows:

> I have a *St. Joan* film coming on with Wendy Hiller as the star—she who did so well in *Pygmalion.* Until this is released I cannot put up a rival Joan against Wendy. If Hepburn can act—and as she has been playing successfully for the Guild I take it that you are satisfied that she can—she would be a formidable rival. I never feel that I have any moral right to lock up a part against anyone who feels called on to play it, and has fairly won an artist's right to try it; but business has its rights too; and when I have given Pascal an agreement on which he must raise $500,000 to film the play I cannot reasonably do

anything that could spoil his claim. So, until the film is released, I am afraid I must hold up the play unless Miss Hepburn can persuade Pascal that her performance would be a help.

On August 30, 1940, I returned to the subject, after discussing it with Pascal's secretary, Miss Baldwin, who preceded him on one of his periodic visits to New York.

When I read these accounts in the papers about air raids, I often think of you and Mrs. Shaw and wonder how you are. I hope it is not causing you to lose too much sleep, because the accounts over here indicate that the raiders fly over London at night and are apparently able to destroy people's sleep more than their property.

I have met Miss Baldwin over here, who is representing Gabriel Pascal, and we talked several times about Katharine Hepburn. Katharine is very very keen to do *St. Joan,* and I am sure will do a good job. I hope something can be arranged but, of course, Mr. Pascal must have his hands full at the moment trying to finish *Major Barbara.* I imagine that the conditions under which this picture is now being made, show how really topical it is.

My best wishes to you and Mrs. Shaw. I wish I could see you both again.

On October 11, 1940, I received a full reply from GBS:

The *Barbara* film is on the extreme verge of completion; and Hepburn is in the running for *Saint Joan,* which is to follow immediately, but must, I think, be made in America, as the raids here add frightfully to the expense through the interruptions of the work, not to mention the risk of the film being destroyed before it can be duplicated. But nothing is settled yet; so this is all private for the present.

I am staying in the country at present, contemplating London from a distance of 30 miles. But as the German pilots cannot navigate as ours do, and, trusting to their instruments, are convinced that they are bombing the Houses of Parliament when they are in fact making me jump by shaking my dwelling with unpleasantly close explosions, the villages in the home counties are wishing they were in New England. However, as far as the bombing getting them an inch forward in the war, the Germans might as well be shooting the moon. Most of the houses they have destroyed we should have destroyed ourselves long ago as unfit for human habitation.

Alas, Katharine Hepburn never made the talking picture of *Saint Joan* and I doubt that she ever will. Ingrid Bergman made a picture of Maxwell Anderson's play about Joan, and it was a ghastly failure—enough to discourage any other picture about the Saint for many years to come, but not enough to discourage Otto Preminger from finally making the picture of Shaw's *Saint Joan* with an untrained actress, who has since done excellent work. The ultimate motion picture of *Saint Joan* still remains to be made.

During the early part of the war I spent much of my time in Washington, D.C., with the National Inventors' Council. After we entered the war this became almost a fulltime job. Moreover, Armina became the acting head of the Washington Stage Door Canteen under Helen Hayes. For several years Armina and I shuttled back and forth between the Theatre Guild in New York and our wartime jobs in Washington. It is remarkable that during this period we nevertheless were able to produce many important plays, including the Rodgers and Hammerstein musical *Oklahoma!,* which was suggested by Theresa Helburn.

During the war, Pascal had a disconcerting habit of thinking up projects which would enable him to secure visas to travel back and forth between London and New York, and we sometimes received unexpected visits by him for somewhat meaningless purposes. He was a welcome visitor to our country home in Weston, but his unconventional habits made him rather a trial as we learned to know him better. One of these was to ask for his breakfast on a Sunday morning at the swimming pool, where he lay stretched out taking a sunbath. Our pretty Irish Catholic parlormaid took one look at him, saw that he was completely naked, dropped the tray and fled to late Mass. But one took these incidents in one's stride. "After all, he's Hungarian," I would explain to Armina.

After the War, in May of 1947, when Armina and I were in London for the opening of *Oklahoma!* at the Drury Lane Theatre, we had a pleasant visit with Pascal at his country place near Denham, where he lived in a beautiful old English farmhouse furnished in Italian antiques, an incongruity of style which was made possible only by Pascal's unique personality, which seemed to blend the two cultures together into a tasteful Anglo-Italian mélange. Present at dinner were several important members of the Irish government, who were negotiating with Gaby for making motion pictures of Shaw's plays in Ireland. I gathered that a large castle was being turned over to Pascal to be transformed into a Hibernian Hollywood. We told Gaby we were going to visit GBS on the following Thursday, and he volunteered to come along with us. This was my first opportunity of seeing GBS and Gaby together, and it was probably as amusing for me to witness GBS laying down the law to Gaby as it was for Gaby to hear GBS reprimand me on the subject of the Theatre Guild and its shortcomings.

After GBS had given me a severe lecture on how to run the Theatre Guild and Gaby a similarly severe lecture on how to make motion pictures in Ireland or elsewhere, he suddenly turned to me as though in distress, and said, "Lawrence, I have no photograph of you. I want to take your picture and I want to take Armina's, too." He then produced a small camera which seemed to require a great deal of adjustment, and then took us out on the terrace. Here he posed us together, but I stopped him and said, "GBS, I want a picture of Armina and myself with *you*." "Who will take the picture?" he said. "Why not Gaby?" I replied. "He's a motion-picture maker." "He doesn't know the slightest thing about photography," said GBS with a twinkle in his eye, "I don't dare trust him." He handed the camera to Gaby with a show of protest, seated himself beside Armina and myself, and proceeded to instruct Gaby in the use of the camera. Later on, I received a postcard from Mr. Loewenstein, who was helping GBS classify his documents at Ayot St. Lawrence, and in it he wrote that the pictures which Gaby took turned out badly, so of course GBS was right as usual.

During the Spring of 1954, I learned from Gaby that he was planning to make a motion picture of the life of Ghandhi, and he had various associates working on the project. In order to finance this, he had to maintain an image of his personal good health which was far from being the case. Unfortunately he did not inform me of the details of his illness, nor was his condition actually known among many of his friends on this side. A few days before his death on July 6, 1954, at the Roosevelt Hospital, we were informed of the fatal nature of his illness by his devoted friends Mr. and Mrs. Edmond Pauker, but we were asked not to call on him at the hospital, as he was already far too ill to recognize callers. Two days later Armina, Terry and I attended the funeral at St. Paul the Apostle's Church, at Columbus Avenue, New York City, where a Memorial Service with High Requiem Mass was performed with considerable pomp and circumstance. At the head of the funeral procession following the casket came his wife and his former wife, both dressed in deep black mourning and walking side by side. To the solemn sounds of the *Te Deum* sung in sonorous tones and to the continuous rise and fall of organ music, Gabriel Pascal was carried to his last resting place. The stage setting consisted of Catholic Church dignitaries chanting in Latin amid myriads of lighted candles, with a dismal audience spread over a wilderness of empty seats. I looked at the faces of those present and recognized many of the most prominent business people of the American theatre and motion pictures, all of whom admired and respected him. Had he died in London, where so many famous actors and actresses who had benefited by his artistry would have surely been present, the occasion would have been far more glamorous. I saw one familiar face at the funeral, dissolved in tears. It was his former secretary, Miss Baldwin, who had come to the church to pay her last respects to Gaby. She had left his service some years before, but was still under the enchantment of the wild adventure of working with him. Unhappily, she did not survive him long. It was only later on that I learned how much he owed to the care of his wife (now Mrs. George Delacort), and a friend, Mrs. Zaya Kingman-Speelman, who helped him during his last illness.

Gabriel Pascal's monument is not the tombstone in the Gate of Heaven cemetery at Mount Pleasant, N.Y., which marks the grave where he was buried, but in the magnificent film of *Pygmalion* which should live eternally, and the world-famous musical *My Fair Lady* which came into being as an aftermath of the *Pygmalion* film.

While the Theatre Guild had little to do with Shaw's ventures in film making, we were active with him in transferring his plays to the medium of radio, and we were also active but less successful in producing certain of his plays on television. Long before the advent of this medium Shaw had often spoken over the radio and was generally pleased with his performances on the air. On one occasion when I called on him, he remarked that he had recently read his one act play, *O'Flaherty, V.C.* over the "wireless" and that he had received a letter from an admiring lady who wrote, "Mr. Shaw, your voice coming over the air sounded as the voice of God!" And GBS, as he told it, smiled as though he really believed it. God with a Dublin accent!

In the year 1945, the Theatre Guild was engaged by the United States Steel Corporation to produce a series of important plays on radio, thanks to the efforts of our friend and attorney, H. William Fitelson. To accomplish this we formed a special department called "The Theatre Guild of the Air," which existed for over eight years. This radio program was ultimately replaced in the year 1953 by a series of one-hour live television plays called "The United States Steel Hour, produced by the Theatre Guild," and its staff consisted of H. William Fitelson as Managing Director, Homer Fickett as Director and John Haggot as Producer, and Armina, Theresa Helburn, and me as supervisors for the Guild. We felt that we would like to produce many of GBS's plays on radio and thereby bring his works to the attention of a far larger audience in this country. I wrote him on June 26, 1945, as follows:

> It looks as though there is going to be a severe theatre shortage in New York next season, and we have to begin to make our plans early.
>
> Because of the theatre shortage, we are going to have a radio program which will, later on, lead to television. We should like to have the right to do your plays over the radio, at your usual rates.
>
> Terry and I are in wonderfully good health, and we hope that you are too. The Theatre Guild is going strong, and we have a wonderful new building, in the hallway of which stands the bust which you loaned me. It has a commanding position, eyeing everybody who goes up the stairs. You will be interested to note that, since your bust was placed in the hall, all dishonest characters, upon passing it, turn tail and fly out of the building without going upstairs.
>
> Please give my best regards to Miss Patch. Armina and I hope to see you both in England during the coming year.

GBS replied that he was skeptical as to whether we could succeed in operating such a program. His attitude placed him in the same boat with most of the advertising agencies, one of which stated that the name of the Theatre Guild on radio would be "the Kiss of Death." Later on they all had to eat their words. Shaw's critical attitude was expressed in his answer to my request by his letter of 9th July:

My plays are mostly too long for radio; and the art of producing plays invisibly is a special one in which the choice of contrasting voices (the vocalists may be as ugly as Satan) is all important. I doubt whether you will find it possible to run the two distinct businesses together, and shall not commit myself to it until my doubts are resolved one way or the other.

Your news of the renovation of the Guild is very welcome. I had written it off as moribund.

In great haste—I am overwhelmed with business on the verge of my 90th year—

GBS at the age of eighty-nine was not taking any chances on the "moribund" Theatre Guild which was then about twenty-six years old.

I replied somewhat tartly with a letter dated August 21, 1945, in which I stated:

Regarding our radio program:

We have engaged the very best radio people in the United States to manage the program, as we would not dream of going into this without good help. Alfred Lunt and Lynn Fontanne are going to do ten shows.

Since this program is supposed to embrace the history of the Theatre Guild, won't you please let us do some of your plays with Lunt and Fontanne and other actors? We would like to have the right to select five plays from the following: *Pygmalion; Arms and the Man; Candida; You Never Can Tell; Saint Joan; The Devil's Disciple; Man and Superman; In Good King Charles's Golden Days; Major Barbara; Too True to Be Good.* For each of the plays which we use, we will pay you the sum of $500. Will you please cable your assent to the above? Practically all of the important authors in England and the United States whose plays we have done in the past are giving us permission to do their plays on the air.

P.S. I saw a reprint of your letter regarding the atomic bomb. I thought everything you said was splendid. We are beginning our program with Robert Nichols' and Maurice Browne's plays, *Wings over Europe,* which prophesied the dire possibilities of this bomb in the year 1926.

When we produced this play, everyone said we were crazy. The artists are always ahead of the scientists, as you will be the first to admit.

To this GBS cabled his consent, which was not a consent at all. The cable read:

AGREED FOR YOUR PICK OF ALL MY PLAYS UNCUT AND UNCOOKED BUT THE LONGEST ARE TOO LONG FOR RADIO.

Since each play on our program could not last longer than an hour, GBS's requirement that we present them "uncut and uncooked" meant that we could not produce most of them at all. However, we did not despair, and made the best of the situation. On September 8, 1945, I replied:

You are very good to let us do your plays on the air. There are a number of one act plays, like *Man of Destiny, Blanco Posnet* and *Great Catherine,* which will do very nicely in an hour. As to some of the others, it seems to us that we might do them on the installment basis; that is, let's say *Pygmalion* or *Arms and the Man.* These could be done the first half one evening and the second half another evening, and I think it might work out quite well, though we might have a little trouble over the act divisions. However, this is our problem, and not yours.

Meanwhile, many thanks. And is it true that you are writing a new play? This would be wonderful.

Since we felt that it might be possible to do Shaw's plays in two parts, I wrote GBS on September 18, 1945, as follows:

Just a line to let you know that our radio show started off as a great success. Enclosed please find the notice which just appeared in *The New York Times* about our first play. The second one also went very well.

I have talked to Alfred and Lynn about your telegram, and our idea of doing some of your plays in two parts, the first half one week and the second half the next. They are very eager to do *Pygmalion,* and the reading part of this will just about fit into two hours, with such emendations as may be necessary for the exigencies of radio. In this way, we ought to be able to get through without "cutting or cooking," which you could not do in a one-hour show.

I heard indirectly that Katharine Cornell might also be interested in doing *Candida*—possibly in the same way—but this is only a rumor.

By doing the plays over the air in this way, we will keep them alive until such time as the income tax permits them to be done in the theatre again.

Once again, we are very grateful to you for giving us your consent to do these plays on the air.

On March 26, 1946, I wrote GBS regarding the *Pygmalion* situation. In view of his early doubts of our ability to handle "two businesses," I could not resist the temptation to "sound off" about the success of the radio program:

It was so wonderful to receive a letter from you in your enchanting handwriting that I hasten to reply.

First, our radio program is an outstanding success. It is listened to by between six and seven million persons every Sunday night, and we are bringing all the great plays of the theatre before this audience. As I cabled you, in the case of *Pygmalion,* this has already been done twice in one-hour versions. And now here's some wonderful news. Katharine Cornell is interested in doing *Candida* on the air.

The reason I am so pleased about the success of our radio program is because most of these millions of listeners are poor people out on farms all over the country who never get a chance to see a stage play. We are giving them an idea of the values of the theatre, using stage actors rather than motion picture actors, and in this way counteracting the pernicious effect of the so-called radio plays and motion pictures, which show little sign of improvement.

In other words, every time a fine play is given on our program over the air, it is a great advertisement for the theatre as an institution.

Our program has already won more awards than any other new dramatic program, and has been rated by a poll as one of the two best dramatic shows in the country. It is generally considered the best acted and contains the best versions. I personally take a hand in making these versions and so does Armina. In other words, we supervise the versions and make quite sure that the radio version contains the essential material of the author's play.

We're getting ready to do Eugene O'Neill's three latest plays, *The Iceman Cometh, Moon for the Misbegotten,* and *A Touch of the Poet;* all of them are tremendously interesting but tremendously tragic. We certainly need a good Shaw comedy for next season. Have you any ideas? It is a long time since anyone has seen a production of *You Never Can Tell.* This play is so charming and entertaining that I think it would make a good revival. What are your ideas? Naturally, with the *Pygmalion* success, everyone wants to do Shaw plays.

P.S. The little daughter Phyllis is now grown up and has two children—We also have a son, Philip, age 19, who is in the Navy.

Because GBS's inexorable dictum that the plays must be presented "uncut and uncooked" made it difficult for us to present many of his plays on "The Theatre Guild of the Air" program, we wanted to persuade him to change his position. Our friend Morris Ernst, who was handling Shaw's legal matters for radio, was going to be in England in the summer of 1946, so I told GBS in a letter of April 24, 1946, of our many problems with him, including cutting, and asked him to discuss them with Morris Ernst:

Our mutual friend, Morris Ernst, is going to be over in England shortly, and I have asked him to take up with you some of the matters about which we have been corresponding, especially the resumption of our old arrangement, which was broken off through no fault of our own, but only because you did not want your plays done over here during the war.

We wrote you several times during the war that we wanted to revive some of your plays, and, in each instance, you refused. We do not think that this should be a reason for breaking an old established relation with us which has gone on for so many years.

We have recently started a Theatre Guild Shakespeare Company, which is doing very well. Perhaps we should make it "Shakespeare and Shaw," or would you prefer the billing "Shaw and Shakespeare"?

We were never able to come to an agreement with GBS on the subject of cutting his plays, and my letter to him of May 20, 1947, ended the correspondence on an ironic note.

When we first started to handle the radio show, everyone said we couldn't do it. Now after two years, we are running the best dramatic program on the air.

Of course, we can't put on any Shaw plays because we're not allowed to shorten them.

I am sending you this booklet which has just been put out by U.S. Steel. On the last page but one, you will see that the Secretary of State, George C. Marshall, and General Eisenhower appeared on the program. Why not you?

The Theatre Guild produced 316 radio plays over a period of eight years. Copies of all of these are to be found in the Theatre Guild Collection at the Sterling Library of Yale University, where many of the recordings of the plays can give future generations an idea of the speaking voices of most of America's best actors and actresses of this era, including a few in Shaw's plays.

I felt that the Theatre Guild should enter television in its very beginnings and should attempt to shape the future of the medium in terms of important plays. Among them of course I wished to include the plays of GBS. As a result, we were the first in the United States to produce a Shaw play on television. This is how it happened.

When I was in London for the opening of *Oklahoma!* early in 1947, I found that Denis Johnston, author of *The Moon in the Yellow River,* which we had presented on the stage in New York, was in charge of the Program Department of the British Broadcasting Company. I saw some television plays in London and realized that while still technically imperfect, the medium would ultimately be capable of bringing the finest works of the theatre into the homes of the people. Terry and Armina agreed and together we decided to go forward.

I explained my ideas to Niles Trammell, John Royal and Warren Wade of the National Broadcasting Company, and

they entered into an agreement with the Theatre Guild to produce a television play each month for seven months, each concern to pay its own expenses. It was our intention that each
play should represent the best we could supply as theatrical
producers, with the assistance of the television experts and
directors provided by the National Broadcasting Company. We
formed a small department headed by our Warren Caro. NBC
supplied Fred Coe as director, and we brought over Denis
Johnston from England to direct our first play. We also decided,
as a matter of sentiment, that we would begin our series with
our first theatre success, St. John Ervine's *John Ferguson,* with
Thomas Mitchell and Joyce Redman in the leading parts. We
had to cut the running time of the play down to one hour, and
the condensation unfortunately brought the emotional situations of the play too close together and consequently turned this
fine Irish drama into a melodrama. The general consensus of
critical opinion was that our first experimental play was far
from successful. I had no quarrel with this appraisal, for we
had to do our experiments in public. I knew, however, that if
we proceeded with the program, we would learn from one play
to the next just what the medium called for, and that improvements would be shown. This turned out to be correct.

Since GBS's dictum that his plays were to be presented "uncut and uncooked" applied to television as well as radio, we
were limited to choosing one of his shorter plays for this series.

We were successful in securing permission from GBS to present *Great Catherine* exactly as written, and we engaged the
brilliant English comedienne Gertrude Lawrence for the title
role. It was directed by Fred Coe and produced by me, and the
acting of Gertie Lawrence, Michael MacLiammoir, David
Wayne and Joan McCracken was excellent. It was not only the
first television play of Bernard Shaw to be performed in this
country, but it also opened the first large studio of the National
Broadcasting Company. A kinescope copy of the televised play
reposes in the Museum of Modern Art, in New York City. It
constituted a perfect television production for the early days of
this new medium.

Our seventh and last production, Thornton Wilder's *Our
Town,* with Raymond Massey acting as Stage Manager, was the
most interesting television play produced in the series. The
eminent critic John Gassner, writing in *The Forum* magazine,
had the following to say on the subject of this production:

Unless I greatly miss my guess, the Theatre Guild's telecast of *Our Town* over NBC on Sunday, June 6th, will go down in history as the day when televised drama was born. It was the first time that a play of quality was televised in the new medium with style and distinction. . . . It turned the limitations of the medium into an advantage, just as the good sculptor takes advantage of the intractability of his materials instead of being defeated by the conditions of his art.

These seven plays were the first to be presented in this country after World War II, and they made television history. Our program was continued as the Philco Theatre of the Air, which was produced by director Fred Coe, who had also worked on our television plays.

In retrospect, it is a pity we have not been able to produce more plays of GBS on our U. S. Steel Hour television program. To do so requires a special talent for comedy direction and playing, a talent very few television directors and actors now possess. This is one of the many reasons why realistic plays predominate in this medium. Another reason is because English comedies are not nearly as popular in this country as American comedies, and are a good deal more difficult to do well. Some of GBS's earlier plays lend themselves to the medium, as well as his most important plays (such as *Saint Joan*), which should certainly be shown on television as special productions or spectaculars. They will need at least one hour and a half to two hours playing time, which makes it impossible to include them in a one-hour program. Until television stops its present practice of cutting down its great heritage of plays from the theatre to fit into "time slots" dictated by commercial advertisers, neither Shaw nor any of the world's great dramatists will be properly represented in this new medium. However, it is only fair to add that this is only one problem in regard to presenting Shaw's plays on television. The subjects of most of the plays are also partly responsible, as well as the unresponsive attitude of the sponsors, the advertising agencies and the present mass television audiences in the United States. Conditions are considerably better in England, where the British Broadcasting Company has built up a following for the plays of Shaw and other important dramatists.

But even under the best conditions, it would not have been

possible for us to please GBS during his lifetime, since he wanted his plays produced on television "uncut and uncooked." Food which is "uncut and uncooked" is often indigestible. Indeed, it has not yet been demonstrated in this medium that it is possible to watch a static conversational play for over two hours without most of the audience's falling asleep or being afflicted with eye trouble. Now that Shaw is no longer able to control the situation, his plays are being cut and cooked for television, but it has yet to be shown that all of these shortened meals are either digestible or palatable for American television audiences.

CHAPTER FIFTEEN

My Fair Lady

THE story of the Theatre Guild's relations with Bernard Shaw would be incomplete without the story of the contributions made by Gabriel Pascal and the Theatre Guild in the early promotion of the musical play *My Fair Lady,* based on Shaw's *Pygmalion.* This work of Alan J. Lerner and Frederick Loewe, which has been acclaimed on both sides of the Atlantic, has attained a deserved popularity all over the world and is rightly regarded as one of the world's greatest musicals.

Theatre managers are often the gadflies who encourage and stimulate artists to create works for the theatre. One such gadfly was Theresa Helburn of the Guild, one of the unsung heroines of this saga, whose brilliant imagination was responsible for the idea of making the famous Rodgers and Hammerstein musical *Oklahoma!* from Lynn Riggs' play *Green Grow the Lilacs*; it was also Miss Helburn who secured the interest of Richard Rodgers in composing the music. It was no novelty for the Guild to take some of its earlier plays and convert them into musicals, selecting the composers, the librettists and the lyric writers. Besides *Oklahoma!,* the Guild's successful musicals included *Porgy and Bess* by the Gershwins and DuBose and Dorothy Heyward, made from the play *Porgy,* and Rodgers and Hammerstein's greatest work *Carousel* made from Molnar's *Liliom*. These may be likened to the biggest fish in the musical theatre, and the stories of how they were hauled in by the Guild's managerial fishermen is theatre history. But what has turned out to be the biggest musical fish of all, possibly artistically, and certainly financially, got away from us, and this is the story of how it happened.

One of the principal actors in the saga of *Pygmalion* was Gabriel Pascal, who had never produced a stage play in his life, much less a musical. But this did not deter him from rushing into action and mowing down all opposition to his desire to make a stunning musical of *Pygmalion*. Death was the one obstacle he could not overcome, but in the end he even triumphed over the grim reaper, for *My Fair Lady* not only appeared on the boards as a result of his early inspiration, but it exceeded all his possible expectations as a popular musical. Moreover, its producers paid a huge royalty to his estate and heirs and are still paying it. It is greatly to be regretted that Gaby did not live to enjoy the triumph of his efforts, in which he was joined by the Theatre Guild and especially Theresa Helburn and myself.

A half-dozen theatre producers had the idea of making a musical of *Pygmalion,* as well as several important composers, but they got nowhere. For it was Gabriel Pascal who held the key to the situation. This was his participation in the moving-picture rights which contained the elaborate royal party scene, which was not in the original play but which Shaw wrote for the motion picture. This scene, Gaby foresaw, would constitute the climax of the musical, as it does in actual fact; and this is why it was impossible for anyone to write a musical from *Pygmalion* without including Pascal.

When enthusiastic individuals such as Theresa Helburn and Gabriel Pascal get together, sparks fly. In six short months, Terry, Pascal and I covered the entire musical field, interviewing book writers, lyricists, and composers. Among these were Leonard Bernstein, Cole Porter, Betty Comden, Adolph Green, Gian-Carlo Menotti and Lerner and Loewe.

Pascal brought the project to the Guild on one of his many journeys to the United States, at a time when we ourselves were corresponding with the British Society of Authors, representing the Shaw Estate, on the subject of making *Pygmalion* into a musical. He had been attempting to carry out the production alone and had discussed the matter with Rodgers and Hammerstein without satisfactory results. Knowing of our long relationship with Shaw and our many discussions about joint Shaw pictures and play productions, he brought up the subject with us in October of 1951. I found myself writing the British Society of Authors the same month that Pascal had invited us to join him in producing a musical version of *Pygmalion*. I wrote that "Mr. Pascal claims that he has the rights, and that he has discussed the matter with Mr. Loesser, who is interested in working on it."

The British Society of Authors wrote me on November 5, 1951:

> Mr. Pascal has not yet acquired the rights to make a musical version of *Pygmalion*. In fact, in association with Hammerstein and Rodgers he did put up a proposal which was quite unsatisfactory from the Public Trustee's point of view, one of the principal objections being that he was requiring more than a five year license.

Negotiations were started by Pascal and the Theatre Guild with the lawyers of the Trustee to find a way whereby a performing license could be legally granted under Shaw's will for more than five years, for it was obviously impossible to interest composers and writers in working on so important a project with a license to perform the play limited for so short a time.

I was in the habit of sending office memoranda to my associates in the Theatre Guild regarding pending projects, and I shall from time to time quote from some of these.

On March 21 I wrote the following office memorandum describing a meeting with Alan Jay Lerner on March 20, 1952, and his lawyer.

C O N F I D E N T I A L

March 21, 1952

From: LL

Re: PYGMALION

I met Alan Jay Lerner yesterday afternoon, and he seemed very excited over the prospect of *Pygmalion*. He did not seem to be too frightened of Pascal.

At lunch that same day with Mr. Lerner, his lawyer said that Rodgers and Hammerstein had refused to do the play because they did not want to have to cooperate with Pascal or give him billing. He assured me that Oscar is now absolutely cold on the play. We were joined later by Fritz Loewe, and also the agent, Dick LaMarr. They have not seen the Shubert [*sic*] film but have promised to look at it as soon as possible.

The next step seems to be as follows:

1. Arrange for Lerner and Loewe to see the film.
2. Settle the deal with Pascal in writing so it is quite clear he does not interfere on the production.
3. Get Lerner and Loewe accepted by the Shaw estate.

Lerner said he would be tremendously eager to have Mary Martin play in it and asked if she was really interested? I said we had been told she was and that she could learn the Cockney accent while she was in London. He said he was going over to London in two or three weeks and would see her there. However, he agreed that his making a deal with us would not depend on Mary Martin. Other names were suggested, including Dolores Grey.

He said they could start right away after he had finished his work in London and would gather material there.

With reference to Rodgers and Hammerstein, I learned subsequently that there were several other reasons why they did not wish to work on the musical.

Lerner and Loewe left for Hollywood the same day I met Lerner (March 21) where they met the enthusiastic Gabriel Pascal and attended a screening of *Pygmalion*. My next office memorandum of March 28 shows what took place between them in Hollywood:

> Mr. Pascal spoke on the phone to LL today about *Pygmalion*. He (Pascal) is showing the picture on Monday to Lerner and Loewe. He claims he has paid $10,000 to the Shaw Estate and that the contract will be ready next week. He says that Carlo Menotti is interested, and I should get in touch with Menotti's friend, Sam Barber, in Mount Kisco. . . . He also asked me if I would consider *The Devil's Disciple* with a big picture star at Westport, then to do it in New York. This all happened in three minutes. I naturally agreed to everything including the doctor's bills for HWF's breakdown.

My reference to my "agreeing to everything including the doctor's bills for HWF's breakdown" was a teasing reference to the fact that our good friend and attorney, H. William Fitelson, was always properly warning us not to engage in too many enterprises at a time, and I feared that forming a company of *The Devil's Disciple* for Broadway with Pascal might give Bill heart failure.

Meanwhile, negotiations were going on with the Shaw Estate, and the lawyers ultimately found a legal formula based on a series of five-year options to reconcile the five-year clause in Shaw's will with the practical considerations. For this our attorney, H. William Fitelson, must be given full credit, for it was his suggestion, and it was accepted by Pascal's attorney, Irwin Margulies, and Edwin A. Davis, of London. Their joint efforts resulted in a license contract dated 30th April, 1952, being granted to Gabriel Pascal Enterprises, Ltd. by the Shaw Estate. It was agreed that Lerner and Loewe should be mentioned only conditionally in the contract, as they had not committed themselves. As a result the Pascal contract with the Shaw Estate contained a clause to the effect that "if within six months after the execution and delivery of the contract, Pascal did not secure a contract *with Lerner and Loewe or some other composer or composers of prestige substantially similar,*" the contract with Pascal could be canceled.

We then all worked like beavers to persuade Lerner and Loewe to agree to do the book, lyrics and music. At the time, while greatly interested in the project, they did not want to commit themselves until they knew whether Mary Martin would play the role of Liza. Lerner's state of mind is explained clearly in a letter addressed to Gabriel Pascal from the Surf-Rider Hotel, Waikiki, Honolulu, dated May 10, 1952, a copy of which exists in the Theatre Guild Collection at the Yale Sterling Library in New Haven.

In this letter, Lerner wrote to the effect that no matter how thrilled he became about the play, he always stopped when he wondered whether he could persuade Mary Martin to play the role of Liza. He wrote that he thought it seemed a perfect marriage. Nor did it bother him that she is American, so far as the King's English as taught to her by Prof. Higgins was concerned. He also thought it would be a great tour-de-force for her from a show-business point of view. He also thought she had naturally that good combination of the little girl and the great lady. He thought that this was one play that should be written *for* her and *with* her, and that if Pascal could persuade her and

Dick (Richard Halliday) to be as enthusiastic as we were, they would gladly fly over and discuss it with her when they had the actual layout completed.

But Alan Lerner was taking no chances in the situation in case Mary did not wish to play the part. He kept the door open as would any good businessman. So he added that if Gabriel Pascal should fail with Mary Martin, then he was to fly right home and persuade Lerner to write it anyhow. He knew it was a superb property, but at the moment he was stuck with Mary Martin in his head and in his heart. He ended by asking Pascal to give Mary and Dick his love and to say he was ready to do anything short of homicide to see Mary as Liza.

The day after the arrival of Lerner and Loewe in New York on May 21, 1952, I had a conference with them. He and Loewe were still excited about the idea of *Pygmalion* but were beginning to consider soberly what would happen if they could not get Mary Martin to play Liza. Armina and I were going to London almost immediately, and it was agreed that we were to wage a campaign there to interest her. What transpired at this interview was set forth in my office memorandum to our attorney dated May 22, 1952, as follows:

To: HWF
Re: PYGMALION
Dear Bill:

At a conference yesterday with Lerner, Loewe and Dick LaMarr, the following transpired: Both Lerner and Loewe expressed themselves as highly excited about the project of *Pygmalion* and stated that they wanted to do it. They already have a scenario. The attached letter was written to be shown to Mary Martin. Lerner does not think we will get Mary Martin. They thought of Deanna Durbin. I suggested Dolores Grey, and Lerner thought well of her provided we had an exciting man. The suggestion was made that this could be George Sanders. Later on, it was suggested that Noel Coward might be suitable for the job.

They were excited about the possibility of doing the show in England first and then bringing another company over here. They can get to work on it practically at once. They want Bobby Lewis to direct . . . but they said they would be willing to accept Jack Wilson in view of his work in *Gentlemen Prefer Blondes* and *Kiss Me Kate.* We

are getting along very well. I asked about our contract.
They said we would have no trouble getting together and
referred me to Irving Cohn. Later on today, Irving Cohn
called me on the phone and said he wanted to know
about whether the five year clause had been straightened
out. I said I thought the proper thing to do was for you
and him to get together, along with Margulies, and have
a conference to straighten out the entire legal situation.
As you know, Pascal told me first of all they wanted 8%
without Mary Martin and 6% with her. Pascal said he had
changed this to 6% and was confident that they would accept this. Terry, Armina and I feel that if the deal can be
set up with these two, we should go into the proposition.
Apparently, they like Pascal and are not worried about him.
They seem to have tremendous enthusiasm which is important.

Meanwhile, in order to convince Lerner and Loewe that Liza
was capable of being played by other singers, in case Mary
Martin did not wish to play the part, we at the Guild decided to
produce *Pygmalion* at our own expense as the opening play for
our summer season at the Westport Country Playhouse. The play
was to be put into rehearsal by Theresa Helburn and directed
by John C. Wilson, our partner in the Westport enterprise.
Dolores Grey was to be engaged for Liza, while the part of
Professor Higgins was to be assigned to Tom Helmore, the English actor. Dolores Grey's name was recommended because she
had recently had a great success in London playing *Annie Get
Your Gun* for over two years, during which she had acquired
an excellent cockney accent suitable for the role.

The scene of our comedy now moved to London, where Armina and I arrived and at once were in touch with Mary Martin, who was playing the part of Nellie Forbush in *South Pacific,*
and her husband, Dick Halliday, who looked after her affairs.
Their reaction to our project indicated that she was very tired
and unwilling to commit herself to anything blindly. We
learned later that she had also had intimations of another offer
from Rodgers and Hammerstein for a new musical, and she had
great loyalty and love for Dick and Oscar who had provided
the role for her in *South Pacific,* in which she was very happy.

What went on between us in London before Pascal arrived
is shown by the document which I prepared over there, and in

which he suggested Rex Harrison for the part of Higgins. We drew up a plan for her which I quote *in toto* as follows:

These are the plans for the musical of *Pygmalion.*

1. Book, lyrics and music by Alan Lerner and Fritz Loewe.

2. Orchestration by: Russell Bennett or equivalent.

3. Direction by Peter Brook or Noel Coward or Jack Wilson or Joshua Logan or equivalent.

4. Scenery by: Cecil Beaton or equivalent.

5. Part of the Professor to be played by Rex Harrison if available. If not, best possible English or American star. Cast up to highest Theatre Guild standards.

6. The business arrangements to be the same as your present, with such changes as would be mutually agreed upon.

7. You would receive top billing.

8. Lerner and Loewe have already agreed that you have the best situations and songs.

9. Lerner and Loewe are working on the musical and will come to London and consult with you from time to time.

10. It is planned to put the musical into rehearsal after December, 1952.

11. Details of Agreement to be worked out by H. William Fitelson.

After several discussions with Mary, I sent a cable to the Guild in New York on June 28 from which I quote the following:

AFTER LONG DISCUSSIONS MARY UNWILLING TO COMMIT HERSELF DOES NOT TURN DOWN BUT SAYS SHE HEARD THREE SONGS PACIFIC BEFORE AGREEING OUR OPINION SHE IS VERY TIRED AND TRYING TO AVOID DECISIONS DICK [HALLIDAY] SAYS SHE REFUSED FERNLEY MUSICAL AND THINKS IF SHE HEARD SOME MUSIC MIGHT AGREE STOP OUR FEELING SHE IS IN NO HURRY WILLING TO RISK LOSING ITS UP TO LERNER LOEWE TO WOO HER WITH SOME SONGS PLEASE TRANSMIT TO PASCAL SEEING REDGRAVE TOMORROW.

Michael Redgrave had been recommended for the part of Higgins, so Armina and I motored out to see him the next evening. We passed through a frightening London fog which was so dense near where he lived that we thought at one moment we were going right over the embankment into the Thames. Apart from this, we spent a delightful evening with the Redgraves but did not succeed in interesting him in the project.

A few days later I spoke over the long-distance phone to Pascal, who was still in New York. According to my memorandum made at the time (June 27), "He [Pascal] said Lerner and Loewe would come to London to play some of their music to Mary Martin. He said I should tell this to Mary. He said he had cabled Rex [Harrison] to see me in Italy. He asked me about the boy to play Freddie who was in *South Pacific,* and I said I would be seeing him."

Rex Harrison now comes more importantly into the picture. (He originated the part of Higgins in *My Fair Lady* in New York and London.) I was to do my best to get him to commit himself to play the part, so I telephoned him in Italy as agreed upon. He told me that he had played in a musical play some years before but was not at all sure whether he could sing well enough at that time to play a heavy singing role.

On July 18, 1952, I sent an office memorandum to New York regarding Rex Harrison, reading:

> These are Rex Harrison's remarks about *Pygmalion:* "I think it is only fair to you and myself, if you are seriously interested in my playing 'Higgins' in a musical version of *Pygmalion,* to wait until some music and lyrics are completed, so that I can hear them and possibly record them myself. After this we could decide whether or not to continue the idea."

Meanwhile, Gaby Pascal arrived in London and decided we had not worked nearly hard enough to persuade Mary Martin to play the part, so he resolved to lay siege to her in his own flamboyant manner. To this end he determined that he would win her over by giving a great party in her honor. We were not too enthusiastic over the idea of the party, but nothing would stop Gaby, who went at everything like a hurricane and swept all obstacles before him.

Pascal, like the magician he was, simply waved the wand of his personality, and hey presto, the party materialized in the stately home of an English lady of title (who shall be name-

less), on a street near Hampstead Heath. She was a patron of
the arts and an old friend of Pascal. She was happy to lend her
palatial mansion for the occasion, but Gaby insisted that, while
he would employ her servants, the refreshments were to be far
more exotic than any English hostess, no matter how sophis-
ticated, would ordinarily provide. So on the day of the party, a
handsome Viennese opera singer, a friend of Gaby's who was
also a magnificent cook, oversaw the operations in the kitchen.
Around midnight a sumptuous buffet was served which included dishes from almost every country in the world—except
England. The repast was particularly notable for its Indian
curry, served in style by an Indian servant of a Maharaja whose
wife, the Maharanee, was, according to Gaby, one of the ten
most beautiful women in the world, a position she filled with
grace and charm. (Gaby told me later that he expected the
Maharaja to stake him to the motion picture of Ghandhi, a project on which he had also set his heart. I am not at all sure, in
retrospect, that Gaby was not trying to kill two birds with one
party.)

Mother India competed successfully with all the other exotic
nationalities present at the affair, for Gaby had hired a group
of Indian dancers, then playing in London, to perform during
the evening. Their colorful costumes mingled with the beautiful gowns of the hundred-odd guests who waited in the ballroom for Mary Martin to arrive after her performance at Drury
Lane. And "odd" was a perfect description of the bevy of
women in low-cut evening dresses and men in black tails and
white ties, which seemed to include large numbers of celebri-
ties from London's theatre and opera world, some executives
and "extras" from the English film studios, and a sprinkling of
blue-blooded English friends of the hostess, one of whom
asked me during supper, "Excuse me, old fellow—er—who is
this chap Pascal? I've never heard of him before." I replied that
he was a magician, which was at least partly true, and the
aristocratic-looking old gentleman who asked me the question
accepted my answer as though it explained everything.

Very few of the guests seemed to know one another, and
Gaby spent most of his time introducing little groups to other
little groups, but they never did coalesce, even under the
warmth of his charming hospitality. As twelve o'clock approached with no signs of Mary, the Indian dancers put on their

stylized performance in the ballroom, while poor Gaby wilted as he watched the time go by. Finally he came up to me with desperation written across his anxious face. "I've just had a telephone call," he informed me. "Mary is quite sick and they have had to send for a doctor," and then he almost collapsed. This was actually the fact, for Mary and Dick were most punctilious and would not have missed the party otherwise. By this time the champagne and tokay were flowing and such a good time was being had on the dance floor that nobody seemed to miss the guest of honor. Nobody, that is, except Gaby, Armina and myself. "The party had failed in its purpose," I thought, "so goodbye to the project unless we can persuade Lerner and Loewe to write it for somebody else." The guests ultimately trickled away, leaving us in the middle of the night buoying each other up with Dutch courage over the success of our unsuccessful party. We finally thanked our gracious hostess and bade her goodnight. Then, as we stepped out into the cool night air, Gaby imbibed the mixture of petrol and oxygen fumes from the departing taxi cabs, and his spirits rose again. "Lawrence," he said, "we shall not give up. I believe we may have to get someone else to play the part of Liza."

The comedy now shifts to Westport, Connecticut, where *Pygmalion* with Dolores Grey and Tom Helmore opened at the Westport Country Playhouse on June 16, 1952. Alan and Fritz were invited to visit the play and they came on the last performance on Saturday night, June 21. Terry entertained them for dinner and they sat with John C. Wilson and her in the theatre. After refreshing their memory of the play by this successful performance, which was put on especially for their benefit, they no longer sat on the fence but enthusiastically agreed to sign contracts for making the play into a musical even if Mary Martin would not commit herself. I asked Jack Wilson (who has since passed away) to write me his recollection on the subject, and he gave me an eye-witness account of the proceedings from which I quote: "The idea of Lerner and Loewe was merely that they should write the music and lyrics and to try and convince them that *Pygmalion* would make a good musical book." He sat next to them in the theatre "and they kept insisting how much they adored the show, adored the production, adored Dolores Grey and adored my direction."

There was, of course, no compulsion on our part or Pascal's

for Lerner and Loewe to accept either John C. Wilson as director or Dolores Grey as the actress in the part of Liza, although
both demonstrated their capabilities. No decisions, however,
were arrived at about casting or direction, and we discussed
various ideas for actresses and directors throughout the rest of
the summer.

Under our arrangement with Pascal, confirmed in a letter
from his attorney, the contract was in his name because of the
motion-picture rights which he controlled, and the production
of which picture was to be "under his personal supervision."
The Theatre Guild was to produce and manage the stage production of the musical in view of our considerable experience
in this field with such successful musicals as *Porgy and Bess,*
Oklahoma! and *Carousel.* Pascal was to be reimbursed for the
money he put up for the Shaw contract from the stage receipts.
We had also been responsible for the expenses of the Westport
production. Thus our arrangement was with Pascal, and we had
no contract with the Shaw Estate, a point which explains why,
later on, Pascal's rights were respected by Lerner and Loewe,
as they were "legal" rights. But for this, it would not have
been possible for Lerner and Loewe to have brought in another
producer instead of the Theatre Guild.

We lost the sum of $1,376.99 for the week of June 16, 1952,
on the production of *Pygmalion* for Lerner and Loewe to see in
Westport. Never in theatre history did so small a loss help to
produce so huge a series of fortunes.

After the performance at Westport, Lerner and Loewe, while
still interested in Mary Martin (whom we continued to woo),
agreed to go ahead in any event, and all the parties concerned
went to work. On my return from Europe, there were a series
of luncheon conferences at the Warwick Hotel on the book.
These were attended by Lerner, Helburn, Loewe, myself, and
our Warren Caro, who took a special interest in musicals. At
one of these luncheons, Alan explained his idea of the Ascot
number, and at another some suggestions which were subsequently adopted were made from our side of the table.

The business negotiations finally culminated in a signed contract between Lerner and Loewe and the Theatre Guild dated
October 28, 1952, reading as follows below. Our right to make
this contract derived from our arrangements with Pascal, and
was never questioned by Lerner or his lawyers.

October 28, 1952

The Theatre Guild, Inc.
23 West 53rd Street
New York City, N.Y.

Re: PYGMALION

Gentlemen:

Your signature under the words "AGREED TO" at the end of this letter will confirm the following as our agreement with respect to the musical version of the above play:

1. Subject to various terms and conditions which have been discussed, Alan J. Lerner has agreed to write the libretto and lyrics and Frederick Loewe has agreed to compose the music for a musical version of the above play to be presented by the Theatre Guild, Inc. in association with Gabriel Pascal.

2. We have composed several of the songs to be included in the musical version and will submit them to you in due course, together with an outline of some of our ideas for the musical version.

3. All parties will enter into a formal agreement on the recommended printed form of the Dramatist Guild of the Authors League of America, Inc. with various conditions subject to our and our respective attorneys' approval as to form and content.

Very truly yours,
Alan J. Lerner
Frederick Loewe

AGREED TO:
The Theatre Guild, Inc.
By Lawrence Langner

A few weeks after the signing of this document, and after the final details were agreed upon and reduced to writing, we were informed that for a number of reasons Lerner would not be able to proceed with the project, and, because of this, the deal was off. Pascal's disappointment at this rupture was intense, for he was not well off and he had invested a great deal of time and money in securing the rights from the Shaw Estate.

Our arrangements with Pascal included an agreement to assign to the joint venture of the Theatre Guild and Pascal the contract with the Shaw Estate. However, after Lerner and Loewe retired from the venture, we made no further attempts to interest other authors or composers, being heartily disgusted with what had happened after so much hard work in New York, London and Westport, and having already canvassed the field with almost all the best music writers.

Pascal died on July 16, 1954, and we attended his funeral. Along with him we buried our hope that we would, at some time in the future, produce *Pygmalion* with him as a musical.

When we learned, from a notice in *The New York Times* of October 10, 1954, less than three months after the death of Pascal, that Lerner and Loewe had secured the rights to make their version of *Pygmalion* with another manager, Herman Levin, Terry and I wrote Lerner a sharply worded letter and he in turn replied with equal force. The upshot of the exchange was that we eventually calmed down, and after our initial disappointment, we faced the facts. Throughout our long careers in the theatre we had never taken any action, legal or otherwise, which would inhibit the creativity of authors. Despite our feelings, we therefore decided that whatever rights we might have had should be dropped, and this is the first publication of the Guild's contract arrangements and correspondence with Lerner and Loewe.

When Terry Helburn, in a draft of her memoirs, made a brief reference to this story, it was decided by her legal executors and myself that it should either be told in its entirety or not at all. Herman Levin demonstrated that with the help of his director, the late Moss Hart, one of the brilliant men of the theatre in so many fields (including playwriting), he was capable of an excellent production of the musical without the additional services of Pascal and the Theatre Guild. The laugh was decidedly on us!

In art, and especially the theatre, the end usually justifies the means. The end in this case was to create a beautiful musical from Shaw's *Pygmalion.* This dream was in the minds of all of us when we labored together in the year 1952, and it was finally made a reality through the enthusiasms of Alan Lerner and Fritz Loewe, who returned to the dream after Pascal's death and achieved the creation of one of the greatest musicals the theatre has ever known. *My Fair Lady* as a work of art has given pleasure to millions of people all over the world, and to this will be added many millions more when the motion picture is made and distributed to the four corners of the earth. The fame of Shaw and his *Pygmalion* has been carried far beyond any wild notion he might have had as to its popularity. The enormous amount of work and travel performed by Pascal and the Guild in the year 1952 and the production of the play in Westport, all helped to get the project started.

But these were merely the preliminaries to the artistic work —the composing, the writing, the scenic investiture, the casting, the direction, the costuming—all these are what mostly mattered, and for these the world is indebted to the group of artists including Alan Lerner, Fritz Loewe, Moss Hart, Oliver Smith, Cecil Beaton, and all the others who helped to select the actors and created and supervised the production—and last but not least, Gabriel Pascal whose dream was enshrined in the motion picture and lives on in the musical. And hovering above all these is the gigantic image of Shaw, whose witty, charming *Pygmalion* inspired the tuneful music and brilliant songs of Lerner and Loewe, to which countless millions have danced and which hundreds of thousands have sung.

Shortly before her death, Theresa Helburn discovered a long-forgotten postcard from GBS, dated April 21, 1939, after she had written him suggesting that *The Devil's Disciple* might be made into a musical play with music by the late Kurt Weill. The postcard contains the following positive admonition:

> My dear Tessie: After my experience with *The Chocolate Soldier,* nothing will ever induce me to allow any other play of mine to be degraded into an operetta and set to any music except my own. I saw a musical version of *The Beggar's Opera* in Moscow by a German composer: probably M. Kurt Weill. He shall NOT touch *The Devil's Disciple.* Make the same reply to all composers. Hands off!!

It is fortunate for the world that this admonition of "Hands Off" was not contained in Shaw's will nor present in our minds when we all were involved in trying to make *Pygmalion* into a musical play after his death. That "Hands off" sounded ominous, and indeed this has proved to be the case.

Howard Taubman, drama critic of *The New York Times,* recently suggested that plays which earned huge amounts might well contribute something to the general good of the theatre, and he mentioned *Oklahoma!* and *My Fair Lady* among these. From the profits of *Oklahoma!* and *Carousel* we were also able to underwrite, or wholly or partly finance, many important plays for several years thereafter, including *Othello, The Innocent Voyage, Jacobowsky and the Colonel, Embezzled Heaven, Foolish Notion,* our Shakespeare Repertory Company which included *The Merry Wives of Windsor* and *The Winter's Tale, The Iceman Cometh,* and *The Silver Whistle.* Moreover, the sale of the motion-picture rights of *Oklahoma!* and *Carousel* largely made possible the gift of $60,000 (later increased to over $100,000) by the three Guild directors for the purchase of the land and the Academy on Elm Street, Stratford, which gave positive impulse to starting the building of the Shakespeare Festival Theatre.

There are so many worthwhile ventures in the American theatre which are in need of financial help that there is great validity to Mr. Taubman's proposal, which we ourselves followed in connection with *Oklahoma!* and *Carousel* long before he made his suggestion. Now that Shaw is being acclaimed as second only to Shakespeare, and since both of them were given to writing on the subject of speech, perhaps Shaw's restless soul might be placated by providing a Pygmalion Hall at the new Shakespeare Student Center at Stratford, Connecticut, which could be devoted to the speech teachings of Shakespeare and Shaw. (There might be some arguments in Heaven on the subject of the billing.) Such a building would help to remind the many thousands of students who visit the Shakespeare Festival Theatre each year of the two masters of the English-speaking theatre, and what they have contributed to the English language —Shakespeare with his magnificent poetry and Shaw with his ebullient prose.

CHAPTER SIXTEEN

Shaw's Alphabet

W H A T a man was Shaw! Inspired by his own *Pygmalion*, in his last will and testament, and while in his early nineties, he disclosed a grandiose plan for revolutionizing not only the English alphabet, but also the spelling, the writing and the speaking of the English language, and he provided the money for doing so. The story of how *My Fair Lady* is contributing to the carrying out of his death wishes, in which he was balked by the British law courts in adversely interpreting his will, is unique in the annals of literature; and its importance is yet to be fully realized by the English-speaking world.

Shaw devised this alphabet plan, leaving explicit instructions in his will as to how it was to be accomplished, and he left the greater part of his fortune at the time of his death (it has more than quadrupled since) so that it might be carried out. Shaw was nobody's fool. He knew that for such an alphabet to be developed and "sold" to the English-speaking world, it would take a good deal of money, and this is the reason why the greater portion of his estate was left for this purpose. It is typical of GBS, both as a thinker and a theatrical showman, that he realized the necessity of spending a great deal of money on "propaganda" to prove the necessity for the alphabet on the one hand and to secure its public adoption on the other. He also realized that a great deal of money should be spent on the actual development of the alphabet, rather than leaving it as a labor of love for those enthusiasts who might wish to spend their time on it without regard to remuneration.

Unfortunately, Shaw's well-thought-out plans were balked by the British courts, which ruled the so-called alphabet trusts to be invalid and at the very beginning made it extremely difficult for the Public Trustee, and also the friends of Shaw who were interested in this subject, to carry out his wishes. That they have been able to do so to the extent indicated by the recent publication of *Androcles and the Lion* in an alphabet made by following Shaw's instructions is a tribute to the devotion and the enormous amount of work done by a group of talented individuals including Sir James Pitman, Mrs. Pauline M. Barrett of Canada, Mr. J. F. Magrath, Dr. S. L. Pugmire, Mr. Kingsley Read, Mr. Alan T. Dodson, Mr. Peter MacCarthy, as well as the work of Mr. C. R. Sopwith, Public Trustee, and others including Sir R. P. Baulkwill, to whom we should all be grateful.

The copy of the so-called "Shaw Alphabet Edition of *Androcles and the Lion,*" recently published as a Penguin book with an introduction by Sir James Pitman and with a copy of the alphabet, indicates at once that the type appears to be readable and practical and certainly does not use up nearly as much space on the printed page as the present alphabet. Since I am no authority on this subject, I cannot express any opinion as to the practicality of the alphabet. It has been received with tremendous interest on this side of the ocean, and at the time of writing, large quantities of the Shaw edition of *Androcles and the Lion* are being sold in this country.

It is of course a great pity that there is not available the very large sum of money which Shaw realized was needed for propaganda for the alphabet. Perhaps it will succeed without this propaganda, but my experience in this connection with innovations and inventions has taught me that they are usually received at first with suspicion, especially when the user is called upon to exercise some skill or to discard old habits and take up new ones. It may therefore prove to be the case that Shaw was quite correct in wanting to spend at least as much effort and money on the propaganda for the alphabet as for the design of it. If it can succeed without this propaganda so much the better, but I feel that the adverse decision of the British courts may well result in leaving this question unresolved. Only time will tell whether, with the pressures of progress behind it, Shaw's revolutionary program will be achieved without the spending of large sums on propaganda and education.

One of the most amazing things about GBS was his sense of timing—a sense which continued into the future long after his demise at the age of ninety-four. Several of the great universities of the United States and England are at the present time carrying out detailed studies along many of the lines suggested by Shaw in his will, in order to examine the time and workhours lost by the use of the present English alphabet, script writing and spelling. The purposes of these studies are many. They are to provide for more rapid teaching methods and more rapid reading and writing; to reduce greatly the time used in stenographic or shorthand work; to save time in dictation; to facilitate spelling; to reduce the amount of paper used in the clerical business of the world; and to save enormous quantities of newsprint.

Shaw was in no playboy mood when he determined to leave the greater part of his hard-earned fortune for his alphabet project. He foresaw that as a result of his project, the world's clerical work could probably be accomplished in far less time than it now takes, giving greater leisure to the reading and writing public and clerical workers; that the resulting standard pronunciation would enable the English language of today to be understood everywhere for future centuries; and that by using standardized symbols, the use of dictating machines and even translating machines might be possible, in addition to the use of such symbols in computers. Moreover, his alphabet and script form would save millions of trees being cut down to make paper and would enable readers to devour literature at an accelerated speed and possibly treble the number of books one might read in a given period. Indeed, the benefits which might accrue to the English-speaking world if the full financial support of those who have benefited by *My Fair Lady* could have been placed behind his bequest staggers the imagination.

Shaw, being a playwright, was greatly interested in the way his words were pronounced on the stage by the actors, and he took up the study of phonetics, to which he contributed some extremely original ideas. As a social scientist, Shaw was also acutely aware of the importance of pronunciation as a measure of class distinction, as well as indicating the geographical origins of his characters. Hence when we note that he states in the Preface of *Pygmalion* that phoneticians are "among the most important people in England at present" we realize how far Shaw was ahead of his times. I personally did not realize the importance of Shaw's interest in the subject when we first produced *Pygmalion,* but while we were doing the preliminary work with Gabriel Pascal on the musical made from Shaw's motion picture by Lerner and Loewe, I sent Lerner a copy of Shaw's will containing his remarks on the subject, and this was made the basis of a scene of teaching phonetics by Lerner which was not in the original play or motion picture but was excellent in the musical. In *Pygmalion* Shaw plainly showed that when Liza spoke like a duchess, she was treated as one, and this was one of Shaw's methods for overcoming the humiliations many people in England undergo merely because their speech reveals their low social positions and origins.

Shaw wrote in the same Preface to *Pygmalion* some laudatory remarks about a Professor Henry Sweet, who was actually a phonetician but, like Shaw himself, constantly fighting the orthodox members of this small fraternity. Shaw stated the following which shows what was in his mind as regards his alphabet and class distinction.

> The English have no respect for their language, and will not teach their children to speak it. They spell it so abominably that no man can teach himself what it sounds like. It is impossible for an Englishman to open his mouth without making some other Englishman hate or despise him. . . . The reformer England needs today is an energetic phonetic enthusiast: that is why I have made such a one the hero of a popular play. . . .

Shaw hastened to add *"Pygmalion* Higgins is not a portrait of Sweet."

Shaw was interested in voice production and phonetic spelling from his childhood on (his mother was a successful voice and diction teacher), but it is only when we read his will on phonetics that we realize how seriously he took this subject throughout his mature life and why he regarded it as of such importance as to make it his major bequest.

I would like to emphasize the point that, irrespective of Shaw's writings, he should be regarded by the English-speaking world as a most generous social reformer by virtue of having attempted to give all his wealth to his government for improving the speech and social status of the masses, as well as for reducing the hours of labor of those engaged in clerical work or in writing of any kind. He has been given little or no public recognition for this contribution.

Like most of his friends in the United States, I did not thoroughly understand what Shaw was driving at in his desire to reform the English alphabet, but I should have had sense enough to know that any project to which he left his wealth (so painfully accumulated in view of his fear of taxes) would be one which should command the greatest respect by all his contemporaries. Most of the people in the American theatre, none of whom could qualify as "phoneticians," regarded Shaw's interest in the alphabet as a personal idiosyncrasy, somewhat similar to his interest in prize fighting. The phonetic spelling in such plays as *Captain Brassbound's Conversion, Major Barbara* and *Pygmalion* was seldom of use to American actors, who were usually informed by their director to "play it with a Cockney accent" or with a North Country or Irish brogue.

Shaw's extraordinary alphabet bequest was perhaps one of the most imaginative gifts any man might make to a country in which he had earned his living for so many years by the use of words and handwriting. Notwithstanding his knowledge of Pitman's shorthand, he could never write fast enough when the creative spirit was on him, so he envisaged an alphabet which not only would simplify spelling and standardize its sound, but could also be written quickly.

Shaw made many appeals to others to help him with his alphabet reform. His final written appeal on the subject before his death sounds both pathetic and (as it turned out later) ineffective. He published and distributed the following to his friends on a printed postcard dated September 9, 1944:

My appeal to existing Government Departments, Colleges, Trusts, Societies, and other relevant agencies to undertake the production of a British alphabet has failed. The need has not been questioned; but the replies are to the same effect: try elsewhere; it is not our job. As, having called attention to its enormous economic importance, and offered to aid its implementation financially, I am far too old and preoccupied to take the work in hand myself, I have finished my part in it by bequeathing to the Public Trust the means of financing any qualified and responsible body, corporate or individual, which will take certain defined steps in its direction. These steps are, in brief, the designing of an alphabet capable of representing at least the 42 sounds of English speech, as listed by the late eminent phonetic expert Henry Sweet, without using more than one letter for each sound, and finally the transliteration and publication of a few English classics, including two of my own plays, in the new characters. Should this bequest have no effect within twenty years following my death, or be made superfluous, as it should be, by government action, my residuary estate will be administered in other public directions.

The matter is now disposed of as far as I am concerned.

Not knowing the detailed reasons why, despite the wondrous bequest in his Will, it was not put into full force and effect as Shaw wished, I investigated the situation. I found the only explanation in this country in an article by Barbara Smoker, Secretary of the British Shaw Society and the Phonetic Association, printed in a mimeographed circular published under the name of "The California Shavian," 9 January 1960:

A reminder about the Chancery Court case of 1957 that set the Shaw alphabet trusts aside might not be out of place here, for some people are under the impression that the Shaw percentage from the fabulous profits made by *My Fair Lady* (based, appropriately enough, on Shaw's one play with a phonetic theme) are all available to finance an alphabet revolution. It is true that more than 500,000 pounds has accrued to the Shaw estate in the past three years, since the 524 pounds Estate Duty was paid off, but a mere 8,300 pounds is to be spent on the alphabet, as the result of a not very generous compromise settlement by the three residuary legatees. Under English law, a bequest must be legally enforceable, and must therefore have a definite beneficiary, either personal or organizational, to take the executors to court if necessary. The only exception to this rule is a bequest whose object is charitable, since charities are officially represented by the Attorney General. But the legal definition of a charity depends, believe it or not, on the categories laid down in the preamble to the Statute of Queen Elizabeth the First! Two of these categories were possibilities for Shaw's alphabet trusts—Education and Public Benefit. The decision of Mr. Justice Harman in 1957 was that the alphabet trusts could not come under either of these two categories of charity, and were therefore invalid. Every effort was made by Shavians to persuade the Attorney-General to appeal against this decision, but he refused to do so. There was no one else in a position to appeal on the charity issue, but the Public Trustee lodged an appeal on the issue that although he could not be forced in law to administer the alphabet trusts, he should be allowed to do so. Before this appeal was heard, the compromise settlement of 8,300 pounds was reached out of court. Immediately, the Public Trustee announced the 500 pound prize competition for a suitable alphabet, allowing a full year for competitors to design and polish their entries. More than 1000 applications for particulars were received, but, as was to be expected, less than half of the applications actually submitted entries.

It is now abundantly clear to all that the main reason why Shaw's trustees were prevented from using the main part of his fortune in carrying out his wishes as regards the reform of the English alphabet was due to the decision of the British Judge J. Harman of the Chancery Division, reported in pages 745 to 759 of the All England Law Reports, March 28, 1957.

Justice Harman's decision seems to indicate that he had a sneaking admiration for Shaw as a wayward Irish genius, but he felt bound to defeat the will by falling back on an old English statute going back to the days of Good Queen Bess. In his decision he gave his views on Shaw in imitation of Shaw himself—wittily but nonetheless destructively. I quote the following from the judgment:

Feb. 20. HARMAN, J., read the following judgment: All his life long Bernard Shaw was an indefatigable reformer. He was already well-known when the present century dawned, as novelist, critic, pamphleteer, playwright; and during the ensuing half century he continued to act as a kind of itching powder to the British public, to the English-speaking people, and indeed to an even wider audience, castigating their follies, their foibles and their fallacies and bombarding them with a combination of par-

adox and wit that earned him in the course of years the
status of an oracle: the Shavian oracle; and the rare distinction of adding a word to the English language. Many of
his projects he lived to see gain acceptance and carried
into effect and become normal. It was natural that he
should be interested in English orthography and pronunciation. These are obvious targets for the reformer. It is as
difficult for the native to defend the one as it is for the
foreigner to encompass the other. The evidence shows
that Shaw had for many years been interested in the subject. Perhaps his best known excursion in this field is "Pygmalion" in which the protagonist is a professor of phonetics: this was produced as a play in 1914 and has held
the stage ever since and invaded the world of the film. It
is indeed a curious reflexion that this same work, tagged
with versicles which I suppose Shaw would have detested,
and tricked out with music which he would have eschewed
(see the preface to "The Admirable Bashville"), is now
charming huge audiences on the other side of the Atlantic
and has given birth to the present proceedings. I am told
that the receipts from this source have enabled the execu-
tor to get on terms with the crushing death duties payable
on the estate, thus bringing the interpretation of the will
into the realm of practical politics.

The learned Judge then goes on to analyze the language of
the will. How dare a man such as Shaw mix his literary style
with the legal style of a reputable firm of British solicitors or
"conveyancers." The learned Judge waxes sarcastic!

The testator, whatever his other qualifications, was the
master of a pellucid style, and the reader embarks on his
Will confident of finding no difficulty in understanding
the objects which the testator had in mind. This document,
moreover, was evidently originally the work of a skilled
equity draftsman. As such, I doubt not, it was easily to be
understood, if not of the vulgar, at any rate by the initiate.
Unfortunately the Will bears ample internal evidence of
being in part the testator's own work. The two styles, as
ever, make an unfortunate mixture. It is always a marriage
of incompatibles: the delicate testamentary machinery devised by the conveyancer can but suffer when subjected to
the *cacoethes scribendi* of the author, even though the lat-

ter's language, if it stood alone, might be a literary master-
piece.

This Will is a long and complicated document made on
June 12, 1950, when the testator was already ninety-four
years old, though it is fair to say that it is rather youthful
exuberance than the circumspection of old age that mars
its symmetry.

But worse than all this, the will contained jokes, and jokes at
the expense of English and Irish "gentlemen" educated at universities. The majesty of the English law as well as that of the
upper classes was (unconsciously perhaps) deeply offended. For
here is what Shaw wrote, and it was obviously in the Judge's
opinion not "the work of a skilled equity draftsman." By this
His Honor meant solicitors or other scriveners of wills, who
were not given nearly so much to showing off their sense of
humor in a will as was the Learned Judge in his adverse decision. The following paragraph (Clause 36) is taken bodily
from the will:

> I desire my Trustee to bear in mind that the proposed
> British Alphabet does not pretend to be exhaustive as it
> contains only sixteen vowels whereas by infinitesimal
> movements of the tongue countless different vowels can
> be produced all of them in use among speakers of English
> who utter the same vowels no oftener than they make the
> same fingerprints. Nevertheless they can understand one
> another's speech and writing sufficiently to converse and
> correspond: for instance, a graduate of Trinity College
> Dublin has no difficulty in understanding a graduate of
> Oxford University when one says that "the sun rohze,"
> and the other "the san raheoze" nor are either of them puz-
> zled when a peasant calls his childhood his "chawldid."
> For a university graduate calls my native country Awlind.

No wonder the Judge pronounced an adverse decision, for
the "jokes" about university men certainly did not represent
GBS at his best, even at the age of ninety-four. There was also
a trace of vinegar in this "joke" such as might have been expected from a self-educated man in discussing university men.

The learned Judge thereafter draws on a host of earlier decisions of the courts (all based on different circumstances, since
no one ever made a bequest to remake the British alphabet be-

fore) to show that Shaw's will was invalid as to the alphabet trusts. Here are some of the reasons given in the decision.

> The research and propaganda enjoined by the testator seem to me merely to tend to the increase of public knowledge in a certain respect, namely, the saving of time and money by the use of the proposed alphabet. There is no element of teaching or education combined with this, nor does the propaganda element in the trusts tend to more than to persuade the public that the adoption of the new script would be "a good thing," and that, in my view, is not education. Therefore I reject this element. . . .
>
> I feel unable to pronounce that the research to be done is a task of general utility. In order to be persuaded of that, I should have to hold it to be generally accepted that benefit would be conferred on the public by the end proposed. That, however, is the very conviction which the propaganda based on the research is designed to instill. The testator is convinced, and sets out to convince the world, but the fact that he considers the proposed reform to be beneficial does not make it so any more than the fact that he describes the trust as charitable, constrains the court to hold that it is. . . .

The learned Judge, by some feat of imagination, found that the alphabet trusts "are analogous to trusts for political purposes" for he adds:

> It seems to me that the objects of the alphabet trusts are analogous to trusts for political purposes, which advocate a change in the law. Such objects have never been considered charitable. . . .

In his final dismissal of the case the learned Judge summed up his conclusions as follows:

> The result is that the alphabet trusts are, in my judgment, invalid, and must fail. It seems that their begetter suspected as much, hence his jibe about failure by judicial decision. I answer that it is not the fault of the law, but of the testator, who failed almost for the first time in his life to grasp the problem or to make up his mind what he wanted.

Can it be possible that the learned Judge found a jibe where none was intended? Those who have read the will may agree with me that Shaw's language in paragraph 39 merely stated what was to happen in case "such trusts *shall fail through judicial decision* or any other cause beyond my Trustee's control." Surely this is one of the softest "jibes" GBS ever jibed. As to failing to grasp the problem or "to make up his mind as to what he wanted," Shaw's explicit instructions as to how to go about educating the public in order to put over the new alphabet, as well as his explicit instructions as to how to create it, show that GBS knew exactly what he wanted. Indeed, it was Judge Harman who failed to grasp the subject, and the consequences of his failure may be with us for many years.

Those interested may wish to refer to the many reasons, official and unofficial, why a compromise of so small a sum as £8,300 (about $25,000) was to be used to carry out Shaw's ideas to reform the English alphabet for which he felt the minimum sum needed was over £300,000. These will undoubtedly be made available to the public as interest in the Shaw alphabet grows.

Shaw, with his peculiar intuitive sense of human nature, must have sensed the possibility that the courts would prevent his funds from being used for the purpose intended. And this is why his will contained a provision that if anything went wrong with the alphabet bequests, the money was to be divided equally among the Irish National Gallery, the Reading Room of the British Museum and the Royal Academy of Dramatic Arts. This resulted in tremendous windfalls to these deserving institutions, the first two of which had contributed something valuable to Shaw's early artistic education. The Reading Room of the British Museum had been haunted by him for years during his long period of penury; and the Royal Academy of Dramatic Arts was a source of youthful acting talent which he cherished and to which he gave more attention than almost any other playwright in England.

From the "compromise settlement" of £8,300 a prize of £500 (about $1,400) was offered by the British authorities to the originator of a new alphabet which met Shaw's requirements. But when all the 467 entries came in and were examined, it was announced by the three official assessors that not one alphabet was suitable, so it was decided to divide the money between four contestants. Finally, a committee was formed to "combine" the best features of these four alphabets and to produce a new one. And then someone was engaged to revise this new one. This has now been completed, almost eleven years after Shaw's death. *Androcles and the Lion* has now been printed in an edition published on both sides of the ocean and containing both the old spelling and the new; and copies are being sold and also given to libraries all over the world.

One of the most amazing of Shaw's instructions in his will on this subject was that a voice, the pronunciation of which would "resemble that recorded of His Majesty our late King George V and sometimes described as Northern English," was to be used as the standard of pronunciation for the phonetic alphabet. Why was the King's voice to be regarded as standard English speech, and the phonetic spelling of the English language to follow his pronunciation? Superficially, Shaw may have realized that to make his spelling popular and palatable, he could base it on the British love for the monarchy, for no loyal Britisher could object to speaking like an English king. But what was Shaw, the dyed-in-the-Fabian-wool Socialist up to in selecting the King, rather than some proletarian speaker such as himself? I believe that his purpose was to use his phonetic spelling to provide a standard speech in which all classes would speak as the King did, and in this way he would be able to abolish "class distinction" in speech. The two greatest barriers between the classes in England (and in this country to a lesser extent) are pronunciation and clothing. Anyone brought up in England knows that we unconsciously place every English person we meet as coming from a particular class or locality by their speech, and Shaw wished to remove this.

All very well for England, but as far as the United States is concerned, are our western cowboys and southern Negroes to speak like English kings? I doubt it. Even if Shaw's bequest of millions of dollars were to be fully used to propagandize his alphabet, I doubt whether it would be as effective in changing English pronunciation as the American movies, which have been successfully disseminating bad American speech and slang for the past thirty years with enlivening results wherever the English language is spoken.

Students of this subject will be interested in the following, which I quote from the London *Times* of January 1, 1960.

There is no outright winner of the £500 prize for a
new alphabet called for by George Bernard Shaw in his
Will, but four outstanding competitors out of the 467
entrants share the money. This was announced yesterday
by Mr. R. P. Baulkwill, the Public Trustee. . . .

The winning alphabets, and therefore presumably the
final one which will emerge from the cooperation of their
inventors, are not modifications of the existing alphabet
but completely new departures, though all are written
from left to right and continue from top to bottom of the
page, and three of the four use exactly 40 symbols to represent different phonemes.

Mr. Pitman (I. J. Pitman, M.P., one of the assessors)
said: "We were astonished by the merit and quantity of
the work produced." The response to the competition had
much encouraged himself and the Public Trustee to proceed with the carrying out of Shaw's wishes.

Mr. Baulkwill said that the compromise reached with
the three charities who were the residuary legatees of the
Will—the British Museum, the Royal Academy of Dramatic Arts, and the National Gallery of Ireland—had
left a sum of £8,300, which would be enough for the
publication with economy and prudent management, especially since there was reason to hope for proceeds from
the commercial sale of *Androcles and the Lion.* . . .

Half the entries came from the United Kingdom, 60
from the United States, 40 from Canada, 11 from India,
10 from Germany, and others from Africa, South America and eastern Europe. Half a dozen came from Ireland. . . .

Mr. Baulkwill commented: "We are launching a ship,
and we don't know where it's going. Some people say that
it won't get off the launching slip; but we are not so de-
spondent."

In his introduction to the Shaw alphabet edition of *Androcles and the Lion,* Sir James Pitman states that he has offered to
publish further material in the Shaw alphabet if there is a demand for it. He therefore asked those who have learned to read
and write it fluently, if they so desire, to write him saying which
of Shaw's works and literature they would like to read in the
printed transcription. He says he can make no promises—other

than to consider any suggestions sympathetically. Time alone will tell to what extent there is sufficient demand for other plays and other material to indicate the ultimate success and general adoption of the alphabet.

I feel sure that with the first step of fulfilling Shaw's wishes now accomplished by creating the alphabet and printing and distributing *Androcles,* the second step for creating the necessary propaganda to cause the alphabet to be adopted in the English-speaking world will surely be forthcoming if necessary. Shaw knew that the actual adoption of the new alphabet would take years of effort and publicity, hence his reason for leaving a large sum for this purpose.

At least a dozen institutions, corporations and individuals have earned, or will earn, huge sums from *My Fair Lady.* (The motion picture rights, according to Harold Friedman, who was involved in their sale, sold for a higher price than any other picture in cinema history.) Only 5 per cent of the combined "take" of the various owners of rights would more than cover the expense of carrying out Shaw's wishes, as regards education and propaganda, to the financial extent of about a million dollars mentioned in his will on a tax-free basis. What better way to express their gratitude? Where there's a will, there's a way!

I look forward to the day when, thanks to GBS's new alphabet and the efforts of the responsible authorities, I shall be able to get through my reading and writing in half the time I now spend on it, and be able to speak the King's English as well as, if not better than, an English king.

CHAPTER SEVENTEEN

Shaw's Aftermath

IN THE chapters which have preceded this, I have attempted to give a factual picture of Shaw's relationship to the Theatre Guild and me, as well as to explain how it felt to be on the receiving end of his entertaining and sometimes highly critical correspondence. I have also attempted to appraise the plays themselves on which I personally worked with my colleagues, and from time to time I have mingled my admiration for GBS with some strictures regarding his infallibility, especially in the field of economics.

The perspective of more than a decade since his death has greatly increased my admiration for GBS as a thinker, as a dramatist and as a man. As his fame grows posthumously, and his plays are produced year after year in all civilized countries, there emerges from the contradictions, the controversies and the confusions of his life a world figure which transcends every other playwright, living or dead, who has written for the theatre since the time of Shakespeare.

This is not to say that Shaw was the greatest dramatist, or even the greatest writer of comedy of this period. Shakespeare, Molière, Ibsen, Chekhov and others have written better plays, but in the realm of creative intellect, scholarship, social philosophy and in the influence he has had on his own and future generations of the world, with the sole exception of Shakespeare, he stands head and shoulders over all the other writers who have ever written for the theatre. Ironically enough, while he often compared himself to Shakespeare more or less as a joke, it has remained for future generations to place him as second only to the great William in the English theatre, and in certain aspects of his writing, at least on the level of the Bard.

Let me hasten to correct a possible misunderstanding. Shaw, while writing magnificent English prose and expressing the most poetic thoughts, could not touch Shakespeare in poetry, in the expression of philosophic thought or in creating dramatic or tragic situations; yet in intellectual perception and understanding of the world and its problems, and how to cure many of them, Shaw was supreme.

Shakespeare in his best moments created great human characters, dramatic situations and magnificent tragedies; far beyond Shaw he was contemplative and philosophical about the meaning of life. But in the main pattern of his writing he served his Queen and later on his King, both in the writing of his historical plays and later on in his comedic plays, most of these being written to please and entertain his masters in the aristocracy, and in pleasing and entertaining them, he has pleased and entertained countless readers and audiences all over the world for the past four hundred years.

On the contrary, Shaw wrote most of his best plays to sting his audiences into making a better world for themselves and for future generations to live in. However, he could not, as Shakespeare could, write tragedies and plays which showed man's despair (*Othello*), or ultimate humiliation (*Macbeth*), or murder and death (*Richard II*), yet neither could Shakespeare write a *Saint Joan,* as Shaw did, in a spirit of affirmation as to the future of the human race.

I have explained in an earlier chapter how Shaw refused to permit his audiences for *Saint Joan* to leave the theatre in a mood of despair over the wickedness of mankind, or in a mood of horror at the burning of a human being. Shaw wrote his controversial Epilogue to show how, years later, Joan's death became a beacon to light up man's faith in the ultimate betterment of the world, rather than to show it as a tragedy of the hopeless perversity of man.

One of the most important of Shaw's accomplishments in the modern theatre was to transfer the theatre of ideas from the small and struggling art theatres to the larger ones (and even the largest). This he did by serving up his ideas with such a sauce of wit, theatrical innovations, delightful and lovable characters, surprises and paradoxical contradictions, that he made palatable to the richest customers of the theatre (those who filled the orchestra and dress circle seats) the most positive and impudent attacks on their morality, their security, their social positions, their politics, their treatment of the poor and even their treatment of one another. And he did this with such charm, such grace and intelligence, that he ultimately converted the larger part of almost an entire generation of the upper and middle classes into a belief that his Fabian Socialistic ideas were both practical and possible and essential to the welfare of the State. There was no need to convert the greater part of the balcony audiences, the teachers, the civil servants and the younger generation of theatregoers. They were already conditioned by Ibsen and by the ferment for social reform which permeated what we would call today "the youth movements" of the turn of the century.

In England, Shaw moved from the confining quarters of the small Royal Court Theatre into the largest theatres of Shaftesbury Avenue; and in New York, from the small Garrick of Richard Mansfield and the Bandbox of Arnold Daly to the theatres of Broadway, such was his gift for entertaining his audiences while feeding them large doses of bitter medicine which they would never have swallowed had he not made it palatable by his comedic genius.

Shaw was impelled by his art and his libido, not to mention his social conscience, to use the theatre to affirm the power of human faith to conquer all phases of the material world, such as government, politics, education, public health, economic security and almost every other obstacle to human progress which must be overcome in order to enable mankind to create a better life on earth. For this, his memory should be blessed forever.

Shaw was a colossal optimist. Because he disapproved of the standard religions of his day, while believing in religion, he created his own, that of Creative Evolution, and he wrote a Pentateuch for it almost as long as the five books of Moses, to explain it to his elite coterie of followers. He disapproved of our existing economic system and created a new one to take its place, in which his own ideas usually transcended those of his followers of the Fabian Society, and were mostly sane and practical while many of those of his colleagues were not.

The range of Shaw's social interests was extraordinary and his knowledge of almost every aspect of human endeavor was greater than any other writer who has ever written for the theatre. It is interesting to note that GBS had no formal university education and garnered his great knowledge of contemporary problems from his many years of conscientious service as a member of the Borough Council of Saint Pancras, Marylebone, by working with and lecturing to all classes of people, and by his omnivorous reading of books from early childhood and through all his penurious days, in the libraries of Dublin and the Public Reading Room of the British Museum in London. He was undoubtedly one of the best-read men of his day. I noted on visiting his study on many occasions that he read the leading newspapers of England, the United States, Canada and some of the continental press, thus keeping himself well informed of what was going on in the various parts of the world.

For the greater part of his life it was Shaw's general habit to raise problems in his plays and provide the solutions in his Prefaces or essays. An example of this is *Major Barbara,* in which he aired so many social problems entertainingly in the play and supplied his answers to them in the Preface. His first play, *Widowers' Houses,* was his only realistic play on the model of Ibsen. It was neither entertaining, popular nor remunerative, so he did not repeat the pattern but fell back on his genius for creating laughter to cover the unpalatable aspects of his social views. This technique of asking questions about current events and providing the answers in his Prefaces served him well in most of his best plays. However, in his late seventies, he began to raise both the questions and give the answers in the play itself, which resulted in some of his worst plays.

In an article appearing in *The New York Times* (Book Section) on May 6, 1962, our most distinguished dramatic critic, Brooks Atkinson, eulogized Shaw under the headline TO GBS THE IDEA WAS THE THING. But with Shaw it was also "the play's the thing." No one constructed better plays or created better acting parts or more notable characters since the days of Shakespeare, and Shaw did not buy his plots and characters from other writers as Shakespeare did. It is fashionable but inaccurate to state that Shaw wrote "ideas" for his characters and not people. His gallery of male and female roles included dozens of memorable acting parts which have become famous in English literature. These include Dick Dudgeon, General Burgoyne, Bluntschli, Sergius, Henry Higgins, Alfred Doolittle, Captain Brassbound, Andrew Undershaft, King Magnus, Captain Shotover, Louis Dubedat, Sir Colenso Ridgeon, Blanco Posnet; as well as unforgettable female roles, such as Eliza Doolittle, Mrs. Warren, Major Barbara, Lady Cicely Waynefleet, Cleopatra, Ellie and the Millionairess. His historical and mythological characters, of which he wrote far too few, included such masterpieces as Caesar, Saint Joan, Androcles, Napoleon, and Catherine the Great; as well as scores of lesser parts. That some of today's American actors tend to be afraid to play in Shaw's plays is due to their own overrealistic acting training. For Shaw, good diction and bravura playing is essential. Because his characters are original, unconventional and paradoxical, they require a sense of style and comedy playing which is extremely rare in the American theatre of today (1962). Moreover, his passion for dealing with social problems often calls for actors with keen mental capacity and satiric bite, also rare in our theatre.

Shaw was the most distinguished playwright of this era to write his plays in terms of needed social reform. He excelled his contemporaries such as Ibsen, Galsworthy, Brieux, Chekhov and Gorki in using laughter and ridicule as his weapons. Since Shaw's stock-in-trade as an author was to attack the prevailing governments and the social ideas under which he lived, it is amusing to speculate how many times he would have been officially disposed of by the authorities for his iconoclastic views had he lived in other periods of history.

For instance, in the time of the flowering of the Greek theatre, he would have undoubtedly criticized the system by which only a single performance was given of the prize festival play in Athens and would have made a nuisance of himself by agitating for at least fifty performances of each of his own plays. He would have severely criticized the Greek alphabet which was then being evolved. He would have argued with Aristotle that a play needed only a beginning, but neither a middle nor an end—and that it could be almost endless, as in *Methuselah*. He surely would have regarded himself as the rival of Aristophanes, perhaps the only satirist who could hold a candle to

Shaw; and he would have agreed with Plato and disagreed with Pericles on the subject of democracy, and as a result of his puritanical attitude on Socrates and the prevailing Greek mode of sex life, he would probably have been given a double dose of hemlock to make sure of getting rid of him.

Had he lived in Rome later on he would have sneered at the Roman playwrights for copying his hits in the Greek theatre and would have ended up a victim of the gladiators for defending Christianity. Later on, Constantine and the early Christians would have thrown him to the lions for attacking the Christian priesthood, and unlike Androcles, he would have found no hungry lion unwilling to eat him.

In medieval times, he would have strongly objected to the Passion plays, referring their authors to his views on religion and puritanism as exemplified in *Three Plays for Puritans* and *Back to Methuselah*. Generations later, in the period of the great Spanish theatre of Lope de Vega and Calderon, he would have attacked the feudalism of the local playwrights and might have been slaughtered in the bull ring for advocating vegetarianism and denouncing bull fighting as unkind to bulls.

Had he lived in the days of Good Queen Bess and James Stuart, he might have ended his days ignominiously on the scaffold, for inciting Shakespeare to write plays attacking the aristocracy and the royal family; and he would surely have urged the actors to throw off their shackles to the English noblemen and admirals who employed them and to work in plays he would write attacking the nobility and praising the town and agricultural laborers. He would have attacked Marlowe on the sadism of *Tamburlaine,* challenged Bacon to endless debates on all subjects, and he would have questioned Sir Walter Raleigh's wasteful gallantry in laying down his cloak for Queen Elizabeth to walk on. But his ultimate death sentence would have been earned by suggesting, as in *The Dark Lady of the Sonnets,* that Elizabeth was not a virgin.

In the days of the Restoration in England and Louis XIV in France, Shaw would have felt more at home, though he would have criticized Dryden for selling two separate plots in a single play, such as *All for Love,* for the price of one theatre ticket instead of two. He would also have felt at home with Congreve and Wycherley, the first as a fellow Irishman and the second as a talented imitator of the Irish, but he would have chided them both for failing to teach the Irish and the English how to improve their way of living after demonstrating their national stupidity. Finally, he would have earned his death sentence for criticizing the unmanly lace-trimmed pants of James II and suggesting that he replace them by "plus-fours."

We will pass over the period after the Restoration and the plays of Oliver Goldsmith, another Irishman who had the bite of satire but without the leaven of social reform, to the period of the so-called modern theatre which, while it began in Russia with Turgenev's *A Month in the Country,* did not hit Western Europe and especially England until the eighteen seventies and eighties.

Why did the English fail to jail or attempt to silence Shaw when he gave them so many good reasons for doing so? I believe that GBS saved himself many times by demonstrating that he was too entertaining and amusing to be put away, either temporarily or permanently.

After Shaw had arrived in London, a witty young Irishman named Oscar Wilde proved conclusively that English society enjoyed being made fun of in the theatre, provided that the playwright was sufficiently witty and gracious enough to indicate that despite their laughable foibles, the ladies and gentlemen of Victorian England were lovable and worthy of imitation by the lower classes. Ibsen set out to demonstrate the many faults of society people in a way which was intense, unflattering and dramatic, but this was of interest mainly to a small audience of intellectuals.

One of Shaw's achievements was to take some of the technique, wit and charm of Wilde and the social conscience of Ibsen, mix them together with the spice of his own Irish imagination, comedic genius and fervor for social reform, and in this way to create a popular theatre for the airing of his social and economic views. It is a tribute to his genius as an entertainer that writing for the same kind of audiences as Wilde, he won over many of these "best people" to his own point of view, so that no matter what social or economic heresies he expressed, no one ever thought of jailing him for them. He was able to write dozens of pamphlets and to make countless speeches against British institutions and society and the governments in power, for which he received only the mildest rebukes. And this was not because the British authorities did not take him seriously. They did on many occasions, but he literally laughed himself out of trouble. He could take up his pen to attack the

Irish, yet the worst that happened to him was that some of his books were burned, which undoubtedly increased their sale. He wrote denouncing World War I during the war, but the English authorities took little notice of his pamphlets and merely stopped taking him less seriously than before.

Paradoxically, only in those countries of which he spoke well from time to time would his life have been in danger had he lived in them permanently. These were the countries where the dictators were in power: Germany, Italy and the Soviet Russia of Lenin and the G.P.U. Hitler would have made short shrift of him in the Third Reich, and so would have Franco in the early days of the Spanish Civil War. And after he changed his point of view about Mussolini, he would not have fared too well with the Fascists. Even in Russia, in the early days, he would not have survived, for he was highly critical of what was going on there; and his later unbounded admiration for Communism and Stalin did not include any unbounded admiration for the silencing of writers and especially playwrights. Had he lived permanently in the United States, it is almost certain that he would have been called before the Un-American Activities Committee of Congress and jailed for his disrespectful answers to their questions. Thus Shaw led a charmed life in his own period of history, and it is not recorded that he ever felt the impact of any greater violence than a few eggs and tomatoes thrown at him to punctuate his Hyde Park oratory.

In the conduct of his business affairs during his later years, Shaw turned over to the British Society of Authors the work of handling all his rights all over the world. Shaw was fortunate in the fact that the Society had an extremely efficient staff, headed by his old and trusted friend Denys Kirkham Roberts, and having for its secretary Elizabeth Barber, a particularly capable woman, a barrister with the highest legal and executive qualifications, who is dedicated to the Society's interests and helped to shepherd her flock of authors through the many vicissitudes they encountered in the turbulent social upheavals of the present century. Notwithstanding all the other calls on her time, as a devoted friend and admirer of GBS, she relieved him of numerous details in administering his plays during his extreme old age, and she has continued to represent his estate with the same faithfulness in carrying out his wishes after his death.

Shaw became a member of the Society of Authors in 1897

and took a very active part in its work during the greater part
of his life. Almost from the beginning, the Society dealt with
amateur licensing and other comparatively minor agency work
for him, as did the Theatre Guild for him in New York. Little
by little he put more on the shoulders of the Society's staff, until at the time of his death they were dealing with all his literary and dramatic business for him all over the world and have
carried on in the same way for his estate since his death.

Naturally, the Society's remuneration for handling the Shaw
business helps considerably with its expenses, which like everyone else's rise every year, while the very reasonable basic annual subscription paid by its members does not. But the prestige value of the representation is of far greater importance
than the financial remuneration for the Society.

Shaw's influence in the Society of Authors was powerfully
reflected in its ultimately successful attacks on the censorship,
its spread of taxation for authors, and the old-age retirement
benefits which came into effect after Shaw's death; as well as
its successful advocacy of reforms in the laws of libel, copyright and obscenity; its improved relations with the British
Broadcasting Company, the British Publishers' Association, etc.;
as well as dealing advantageously with the complications aris-
ing from television, records, movies and radio, and conduct-
ing about forty law suits each year for authors. While administering Shaw's plays is only a small part of the work of the
Society, so many productions have been made in so many countries since his death that it would take weeks to tabulate them.
And since copyright in Great Britain and many other foreign
countries runs for a period of fifty years after the death of the
author (and can run even longer in the USA) this work for
Shaw's estate will not terminate until the year A.D. 2,000!

The work still to be done by the staff of the British Society
in handling GBS's plays and books remains enormous. Many of
the plays are as popular as ever with professionals and amateurs. There is a huge demand for them all over the world in
printed editions. There are long-playing records of a number of
them, and they are continually being performed on radio and
television in many countries. *Dear Liar,* the Shaw/Mrs. Patrick Campbell correspondence which Katharine Cornell and
Brian Aherne, and Jerome Kilty and his wife, presented on the
stage in the USA and England, was arranged for by the Society,
with German, French and Dutch versions currently running

and others planned. Motion pictures of Shaw's plays made and released since his death are *Arms and the Man* (German), *The Devil's Disciple, The Millionairess, Mrs. Warren's Profession* (German) and *Saint Joan,* and more are contemplated. A large part of the work of the British Society is concerned with the publication in hardback and paperback books of all of Shaw's works, and in great quantities; to say nothing of the work involved in connection with his alphabet project.

Shaw's Corner, the house at Ayot St. Lawrence which Shaw bequeathed to the nation, is a fairly undistinguished red brick villa which was once the new rectory of the village. From it Shaw wrote and preached far more sermons than any previous clerical occupants. It was bought when he was fifty, in the year 1906. According to a pamphlet published by the British National Trust,

> At Ayot St. Lawrence there is a tombstone to "Mary Anne South, Born 1825. Died 1895." "Her time was short" the tombstone further records, no doubt measuring some seventy years in terms of eternity. The discovery of this tombstone—or so the story goes and it is apparently a true one—prompted the dramatist to buy The Old Vicarage, envisaging in a parish so favourable to longevity a full and fruitful old age. He was not deceived. Ceaselessly active, and creative to the last, he lived at Shaw's Corner until the age of ninety-four and died there in November 1950. Shaw's Corner was left to The National Trust in 1944, and the rooms where the dramatist worked and lived are now preserved for the nation.

While Shaw generously bequeathed the house to the nation, he made no provisions for its upkeep in his will. Consequently, a group of his friends formed a committee under the chairmanship of Ivor Brown to raise £250,000 for this purpose. After collecting only £407, the committee was disbanded. Most people thought the Shaw estate was rich enough to maintain the building but did not know that its funds could not legally be used for this purpose. The building is now supported by the British National Trust, and visitors are permitted to view the Shaw home on payment of two shillings for adults and one shilling for children. I feel sure that had Shaw been consulted, he would have charged ten shillings for children to keep them out, and prevent them from being bored, and he would have admitted the adults for nothing, on the ground that it might possibly improve their minds and should therefore be part of the national educational program. But wiser heads than his have decreed otherwise.

Blanche Patch, Shaw's helpful and devoted secretary for over thirty years, still lives in London on the pension which Shaw left her. Realizing the vast sums the residuary legatees are reaping from *My Fair Lady,* some people mistakenly think that some or most of it goes to her. She wrote me recently, "The privilege of working for GBS was a great thing for which I am thankful." I echo her sentiments.

The Theatre Guild itself was remembered in Shaw's will by what may be termed an Irish bequest; that is, instead of leaving us anything, he arranged to take something away from us!

We were mentioned in connection with the bust of GBS by Paul Troubetzskoy which he had loaned to me years before, in a passage in the will referring to various institutions to whom he had loaned pictures and statues of himself. Regarding these, he stated:

> I bequeath all of them . . . to the several institutions in whose custody they stand, save that in the case of the said Theatre Guild which is not in its nature a permanent institution I direct that on the Guild's dissolution or the winding up of its business from any cause during the special period the bust shall pass to the Metropolitan Museum in New York City or failing its acceptance for immediate or future exhibition in that institution to the next most eligible (in my Trustee's opinion) American public collection willing to accept it.

With so many things for Shaw to remember in his will, the fact that the bust was first displayed at the Guild Theatre, and later in the Foyer of the Theatre Guild building at 245 West 52nd Street, New York City, might well have been forgotten by any ordinary mortal, especially as he possessed a duplicate bust. Not so GBS. If God can remember the fall of a sparrow, Shaw could remember the loan of his bust. We moved it into our new Theatre Guild building at 27 West 53rd Street, where it was no longer located in the foyer, for fear someone might steal it, and as an alternative to chaining it to the wall, it was placed in my private office opposite to where I sit at my desk, so I have the feeling that in spirit he is watching over me.

However, I cannot be in his good books just now, for not too long ago another Dublin playwright, Brendan Behan (of whom GBS would certainly have disapproved on half-a-dozen puritanical counts) came to my office and sat in the shadow of Shaw's bust. "What's that doing here?" he asked. I explained that for many years GBS had made his home with us in this country.

"Well," he said, with a happy smile, "if you're good enough for Shaw, you're good enough for Behan!" With that he arranged for us to produce his next play, *Richard's Cork Leg*.

To paraphrase Shaw in *John Bull's Other Island* regarding the Irish, "Oh, the dreaming, the dreaming, the dreaming!"

Much discussion took place after Shaw's will was published as to the meaning of his instructions regarding the disposition of his mortal remains. This part of the will reads as follows:

> I desire that my dead body shall be cremated and its ashes inseparably mixed with those of my late wife now in the custody of the Golders Green Crematorium and in this condition inurned or scattered in the garden of the house in Ayot St. Lawrence where we lived together for thirty five years, unless some other disposal of them should be in the opinion of my Trustee more eligible. Personally I prefer the garden to the cloister.

It is assumed that by "the cloister" was meant Westminster Abbey, in the cloisters of which many of Britain's great figures of literature were interred. Not all the great writers who are buried in the Abbey were conforming churchmen, nor is the question of orthodoxy of Christian belief a determining factor for such burial. I believe the time may come when the people of England will realize that the catharsis of criticism which Shaw administered with such telling effect to so many stuffy and obsolete British institutions and customs, as well as the works of art and literature which he created, will entitle his mortal remains to a place beside the greatest men of Britain, of which Ireland was a part at the time of Shaw's birth. When that time arrives, I hope that the authorities of the Church of England will dig up some of the earth from the garden at Ayot St. Lawrence, place it in an urn and deposit it in the cloister. In this way, some of Shaw's ashes, along with a portion of the ashes of Charlotte Shaw, who worked at his side, will be preserved among the remains of the greatest men of England.

In conclusion, I believe that Shaw's influence and Shaw's plays will continue to live on as long as the theatre lives on, and this I believe to be as long as the life of humanity itself. Whatever the future holds for the theatre, whether it will exist by reason of government subsidy or by some new form of communal action, it should never be forgotten that Shaw's plays had their being and flourished in an era of the so-called "commercial" theatre, when managers produced these plays for possible profits and audiences bought and paid for their tickets and authors were relatively free to speak their minds, because the theatres and managers operated without government subsidy or control.

It should also be remembered that many of Shaw's plays would have had the greatest difficulty in finding their way to the stages of countries where writers were not permitted to attack their governments and existing social or religious evils. The unsubsidized artistic managers, such as Vendrenne and Barker in London and the Theatre Guild in New York, carried on the business of producing the plays of Bernard Shaw and plays of artistic caliber by other authors with the clouds of bankruptcy always gathering on the horizon, but it did not deter them. The sharp keen joy of participating in the birth pains of Shaw's masterpieces was an exhilarating adventure, never to be forgotten by those who experienced it. If I have been able to communicate some of the feelings we enjoyed to oncoming generations, I shall have achieved in large part the purpose of this book.

Part Three

ADDENDA

ADDENDUM A

WANTED: A NEW SORT OF THEATRE
FOR AN OLD SORT OF PLAY
BY BERNARD SHAW

*This article was written by Bernard Shaw and given to the Thea-
tre Guild as his contribution toward the cost of building the
Guild Theatre, now ANTA Theatre. It was given by Lawrence
Langner to* Theatre *magazine of New York, with which he was
associate editor at the time, and was published by them.*

AND

*A Letter from Bernard Shaw to Lawrence Langner Giving Him
Instructions as to How to Sell the Article, or to Give It Away to
the Best Advantage*

ADDENDUM B

PROPOSED AGREEMENT BETWEEN
THE THEATRE GUILD AND BERNARD SHAW,
WITH COMMENTS IN SHAW'S HAND

AND

ORIGINAL AGREEMENT BETWEEN
THE THEATRE GUILD AND BERNARD SHAW
FOR THE PERFORMANCE OF
HEARTBREAK HOUSE

THERE is no doubt at all in my mind that the Theatre Guild should have a new theatre. And by a new theatre I mean a new theatre, and not another old theatre. The nineteenth century has left our cities stuffed with pestiferous playgoer barrels in which the unfortunate playwrights and actors were expected by sheer force of entertaining power to set up an attraction that would counterbalance the greatest discomfort of the greatest number. There is a tradition of discomfort in the theatre, dating back to a time when ground rents, which now make it compulsory, were comparatively negligible. In Shakespear's time it seemed a matter of course that playgoers should stand staring at the stage without a roof over their heads as they do still at a Punch and Judy show. A seat was a privilege to be hired as one hires a trestle at a race to look over the heads of those in front. To this day in the Italian theatres you pay for ingress to the theatre, and then pay for your seat in addition as a separate transaction. In Pepys' time the money was still collected from the spectators, Punch and Judy fashion, at the end of the first act. Within my recollection Shakespear's seatless groundlings were provided with plain wooden benches only, though, to be sure, they were roofed in. There were no stalls; and there was half price after nine o'clock. In the old Theatre Royal, Dublin, a first rate house of its kind, there was, besides the dress circle and the undress circle for the aristocracy and the bourgeoisie at four shillings and three shillings, the pit at two shillings, a middle gallery at eight-eenpence and a top gallery or gods at sixpence. Nobody dreamt of comfort, or expected it, though in the circles there was grandeur, consisting of red stuffed upholstery on the narrow benches. It was the business of the play and of the actors to hold you spellbound and forgetful. And this was not for a mere two-and-a-half or three hours. The first time I was ever in a theatre the program consisted of a farce, Tom Taylor's drama, Plot and Passion, in three acts, a grand Christmas pantomime, and probably another farce which I was not allowed to wait for. Most of the spectators were seated on narrow planks, without cushions, sides or backs; but they stuck it out like the French at Verdun, except that they did it voluntarily and paid for the privilege. Such feats of endurance are not things of the past. They are surpassed every season in London by infatuated people who wait at the theatre doors for eight, twelve, and sometimes actually twenty hours to secure front places on occasions like the return of Melba the other day, creating unmentionable problems of provision and sanitation. Every night the devoted theatre queues may be seen in London beginning to form three hours before the opening with extraordinary provocation.

Having discovered that people will perform these feats of self-torture as resolutely as the Indian fanatics who swing on hooks, or the early Christian ascetics, the theatre managers and their architects have naturally concluded that comfort is thrown away on playgoers. A theatre is therefore regarded as a palace of enchantment, but not as a prosaically comfortable place. If criminals were crowded together in our prisons without proper ventilation and elbow room as playgoers are in our theatres there would be an agitation against the cruelty of the authorities. In many London theatres the three dollar stalls are so closely packed that the back of each stall overhangs the knees of the person in the stall behind it. The gymnastics of the later comers who have to choose between pulling over the stall in front of them as they cling to it and crashing into the lap of the already seated behind them are familiar to every playgoer.

I am in favor of making the playgoer comfortable. I admit that once you get him into the theatre he will endure anything, and that if you give him good drama and acting you give him, in effect, a chloroform that would make him forget St. Lawrence's gridiron if he happened to be sitting on it. But the difficulty is to get him in. If a good play makes him forget his discomfort, a bad one makes him remember it and fear it next time. He craves for the comfort of the cinema theatres, the best of which are made very comfortable because, as they are seldom full, nor ever expected to be full, and pay quite handsomely when they are what the manager of an ordinary theatre would call empty, the temptation to pack the seats together without regard to the comfort of the sitters is less strong than the desire to court their custom. Besides, the cinema relieves the spectator of all preoccupying and worrying self-consciousness—about his dress, for instance—whereas the ordinary theatre, the moment it takes its glaring lights off the actors, turns them full on to the blushing spectators. This factor in the success of the cinema is of enormous importance; but it is so little talked about that I should not be surprised if some idiot were to invent a means of making the screen visible in a fully lighted auditorium, and be hailed as a deliverer by the industry he was trying to ruin.

For the moment, however, people go to the picture palace oftener than to the theatre because they are more comfortable and less conspicuous there; and to meet this competition we of the regular theatre need to demolish most of our existing play-

houses and replace them with structures in which the audience
is comfortable and obscure, and the stage blazingly conspicuous.
(But there is another condition to be fulfilled. The cinema has
restored to the stage the dramatic form used by Shakespear: the
story told with utter disregard of the unity of place in a rapid
succession of scenes, practically unlimited in number, uninterrupted by waits, and just as short or as long as their dramatic
interest can bear. In this free, varied, continuous manner almost
anyone who can tell a story well can also write a play. The
specific ingenuity needed to force the story into the strait waist-
coat of three or five acts, with one unchanging scene to each, is
no longer needed. The classic unities have their value for those
who can handle them, and are indeed inherent in drama at its
highest concentration; but they were originally only products
of the mechanical conditions of the ancient Greek theatre; and
to impose these conditions, or still worse, the conditions of the
scenic theatres of the XVII-XIX centuries on all playwrights,
is to deprive the theatre of the services of many most entertaining novelists and fabulists of one kind or another, and to put a
premium on the mental defects of playwrights who have what
is called a sense of the theatre, which usually means that they
have lost all sense of anything in nature but the stage.

No theatre is likely to be generally useful in the future unless
its stage is so constructed that it can present a play in fifty scenes
without a break. I do not mean that there should be no break,
as fifty scenes might be too much for the endurance of the
audience; but I do mean that the suspension of the performance
for ten minutes or so should be solely for the relief of the
spectators, and not a mechanical necessity. If I am right, most
of our existing theatres will become unlettable as playhouses. I
hope they will; the sooner the better.

My next play will be a chronicle play which will be imprac-
ticable without a Shakesperian stage. I do not know whether it
will be in fifty scenes or fifteen or five hundred; but in writing
it I shall ignore the limitations of the XIX century scenic stage
as completely as Shakespear did. I shall have to depend on the
Theatre Guild of America for a performance of it, just as I had
to depend on it for a performance of Back to Methuselah. But
I want the Guild to build a new theatre for it; and I should
hesitate to ask them to do so if I did not believe that the sort of
theatre my next play needs will soon be the only sort easily
saleable or lettable for popular theatrical purposes. The specifi-
cation is simple enough. The auditorium must combine the

optics and acoustics of a first rate lecture theatre and a first rate circus. There must be a fore-stage extending on occasion to the occupation of all the floor level (what is called a ring in an equestrian circus) and the back stage must be easily curtained off and provided with modern machinery capable of doing its work noiselessly whilst the play is proceeding on the forestage. That the stage lighting should be modern, and if possible planned by persons who have never seen footlights, and wonder what on earth they can have been when they read about them in books, goes without saying. Mr. Lee Simonson knows all about that.

The general effect during a performance should be the reverse of the XIX century effect. In it the important spectacle was the evening dress and diamonds of the members of the acting manager's free list, occupying the stalls and boxes to the exclusion of the outsiders who get into a theatre by paying (a thing any nobody can do), the stage being a mere hole in the wall at the narrow end, through which you peeped at a remote *tableau vivant* resembling a pictorial advertisement of the best rooms in the latest hotel.

In the new theatre of the Guild, the audience must pay and not be seen, as good children should be seen and not heard; and it should be impossible for a person entering during a performance to have eyes for anything but the all-dominating stage. The stage must be in general conception a tribune, and not a ridiculous peepshow with painted canvas profiles pretending to be natural scenery.

Let me, however, warn all the vulgar theatre builders and planners—meaning mostly those who consider the Theatre Guild an asylum for freaks and cranks—that though they may possibly find many authors able to write effectively for this new old sort of theatre who cannot write for the theatre of Scribe and Sardou at all, they must not imagine, as so many film companies have done, that playing about with the latest lighting systems, and shewing what hydraulic lifts and electric turntables can do, will interest any audience for more than the first half minute. The old formula of two trestles, four boards, and a passion still holds, and will hold until we grow out of playgoing altogether, provided the passion be passionate enough; for the best in this sort are but shadows, and the worst no worse if imagination mend them, as Shakespear found.

My own practice varies, as far as the mechanical conditions allow me, from the ultra-classic to the ultra-operatic. In certain

plays of mine I have voluntarily accepted the strictest unity of
time and place for a three hours action, as if I were Sophocles:
in others I have thrown the unities to the winds, and not only
presented my play in three or five acts, but divided those acts
into scenes. But that does not concern the spectators, who neither
know nor care how I do it: it is the what, not the how, that they
look to. Still, though the mechanical conditions count for nothing with them (for they see a play as in a dream, and are only
awakened and annoyed by having the physical conditions of the
uncomfortable place they are packed into thrust on their notice)
none the less the playwright and the actors must work subject
to those physical conditions and know how to turn them to
account. The novelist, who writes in a dream almost as completely as the playgoer sees the stage in one, often cannot write
an actable play for this reason. If I were to forget the physical
conditions of the theatre and the physical reality of the actor
for a moment, my plans would become partly ineffective, partly
impossible. Thus I am tied down to what can actually be done
with the theatre as it stands; and if you perform my plays in any
sort of theatre but the one they were written for, you may have
to mutilate them more or less horribly to make them practicable.
That is what happened to Shakespear when the Elizabethan
stage was supplanted by the operatic scenic peepshow stage. The
Shakespearicidal result of that proves that when you have to
choose between mutilating the play and rebuilding the theatre
you had better rebuild the theatre.

Also, it is evident that if the Theatre Guild can give me another sort of theatre I can write another sort of play, quite as
good as, and fresher in form than the old ones, but impossible
of performance in the old XIX Century theatres. Wagner, after
composing operas for the old opera houses, composed The Ring
for a theatre that did not exist, and thereby forced it into existence. But his Bayreuth theatre would be of no use to me for my
chronicle play, which I am writing for a theatre that does not
yet exist in New York, but which the Theatre Guild will have
to design and build for the purpose. Whether my play will have
the compelling force of The Ring I do not know; but at least if
my New York congregation will not provide the Guild with
funds for the theatre the play shall be there to tantalize them;
and they may find themselves in the almost inconceivably retro-
grade position of being behind London after leaving London
nowhere by tempting the Guild to produce Back to Methuselah,
an exploit, still unique, which so amazed me that I have hardly
yet recovered my breath after it.

THE MALVERN HOTEL,
MALVERN.

My dear Langner

The enclosed article is for the Guild at your request. And now you have to consider what you will do with it. It contains about 2500 words. The "first serial right" of it is worth $1750 at my current (Hearst) rates. If you take it to my American literary agent, Paul Reynolds of 75 Fifth Avenue, he will probably be able to to sell it for a sum which would leave the Guild $1500 after deducting his commission. You could put this to the credit of the Building Fund; and after the article had appeared in the papers of the purchasing syndicate, and these had become back numbers, you could reprint it as a circular and send it round with your appeals to your hearts content. It seems to me that this might be the best course from the point of view of publicity no less than of money, even though it would restrict the press publicity to one set of papers, Hearst's or some others.

The alternative is to make all the papers in the states a present of the article on condition that they published it along with the appeal of the Guild. There is a great deal to be said for this: in fact I should recommend it if the possible $1500 is of so little consequence in view of your resources and prospects that you are prepared to spree it on the extra ~~extra~~ circulation of the advertisement without thinking twice about it. On the 23rd April (Shakespear's birthday) a somewhat similar appeal on behalf of the Stratford theatre was let loose in the same way. But you must, unlike Stratford, attach the condition of the Guild's appeal to the otherwise free use of the article, because newspapers are apt to undervalue what they get for nothing.

Your telegram announcing the apparent success of the D's D. has just arrived. But I believe nothing but box office returns. Caesar is quite another pair of shoes. It needs a classic ~~actor~~ actor: you can find ten Dicks and fifty Bluntschlis more easily than one Caesar. However, I am all for it if the man can be found.

Have you ever thought of the Don Juan in Hell scene from Man & Superman as a separate show? At the Court Theatre here years ago, with wonderful dresses by Ricketts against a dead black stage, it was unexpectedly successful in holding the audience.

Tell Terry that I quite understand about Calvert, and that if Louis Untermeyer will send me a note of his whereabouts when he arrives in London I will see him for her sake if I am within reach.

ever

G. Bernard Shaw.

MEMORANDUM OF AGREEMENT made and entered into this *24ᵗʰ* day of *August* one thousand nine hundred and *twenty* between *Theatre Guild Inc. of 65 West 35ᵗʰ Street, Borough of Manhattan, City, County and State of New York* (hereinafter called the Manager) of the one part and GEORGE BERNARD SHAW of *10 Adelphi Terrace W.C.2 in the County of London in England* (hereinafter called the Author) of the other part WHEREBY IT IS DECLARED AND AGREED AS FOLLOWS.

1. The Author being the sole owner *of a play* written by him and entitled *Heartbreak House* hereby licenses the Manager to perform the said play in the English language in the United States and the Dominion of Canada from the *sixth* day of *November* one thousand nine hundred and *twenty* until the *thirtieth* day of *June* one thousand nine hundred and *twentythree* subject to the terms and limitations hereinafter set forth.

2. The Manager shall produce the said play at the *Garrick Theater in New York City* in the style customary for first-rate modern productions not later than the *thirtyfirst* day of *December* one thousand nine hundred and *twenty* for an uninterrupted series of at least *fortyeight* consecutive performances.

3. All performances under this Agreement shall be given at the best available theatres in the style customary for first rate modern productions and shall be announced as presented by the Manager.

4. At least *fortyeight* performances of the said play shall be given by the Manager in each year during the term of this Agreement.

5. The Manager shall pay to the Author FIFTEEN PER CENT. (15%) of the gross receipts at every performance given under this Agreement when such receipts exceed fifteen hundred dollars ($1,500); TEN PER CENT. (10%) when they exceed five hundred dollars ($500) and do not exceed fifteen hundred dollars; SEVEN AND A HALF PER CENT. (7½%) when they exceed two hundred and fifty dollars ($250) and do not exceed five hundred dollars; and FIVE PER CENT. (5%) when they do not exceed two hundred and fifty dollars ($250) it being understood that when the specified sums are exceeded the corresponding higher percentages are to be paid on the entire gross receipts and not according to the American custom of different percentages on the successive increments; and it is further understood that the Manager may calculate the percentage on the average of the gross receipts during the week instead of on the actual receipts at each particular performance. PROVIDED ALWAYS that if the said play be omitted from any performance given by the company within the week the gross receipts shall not be averaged in calculating the percentages for that week.

6. Should the Manager fail to produce the said play in compliance with Clause Two of this Agreement or should the said play be withdrawn from consecutive performance on *its* first production before the total payments made or due to the Author under the foregoing clause amount to Two thousand five hundred dollars ($2,500) the Manager shall thereupon pay to the Author a sum sufficient to bring the total sum payable to him

up to Two thousand five hundred dollars ($2,500) PROVIDED that this clause shall not operate if the gross receipts in any two successive weeks shall have averaged less than six hundred dollars ($600) per performance and if the Manager's part of this Agreement shall have been carried out in all other respects.

7. The percentage shall in all cases be calculated and paid on the full prices of admission as announced at the box office and not on cut rates or net returns from persons selling seats on commission.

8. The Author shall not during the term of this Agreement license any person other than the Manager to perform the said play in the English language in any town or towns in the United States of America or in the Dominion of Canada without first offering the Manager by notice in writing an opportunity of undertaking to perform the plays before the expiration of this Agreement in the town or towns in question on the terms set forth in this Agreement. In the event of the Manager giving such an undertaking the Author shall not during the term of this Agreement license any person other than the Manager (save as provided in Clause Fourteen of this Agreement) to perform the said plays in the town or towns so specified. But if the Manager having given such an undertaking wilfully fails to carry it out the Author shall be entitled to claim and receive from the Manager as liquidated damages such sum as he might reasonably have expected to gain had the Manager carried out the said undertaking. PROVIDED ALWAYS that the Author shall not in any case license any other person than the Manager to perform the said plays in the said States and Dominion before the twentyfifth ~ day of March ~~~ one thousand nine hundred and twentyone .

9. The Manager shall in the course of every week mail to the Author at his address in London detailed returns and accounts of the receipts at the performances given under this Agreement during the immediately preceding week, setting out the number of seats taken and paid for in each separate part of the house and the total gross receipts at the full nominal price as announced at the box office, without any deduction for agent's commissions or shares taken by theatre lessees or others; and payment of the percentages due on the gross receipts so returned shall accompany the said returns in the form of a draft on an English firm of bankers in London.

10. The Manager shall if required give to the Author or to his duly accredited Agent or Accountant access to all books papers vouchers and other documents necessary for the verification of the said returns.

11. The Manager shall not in any performance of the said play ~~~ given under this Agreement wilfully make or allow any alterations transpositions interpolations or omissions in or from the text as printed in the current authorized edition or in the prompt copy (if any) supplied by the Author; nor shall the Manager wilfully do or allow the performers to do anything that would have the effect of misrepresenting the Author's meaning either for better or worse.

12. The name of the Author shall appear in its customary public form of Bernard Shaw with due prominence on all playbills programs and advertisements published by the Manager or the Manager's Agents in which the titles of the plays are mentioned.

13. No performance given under this Agreement shall depart from the old-established order of theatrical performances as distinguished from modern cinematographic performances nor shall any performance or rehearsal given under this Agreement be recorded for the purposes of reproduction or for any other purpose by the cinematograph phonograph or other recording or reproducing instrument without the consent in writing of the Author on terms to be agreed upon, which consent the Author shall be free to withhold altogether if he chooses to do so.

14. In any town in which the said play shall have been performed once or oftener by the Manager or in which the Manager has not after due notice given an undertaking to perform under Clause Eight of this Agreement the Author shall be free to license performances of the said plays by amateurs notwithstanding anything to the contrary contained or implied in this Agreement.

15. Should the Manager at any time by   self or anyone acting on   behalf wilfully fail to fulfil or comply with any of the clauses and conditions herein set forth (save with the written consent of the Author) or should   retire from business as a theatrical manager or should   commit an act of bankruptcy the licence to perform contained in Clause One of this Agreement shall thereupon cease and the Author be free to license any other person to perform the said play notwithstanding anything to the contrary contained or implied in any other part of this Agreement.

16. If the Garrick Theater is needed for other trans in the repatory of the Theater Guild before the gross receipts under this Agreement have fallen below six thousand dollars ($6000) a week for the latest two successive weeks the Manager shall transfer the performances to another theater of the same class in New York City.

17. The Manager having paid to the Author two thousand five hundred dollars ($2500) receipt of which the Author hereby acknowledges may deduct this sum from the percentages to be paid under Clause Five of this Agreement or reckon it as a discharge of his undertaking in Clause Six.

AS WITNESS OUR HANDS this _Twenty-fourth_ day of _August_ nineteen hundred and _twenty_ .

WITNESS to the signature of
GEORGE BERNARD SHAW.

G. Bernad Shaw

J. m. Barrie
Author
Adelphi Terrace House
Strand
London. W. C

WITNESS to the signature of

Benj. H. Stern
Lawyer.
149 Broadway
N. Y. City

Theatre Guild Inc
By Lawrence Langner
Treasurer

This is the sort of thing you may expect if the Theatre Guild decides to do business with me. It is only a sample, not a draft.

MEMORANDUM OF AGREEMENT made and entered into this   day
of   one thousand nine hundred and sixteen between ~~_____~~ in the city of New York hereinafter called the Manager of the one part and GEORGE BERNARD SHAW of 10 Adelphi Terrace in the county of London in England hereinafter called the Author of the other part WHEREBY IT IS DECLARED AND AGREED AS FOLLOWS.

1. The Author being the sole owner of a play written by him and entitled ~~_____~~ ~~_____~~ hereby licenses the Manager to perform the said play in the English language in the United States and the Dominion of Canada from ~~the date of the Presidential Election in~~ ~~_____~~ until the thirty-first day of July one thousand nine hundred and nineteen subject to the terms and limitations hereinafter set forth.

2. The Manager shall produce the said play at the ~~_____~~ Theatre in New York City in the style customary for first-rate modern productions not later than the tenth day of December one thousand nine hundred and sixteen for an uninterrupted series of at least fifty consecutive performances.

3. The Manager shall pay to the Author FIFTEEN PER CENT. (15%) of the gross receipts at every performance given under this agreement when such receipts exceed fifteen hundred dollars ($1,500); TEN PER CENT. (10%) when they exceed five hundred dollars ($500) and do not exceed fifteen hundred dollars; SEVEN AND A HALF PER CENT. ($7\frac{1}{2}$%) when they exceed two hundred and fifty dollars ($250) and do not exceed five hundred dollars; and FIVE PER CENT. (5%) when they do not exceed two hundred and fifty dollars ($250) it being understood that when the specified sums are exceeded the corresponding higher percentages are to be paid on the entire gross receipts and not according to the American custom of different percentages on the successive increments; and it is further understood that the Manager may calculate the percentage on the average of the gross receipts during the week instead of on the actual receipts at each particular performance. PROVIDED ALWAYS that if another play by another author be performed by the company within the week instead of the said ~~_____~~ the gross receipts shall not be averaged in calculating the percentages.

4. Should the play be withdrawn from performance in New York on its first production before the total payments made or due to the Author under the foregoing clause amount to Two thousand five hundred dollars ($2,500) the Manager shall thereupon pay to the Author a sum sufficient to bring the total sum payable to him up to Two thousand five hundred dollars ($2,500). ~~_____~~ ~~_____~~ ~~_____~~ ~~_____~~

5. The percentage shall in all cases be calculated and paid on the full prices of admission as announced and charged at the box office and not on cut rates or net returns from persons selling seats on commission.

6 The Author shall not during the term of this agreement license any person other than the Manager to perform the said play in any town or towns in the United States of

America or in the Dominion of Canada without first offering the Manager by notice in writing an opportunity of undertaking the perform the play himself before the expiration of this Agreement in the town or towns in question on the terms set forth in this Agreement. In the event of the Manager giving such an undertaking the Author shall not during the term of this Agreement license any person other than the Manager (save as provided in Clause Twelve of this Agreement) to perform the said play in the town or towns so specified. But if the Manager having given such an undertaking wilfully fails to carry it out the Author shall be entitled to claim and receive from the Manager as liquidated damages such sum as he might reasonably have expected to gain had the Manager carried out his undertaking. PROVIDED ALWAYS that the Author shall not in any case license any other person than the Manager to perform the said play in the said States and Dominion before the ~~~~~~~~th day of ~~~~~~h one thousand nine hundred and ~~~~~~~~~~~~.

7. The Manager shall in the course of every week mail to the Author at his address in London detailed returns and accounts of the receipts at the performances given under this Agreement during the immediately preceding week, setting out the number of seats taken and paid for in each separate part of the house and the total gross receipts at the full nominal price charged at the box office, without any deduction for agent's commissions or shares taken by theatre lessees or others; and payment of the percentages due on the gross receipts so returned shall accompany the said returns in the form of a draft on an English firm of bankers in London.

8. The Manager shall if required give to the Author or to his duly accredited Agent or Accountant access at all reasonable times to all books papers vouchers and other documents necessary for the verification of his returns.

9. The Manager shall not in any performance of the said play given under this Agreement wilfully make or allow any alterations transpositions interpolations or omissions in or from the text of the play as printed in the current authorized edition; nor shall the Manager wilfully do or allow the performers to do anything that would have the effect of misrepresenting the Author's meaning either for better or worse ~~PROVIDED ALWAYS that the interruption of the play by two intervals for the convenience of the audience if described as such in the program and not as divisions of the play into acts shall not be deemed a breach of this clause.~~

10. The name of the Author shall appear in its customary public form of Bernard Shaw with due prominence on all playbills programs and advertisements of the play published by the Manager or his Agents in which the title of the play is mentioned.

11. No performance given under this Agreement shall depart from the old-established order of theatrical performances as distinguished from modern cinematographic performances nor shall any performance or rehearsal given under this Agreement be recorded for the purposes of reproduction or for any other purpose by the cinematograph phonograph or other recording or reproducing instrument without the consent in writing of the Author on terms to be agreed upon, which consent the Author shall be free to withhold altogether if he chooses to do so.

12.   In any town in which the play shall have been performed once or oftener by the Manager or in which the Manager has not after due notice given an undertaking to perform under Clause Six of this agreement the Author shall be free to license perform- ances by amateurs notwithstanding anything to the contrary contained or implied in this agreement.

13.   Should the Manager at any time by himself or anyone acting on his behalf wilfully fail to fulfil or comply with any of the clauses and conditions herein set forth (save with the written consent of the Author) or should he retire from business as a theatrical manager or should he commit an act of bankruptcy the license to perform contained in Clause One of this agreement shall thereupon cease and the Author be free to license any other person to perform the said play notwithstanding anything to the contrary contained or implied in any other part of this agreement.

AS WITNESS OUR HANDS this   day of
nineteen hundred and sixteen.

WITNESS to the signature of
GEORGE BERNARD SHAW.

WITNESS to the signature of *~~illegible~~*

~~To the above clauses I shall probably add one obliging you not to break the run as long as the receipts exceed a certain figure, but allowing you to transfer to another theatre when this comes into conflict with your obligation to produce five (is it?) plays every year.~~

ADDENDUM C

LIST OF SHAW PLAYS PRODUCED BY THE THEATRE GUILD

AND

LIST OF SHAW PLAYS PRESENTED AT THE WESTPORT COUNTRY PLAYHOUSE

THEATRE GUILD PLAYS

HEARTBREAK HOUSE	*November* 1920
BACK TO METHUSELAH	*February* 1922
THE DEVIL'S DISCIPLE	*April* 1923
SAINT JOAN	*December* 1923
CAESAR AND CLEOPATRA	*April* 1925
ARMS AND THE MAN	*September* 1925
THE MAN OF DESTINY	*November* 1925
ANDROCLES AND THE LION	*November* 1925
PYGMALION	*November* 1926
THE DOCTOR'S DILEMMA	*November* 1927
MAJOR BARBARA	*November* 1928
THE APPLE CART	*February* 1930
GETTING MARRIED	*March* 1931

TOO TRUE TO BE GOOD   *April* 1932

THE SIMPLETON OF THE UNEXPECTED ISLES   *February* 1935

YOU NEVER CAN TELL   *March* 1948

THE MILLIONAIRESS   *October* 1952

WESTPORT COUNTRY PLAYHOUSE PLAYS

YOU NEVER CAN TELL   *August* 1935

FANNY'S FIRST PLAY   *July* 1936

THE MILLIONAIRESS   *August* 1938

CAPTAIN BRASSBOUND'S CONVERSION   *July* 1940

THE DEVIL'S DISCIPLE   *July* 1950

THE PHILANDERER   *July* 1951

PYGMALION   *June* 1952

THE SHEWING-UP OF BLANCO POSNET   *June* 1954

ACKNOWLEDGMENTS

I DESIRE to thank many friends connected with the Theatre Guild and the Sterling Library of Yale University for their help in verifying much of the information in this book; and my thanks are especially due to Romney Brent, who appeared in many of Shaw's plays; Professor John Gassner of Yale University; R. William Fitelson and Floria Laskey; and Mary Lou Albright and Jerry Kieffer of the Theatre Guild for their patient research and general support. I am also indebted for photographs to Florence Van Damm; Fred Fehl, James T. Babb, John Ottemiller, Donald Gallup and F. S. Ludwig of the Yale Sterling Library; and to Gala Ebin for assisting me in selecting photographs and writing captions.

I am also indebted to the Shaw Estate and most particularly to the British Society of Authors and its secretary, Elizabeth Barber, for information and permission to use certain material; and to Barbara Smoker of the British Shaw Society for permission to reproduce a part of her article on the Shaw alphabet.

Finally, I am indebted to Hiram Haydn and Herman Ziegner of Atheneum Publishers for their editorial assistance, and for the selection of illustrations.

INDEX

LAWRENCE LANGNER

———————◄◆►———————

BORN IN SWANSEA, Wales, in 1890, Lawrence Langner came to this country in 1911 as a patent specialist. Three years later his interest in the theatre led him to help organize the Washington Square Players, and subsequently he founded the Theatre Guild in 1918. As director of the Theatre Guild, he had been the guiding force in that organization until his death on December 26, 1962. He was active in the production of more than 450 plays for the Westport Country Playhouse and the Theatre Guild. Included in the productions for the Guild were the first presentations in this country of many of the plays by Bernard Shaw, Eugene O'Neill, Turgenev, Molière, Pirandello, Werfel, Chekhov and Goethe.

Then in 1951 he founded the American Shakespeare Festival Theatre and Academy at Stratford, Connecticut. He was also a playwright and produced many plays for radio and television.

Besides his autobiography *The Magic Curtain,* 1951, Mr. Langner was the author of *The Importance of Wearing Clothes,* 1959, and *The Play's the Thing,* 1960.